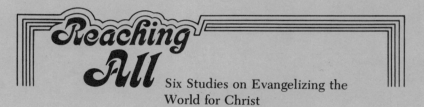

Reaching All

Six Studies on Evangelizing the
World for Christ

**Taken from the International Congress
on World Evangelization.
Lausanne, Switzerland**

WORLD WIDE PUBLICATIONS

MINNEAPOLIS, MN

ISBN 0-89066-251-7 495

Acknowledgements

International Reference Committee:
Saphir Athyal, India
Samuel Escobar, Argentina
Chua Wee Hian, England
Warwick Olson, Australia
Gottfried Osei-Mensah, Kenya

Editor: Paul E. Little

Composition and Instructional Design:
John M. Dettoni, Ted Ward

Copy Editors: Roger Palms, Margaret Ward

Photographs: Russell Busby; Åke Lundberg;
Food for the Hungry

Layout and Cover Design: Ray Orosz

Library of Congress Catalog Card Number: 74–78959

A Word to Group Leaders

1. Each chapter is a series of studies on one topic.
Your class or study group can begin with any chapter. Let your group help to decide which chapter
or chapters to study.

2. Order a book for each member of the class or
study group.

3. Notice that each chapter is divided into six sections. Each section begins with a key word. Your
group can use one or two of these sections for one
study session or class hour. As you read each chapter, think carefully about whether your group
would prefer to discuss one section or two sections
each time they meet. (If you decide on *two* sections
per meeting, one chapter will be used for three
meetings.) Most weekly classes, such as Sunday
School, will want to use two chapters, one after the
other, to serve as a full quarter of studies. In this
sort of use, one section of the chapter can be
studied and discussed each week.

4. You may pick any of the three columns to use
with your group. If you have time, you may want to
use any two of the columns. The left-hand column
uses almost no big words without explaining them.
The right-hand column is much more detailed; it is
designed primarily for more advanced individuals,
study groups and theological schools. The middle
column is neither simplified nor complex. This
middle column has been especially designed for
laymen.

5. Encourage the students to read an assigned section of the chapter in advance. Ask one person to
be prepared to *review* the text (but *not* the study
questions).

6. Assign several others to be prepared to ask the
discussion questions and offer their own ideas after
listening to others share theirs. Read aloud each
question. If time is very limited, break the group
into sub-groups and assign to each a series of ques-

tions to answer and report back to the entire group.

7. The leader should let the chapter do the teaching. As the leader or teacher, you should resist the temptation to explain the readings. Instead urge the participants to reread when necessary and to seek clarification through thinking and discussion.

8. The leader's role is to *help* the group think, discuss and decide what the material means. Your role is that of a facilitator, not an "answer-man." Help the group to clarify the ideas and issues and decide upon answers and solutions. Encourage the group to find ways to *do* what it decides it should.

9. The discussions are designed to help the participants explore ideas and to think together about their own part in evangelization. It is not necessary to try to convince them through argument.

10. Please use the discussion questions in the sequence given; don't skip around. Each question is built on the responses that were given to a previous question.

11. Whenever you are tempted to "make a speech," ask a question instead! Keep this list of sample questions handy:
—"Bob, would you please summarize what we've been saying?"
—"Frances, what do *you* think?"
—"What did the author say about this matter?"
—"What new thought or ideas has the author suggested to you?"
—"Before we go to the next question, how does what we are discussing relate to what the authors are saying?"
—"How can we determine the answer to that question?"

—"Does anyone have another viewpoint on that question?"

12. If several days come between sessions, spend a few minutes each time in sharing how the discussions and decisions at the previous session affected the group, individually and as a whole. Pray for continued effects from the studies. Close the session in group prayer (or short sentence prayers), focusing on that day's decisions for action.

Contents - 1

Acknowledgements

Authors and papers of the International Congress on World Evangelization used in this chapter are as follows:

N. P. Anderson, "Biblical Theology and Cultural Identity in the Anglo-Saxon World";

Peter Beyerhaus, "Evangelism and the Kingdom of God";

Billy Graham, "Why Lausanne?";

Michael Green, "Methods and Strategy in the Evangelism of the Early Church";

Harold Lindsell, "Universalism";

Donald McGavran, "Ten Dimensions of World Evangelism";

C. René Padilla, "Evangelism and the World";

Francis Schaeffer, "Form and Freedom in the Church";

John R. W. Stott, "The Nature of Biblical Evangelism";

Susumu Uda, "Biblical Authority and Evangelism."

What do we believe about evangelism? What is the theological basis for our beliefs? A major emphasis of the International Congress on World Evangelization was the relationship of theology to evangelism. Several speakers at the Congress restated evangelical theology with particular reference to our task of worldwide evangelism today. In this study we shall examine what these evangelical leaders taught about several basic evangelical doctrines and their implications for our roles in evangelism.

Authority

The authority of the Bible is basic to Christian theology. Theology should flow from the Scriptures. The Bible speaks to us with definite and straightforward power from God; we need to listen and obey. In his opening remarks at the Congress, Billy Graham stressed the importance of the authority of the Bible.

Graham

I am more and more convinced that missions and evangelistic efforts are only successful when they are under the authority of the Scriptures. Only when evangelism is biblical is it true evangelism.

We have met in Lausanne as evangelicals united by our firm belief in the authority of the Bible. We shall not compromise on basic biblical truth. If there is one thing the history of the church in this century should teach us, it is the importance of a biblical theology of evangelism. That must never be blurred. We must hold that the entire Bible is the Word of God. It is authoritative and demands faith and obedience to all its declarations. It is inspired and infallible. It contains everything necessary to the faith and practice of Christians. Apart from the Scriptures we cannot know about the eternal purposes of God, entertain hope for immortality, or rejoice in the certain victory of good over evil. It is from this Bible, plainly understood, that the theology of evangelism must be forged.

5

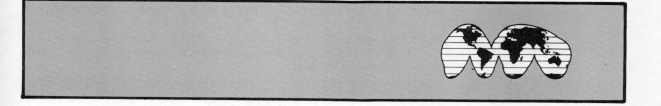

● The first and most basic question in Christian theology is: What do you believe about the Bible and its authority? Why is this so important?

What does it mean to accept the Bible as your authority? How does a person demonstrate that the Bible is his authority in life?

●● What did Billy Graham mean when he said, "Only when evangelism is biblical is it true evangelism"?

Why is the authority of Scripture essential to evangelism? What kind of evangelism is carried out by those who reject the authority of Scripture? How does this differ from evangelism practiced by people who accept the authority of Scripture?

●●● What are the basic philosophical reasons for starting with the authority of the Bible when developing a theology of evangelism?

What can happen to evangelism if the authority of Scripture is diminished or rejected?

Prepare a page for your own notes on the following question and others that will come later in this chapter: What are the practical aspects of a *theology* of evangelism?

Susumu Uda, a professor of theology at Japan Christian Theological Seminary and a member of the Reformed Presbyterian Church, gave five reasons why the Bible is necessary for evangelism.

6

Uda

Whenever in the course of the church's long history the question "What is to be believed?" arose, it was to the Bible that the church turned. We ought to be clear about the fundamental factors which make the Bible, God's written revelation, most necessary.

1) How do we know of our lost and sinful condition and the love of God in Jesus Christ? The Heidelberg Catechism gives a simple, penetrating answer, "Out of the law of God." Since man has sinned, he has become a "willing slave" of sin and thereby spiritually incapable. But from the moment man sinned, God began to show His saving grace. In order that men, blinded by sin, may learn correctly His will, works, and ways with respect to this saving, restorative work, God's special communication to them became necessary (2 Timothy 3:17).

2) The necessity of God's written special revelation appears also with respect to man's inability to interpret *nature* correctly. We may listen to the "harmony of the spheres" and still not understand God's revelation in nature. As sinners, we are in need of a clarifying lens or window through which we can understand the real meaning and purpose of God's creation.

3) Since God is above all things and greater than the whole of His creation, man cannot adequately think of God and properly describe Him in concepts he originates in himself (Job 36:26; 1 Timothy 6:15-16). Only through revelation is God authentically known. For this reason, too, God's written special revelation is necessary.

4) The Christian view of *God as a person* points to the necessity of God's special communication. Bernard Ramm describes it as follows, "As man stands before this Person, the Person of God, he

discovers that he cannot open up the discussion. Under what terms could such a conversation be opened up? . . . What are the connecting ligaments between the human and the divine mind? If we are ready to converse, is God ready to listen? Perhaps God has called to us and we have not heard? If we call, must God answer? Here man stands before the sovereign Person, the transcendent Person! *If there is to be a conversation this Person must initiate it* . . . In the divine readiness this sovereign Person does speak! He does open up the conversation! *And this conversation springing from the readiness of this Person is special revelation"* (From Bernard Ramm: *Special Revelation and the Word of God*, Eerdmans, 1961, pg. 25). And we simply add that this conversation is now embodied in the Bible.

5) The church on earth often comes under the temptation of evil to shift to degenerate forms of faith and worship; therefore, renewal is constantly needed. But from what source should renewal spring? Psalm 119:50 informs us that the way the Spirit of God renews life is by applying the Word of God. Thus the written special revelation is most necessary.

If we did not have the Bible, how much would we know about God, Jesus Christ, God's love for us, our sinfulness and need for Jesus as Savior?

Why is the Bible so central to evangelism?

What does the Bible tell us about man and his relationship to God? How much would we know without it?

How important is the Bible for evangelism?

What knowledge of God would we have without the Bible? What makes biblical revelation so vital to evangelism? Is any one of Uda's points more basic to a biblical understanding of evangelism than any other?

Uda also showed the basis for accepting the authority of the Scriptures.

The real issue before the entire church and every individual Christian today is, "What is our attitude toward the Bible?" The most popular approach to this question today is to submit the Bible to so-called scientific examination by "experts," to abide by that testimony, and to judge the Bible by whether or not modern man thinks it relevant to this day.

What is the evangelical view of the Bible? To be sure, the evangelical approach should not preclude scholarly research and serious discussions about the contemporary relevancy of the Bible. But the evangelical approach gives first priority to the *self-testimony* of the Bible. As every man has a right to speak for himself, and testimony to oneself should not be ruled out as improper, so it is with the Bible.

It has been the faith of the people of God from the very founding of the church until today that the Bible is the Word of God in such a sense that whatever it says, God says. The biblical warrant for this attitude of entire trust in the Bible is the *inspiration* of God the Holy Spirit.

In 2 Timothy 3:16, Paul says, "All scripture is given by inspiration of God." The word which calls for our special attention is the Greek word for "inspiration." This word does not say that Scripture is "breathed into by God" or is the product of the divine "inbreathing" into its human authors, but it is breathed out by God — "God-breathed," the product of the creative breath of God. The "breath of God" in the Bible is a symbol of the almighty and irresistible outflow of His power. In a word, the text explicitly teaches the divine origin of "all Scripture."

This same truth is expressed also in 2 Peter 1:16-21. Peter is assuring his readers that what had been made known to them of "the power and coming of our Lord Jesus Christ" did not come through "cleverly devised myths." He presents to them the testimony of eyewitnesses. And then he says that they have even better testimony than that of eyewitnesses. It is "the prophetic word" which is "more sure." He emphatically states that Scripture does not owe its origin to "the impulse of man," but its origin lies in God, "Men moved by the Holy Spirit spoke from God." The Greek word, "pheromenoi," for "moved" is a remarkable word. It means "brought," "borne," or "carried along." That is, the Holy Spirit lifted them up and carried them along, and thus they spoke. They were borne or carried along under the determining influence of the Spirit and not by their own power. As a result of the inspiration by the Holy Spirit, the Bible possesses divine authority and trustworthiness.

Further, we hear the most definitive word about the authority of the Bible from the lips of our Lord Himself. In Matthew 5:18, Christ says, "Not an iota, not a dot, will pass from the law until all is accomplished." As the previous verse shows, Christ is here referring to the sacred writings of the Jews as a unit. But He says very positively that this book is perfect to the smallest detail.

John's Gospel also refers to Jesus' complete trust in the Bible, "The Scripture cannot be broken" (John 10:35). The concept of breaking a law was well understood by the people of that day. If a man breaks a law, he is guilty, and so he is liable for punishment. The Scripture, however, possesses an authority so great that it cannot be broken. What the Scripture says will stand steadfast and cannot be annulled. If the Scripture speaks, the issue is settled once and for all.

This high view of Scripture was indeed held by the Jews, by the early church, and by the church throughout the centuries. Standing on the promises of God found in the revealed Word of God has certainly been the essential characteristic of the faith of God's people.

●

Can we trust the Bible? Why?

How much of the Bible is to be trusted? If you were to accept only parts of the Bible as authoritative, how would you decide which parts to accept and which parts to reject? What problems does such an approach create?

How much of the Bible do you accept? What is required in your own life for God's Word to have an effect on you?

How does the authority of the Bible make the task of evangelism clearer to you?

●●

What do you think is the *key* reason for accepting the authority of the Bible? What are some other reasons for accepting its authority?

In what ways does the Bible speak for itself about its own authority?

Is there any way to discover the Bible's authority, other than appealing to its own statements?

In what ways does clarifying Scriptural authority also clarify the task of evangelism?

●●●

What is the basic assumption in Uda's approach to using the Bible as a self-testimony to its own authority? Some have called this approach circular. Do you agree? Why or why not?

Can you provide evidence for the authority of Scripture from sources other than Scripture?

Is it possible for a person to accept some portions of the Bible and reject others and still maintain a consistent and coherent attitude toward Scripture?

If the Bible is the authoritative Word of God, how much of it is actually and practically the authority in your life?

9

Donald McGavran, former missionary, author, and professor at the School of World Mission of Fuller Theological Seminary, Pasadena, California, joined Uda in declaring that the Bible is basic in matters of salvation and sanctification.

Uda   McGavran

While the Scriptures of men and the writings of their philosophers and teachers certainly contain many good things, we hold that the Bible alone is the inspired Word of God. It alone is a sufficient rule of faith and practice. It is the standard, the perfect yardstick, by which all other writings about salvation and morals are to be judged. As world evangelism proceeds in love toward all men, truth compels Christians to be clear on this point.

The problem of authority is always the most fundamental problem that the church faces. The choice regarding the foundation of faith determines the road to be traveled.

Now is the time for the church of Jesus Christ to give heed to the truth expressed in the words of Christ's high-priestly prayer, "Sanctify them through thy truth; thy word is truth" (John 17:17). So long as the church holds to the authoritative Word of the sovereign God, she is, in fact, the church of the living God.

How does accepting the Bible as God's truth help to make us holy (sanctified) people?

Can any other authority be substituted for the authority of Scripture?

Why is God's truth so important for evangelism?

What kind of authority is there for evangelism if the Bible is not *the* authority?

Why can God's Word make us holy people (sanctified)? How does this relate to what a Christian should do and be?

How does it relate to what you and your group should do and be in evangelism?

What are the practical results for evangelism of a biblical view of the trustworthiness and authoritativeness of Scripture?

Add notes to your list as suggested at the beginning of this unit.

Kingdom

The evangelistic message of Jesus and His disciples had its roots in the Old Testament. This rich background known to the Jews of Jesus' day was the focus of a paper by Peter Beyerhaus at the International Congress on World Evangelization.

Beyerhaus, a Lutheran theologian from Germany, called attention to a term in the Gospels which was part of Jewish thought for several centuries before Christ. "The Kingdom of God" meant to the Jews that God was going to set up His reign on earth and rule from Jerusalem. Jesus used "The Kingdom of God" in the Gospels to refer to His reign or Lordship in each believer's life, and also to the eventual rule of God over all things in fulfillment of the Old Testament promises.

The Gospel which Jesus preached to the Jews was "good news"! It announced the fulfillment of Israel's central hope, the final establishment of God's messianic rule.

The proclamation of the Kingdom of God forms the heart of the evangelistic ministry of Jesus (Matthew 4:17) and His apostles. Jesus points to the Kingdom as the very reason for His coming, "I must evangelize about the Kingdom of God in the other cities also; for I was sent for this purpose" (Luke 4:43). Why did Jesus choose this idea of God's Kingdom as His favorite theme? The German scholar Wilhelm Bousset has rightly stated, "The sum total of everything which Israel expected of the future was the Kingdom of God." Jesus, therefore, did not introduce a new idea when speaking about the Kingdom. Rather, He referred to the most important concept of Israel's belief and hope. The Old Testament had left the Jews with one basic problem: on the one hand Israel had always believed and confessed that her God *is* already the sovereign ruler over His whole creation; on the other hand Israel observed that other nations did not recognize God's rule.

God, however, did not give up His intention to make the whole earth the place of His glory and to use Israel to establish His rulership over all nations. The day will come when God again will demonstrate His power and manifest Himself as the supreme king of the earth. He will intervene in the course of history and change the lot of His people. This will be on "the Day of the Lord."

The Day of the Lord indicates the great series of eschatological events [those events that are associated with the end of this age] when God finally will restore His people Israel both spiritually and physically. God will pour out His *Spirit* on His people to bring about a spiritual regeneration (Ezekiel 37:9-10, 39:29; Joel 2:28-29; Zechariah 12:10). He will send the *Messiah* to be the agent of salvation. Through Him God will establish His reign of peace on Mount Zion. This rule will extend to all nations on earth (Isaiah 2:1-5, 9:1-7, 11:1-16). Voluntarily, the kings will come to Jerusalem to worship the God of Israel and to accept His laws. And thus they will live in peace, justice and prosperity. This is what the term, the "Kingdom of God," meant to the Israelites.

The word "evangelize" is used for the first time in its typical biblical meaning in Isaiah 52 and 61. The prophet received a vision which he was urged to proclaim to his people. He saw the Lord return to Zion and take up His universal reign (Isaiah 52:7-8). It is a marvelous message of eschatological salvation which forms the content of this evangelism, "The Spirit of the Lord is upon me, because the Lord has anointed me to evangelize (that is, to bring good tidings to) the afflicted; He has sent me to bind up the brokenhearted, to proclaim liberty to the captives. . . to proclaim the year of the Lord's favor, the day of vengeance of our Lord; to comfort all who mourn" (Isaiah 61:1-2).

The same prophetic understanding of evangelism, announcing the Kingdom of God is taken up in the Gospels.

●

Why was it easy for the Jews of Jesus' day to understand His message? Did their understanding always lead to belief?

What do Isaiah 52 and 61 suggest that the people might expect of Jesus?

The "Kingdom of God" is God's ruling; the "Day of the Lord" is all of the events that lead to the rule of God over all things. How is evangelism today related to the "Kingdom of God" and the "Day of the Lord"?

● ●

Why did Jesus use "Kingdom of God" as a central part of His evangelistic message?

How does Jesus' message of the Gospel compare to the Old Testament idea of "good news" as found in Isaiah 52 and 61?

In what way is evangelism related to the "Day of the Lord" and to the "Kingdom of God"?

● ● ●

In what way is the "Kingdom of God" the basic evangelistic concept of both Old and New Testaments?

What was Israel's understanding of the "Kingdom of God"?

In what way is the "Day of the Lord" related to the "Kingdom of God"? How are the "Kingdom of God" and the "Day of the Lord" related to evangelism today?

Beyerhaus stated that Jesus introduced some new elements to an understanding of the Kingdom of God: its focus on Himself, its spiritual reality, and its emphasis on the creation of a new community.

1) *The Kingdom proclaimed in New Testament evangelism is centered in Jesus Christ.*

In His first sermon in the synagogue of Nazareth, Jesus identifies Himself with the messianic prophet of Isaiah 61:1 — "The Spirit of the Lord God is upon me, because the Lord anointed me to evangelize the afflicted." His startling comment on this famous text is, "Today this scripture has been fulfilled in your hearing!" This does not mean that the Kingdom as it was expected so eagerly by the Jews is already totally established by the work of Jesus. There is not that drastic change in history and nature yet which will mark the peace of the messianic Kingdom. But His proclamation and His works demonstrate vital elements of it. They are not the Kingdom in full, but they are signs which point to Jesus Himself as the bringer of this Kingdom. In fact, He is the most important and central element of the Kingdom. All the gifts of the messianic Kingdom are contained in the person of Jesus Christ and mediated through His messianic ministry. It is a ministry rather different from the spectacular political expectations of the contemporary Jews, especially of the Pharisees and the Zealots. They could not understand the vicarious death of the Messiah (Matthew 16:21-27). This appeared scandalous even to His own disciples, although it had been predicted in Isaiah, especially chapter 53. But this was the way the Kingdom of God was to be ushered in according to the plan of God.

All evangelism carried out by the apostles and the early church was Christ-centered. The central place which Jesus in His evangelism gave to the Kingdom is, in the writings of Paul and John, filled by Jesus Himself.

Christ must remain the center of *our* evangelism as well. We must preach the authentic Christ as He is proclaimed and taught in the apostolic writings of the New Testament. One great danger in the church's mission today is the ignoring of God's way in both the Old and the New Testament. The Old Testament's descriptions of the gifts of the Kingdom, liberation, and peace cannot rightly be separated from Christ as the bringer and the Lord of the Kingdom. He is the way in which the restoration of God's rule over men is accomplished.

2) Christian evangelism preaches a Kingdom that is realized by spiritual regeneration.

The second distinct point in the New Testament understanding of the Kingdom is that its deepest nature is *spiritual*. This does not renounce the expectation that it one day will also come with visible force, "with power and great glory" (Matthew 24:30), and that it will reshape the whole physical world as well. But its basic structure is not physical (Romans 14:17). We may *define* the New Testament understanding of the Kingdom as follows:

The Kingdom of God is God's redeeming Lordship, successively winning such liberating power over the hearts of men that their lives and thereby finally the whole creation become transformed into harmony with His divine will (see Romans 8:21).

This is the reason why the Kingdom of God could never be established by political action. And since sinful man by nature is opposed to the will of God, it cannot even be brought about by moral education. The acknowledgement of God's rule presupposes a miraculous change of heart which can be achieved only by an intervention of God Himself.

Suffering under injustice and oppression in the present state of world affairs, and the cries for liberation and peace, are needs which burn on the hearts of conscientious people at all times and in all cultures. Today the quest for total *renewal* is resounding with even greater vigor than before. Some churches are responding to it through church renewal movements. But the crucial question is "renewal which way?" Is it through a return to the Word of God?

The *renewal* which God has to offer is a radical one. It is the renewal of our mind by being regenerated and transformed to the mind of Jesus Christ (Romans 12:2). This offer by far exceeds all other human solutions. And the offer is made through evangelism. The total ministry of Jesus consisted of teaching, evangelizing and healing (Matthew 9:35, 10:7–8). Evangelism has one specific function in this total missionary ministry: it is to decisively ignite the desire for new life in Christ. And as soon as this life is born, it will be expressed through works of love (Galatians 5:6).

It should not be argued that spiritual renewal remains internal or individualistic. Some evangelicals have been tempted to reduce renewal to this dimension. But such a small view is not the true evangelical understanding of the gifts of the Kingdom.

3) *Evangelism leads into the church as the new messianic community of the Kingdom.*

One of the questions in New Testament theology is the relationship between the *Kingdom of God* and the *church*. The messianic Kingdom presupposes a messianic community. This community is the specific people of God, destined to exercise the messianic ministry to the rest of the nations.

The *goal of evangelism* is not only to make individual believers but also to persuade these believers to be incorporated as responsible members into the church as God's messianic community. In the total task of mission, the work of evangelism is continued by the planting of local churches in each nation. Even where Christians are a small minority, they are to be regarded as the first fruit of Christ's saving love for the whole people and are established in order to be self-multiplying.

14

●

Is the rule of Jesus in our lives *spiritual* or *physical*?

What are several ways that people make something other than Christ the center of the Gospel?

In what way is Christ the center of your witness?

Is it correct to say that the spiritual nature of the Kingdom of God *must* also be demonstrated in our actual daily lives?

How do you show by your actions that Christ rules your life?

Why is the church the present form of the Kingdom of God today? In what way is your relationship to the local church important to you?

● ●

How can Christ become the center of your evangelistic message?

Why is it correct to say that although the Kingdom of God is basically spiritual it must also have physical and external dimensions?

If Christ reigns in your life, how does this affect what you do, think about, and want to be?

What makes the spiritual aspects of the Kingdom of God so important to evangelism?

How does evangelism lead to the church as the messianic community?

How important is the church to you? How can you make the messianic community more important?

● ● ●

How are the Old Testament and the New Testament concepts of the Kingdom of God related?

How is the spiritual nature of the Kingdom of God demonstrated in practical, everyday life?

What is the relationship between the Lordship of Christ and the spiritual dimension of the Kingdom of God?

What is the basis of the argument that making individual believers is not the final goal of evangelism? How does the Kingdom of God idea relate to this argument?

How does the church's role in the world affect evangelism?

The return of Christ to establish His Kingdom is a final aspect of the Kingdom of God.

Beyerhaus

One primary function of the church will continue. Nobody will stop it until it has reached its goal. "And this Gospel of the Kingdom will be preached throughout the whole earth, as a testimony to all nations, and then the end will come" (Matthew 24:14). This prophecy puts Christ's commission to evangelize the world into an eschatalogical context. Evangelism is the chief contribution of the church to hasten the visible establishment of Christ's Kingdom on earth. Only when this work is complete will Christ come to redeem the groaning creation from its present bondage.

Evangelism comes to men with a present offer based upon Christ's victory on the Cross, and with an eschatological promise based on the final victory of His return. This tension within the historical movement of God's Kingdom is the driving dynamic of evangelism. It offers God's grace in Christ and new life in the Holy Spirit now. It promises total redemption of our bodies and of the whole creation in the Kingdom of Glory to come. Paul says that the whole "creation waits with eager longing for the revealing of the Son of God; . . . because the creation itself will be set free from its bondage to decay, and will obtain the glorious liberty of the children of God" (Romans 8:19-20). This will take place at the return of Christ. He will transform His militant church into His triumphant church, to reign together with Him in His messianic Kingdom of universal peace (Matthew 19:28-29; Luke 22:28-30; 1 Corinthians 6:2).

15

●

How does evangelism relate to the return of Christ? What is the Christian's ultimate hope? How do you think this hope can best be communicated to people today?

●●

What is the connection between the coming of Christ and evangelism?

How do the present and future aspects of the Gospel motivate Christians to evangelize?

●●●

How are the Kingdom of God and the return of Christ related to the evangelistic task of the church?

What do you understand by Beyerhaus' conclusion that the driving dynamic of evangelism is the tension between the Cross and the return of Christ?

We have seen that Jesus' message had its roots in the Old Testament idea of the Kingdom of God. We have also seen that Jesus brought some new emphases to the understanding of the Kingdom. These New Testament emphases make a difference in our work of evangelism. List several ways that evangelism should be affected because of Jesus' teaching on the Kingdom. Take a look at your own witness to the Good News. Does it show what Jesus taught about the Kingdom?

Message

What is the essential content of the Gospel message? This question was on the minds of the delegates at the International Congress on World Evangelization. Francis A. Schaeffer, speaker, writer, and founder of L'Abri Fellowship in Switzerland, emphasized the importance of correct content.

We must have clear doctrinal content concerning the central elements of Christianity. There is no use talking about meeting the threat of the coming time or fulfilling our calling in the midst of the last quarter of the twentieth century unless we consciously help each other to have a clear doctrinal position. We must have the courage to make no compromise with liberal theology and especially neo-orthodox existential theology.

Christianity is a specific body of truth and we must hold to that truth. There will be borderline things in which we have differences among ourselves, but on the central issues there must be no compromise.

We must be very careful not to fall into the cheap solution of moving people to make decisions without understanding the content of those decisions. People have come to L'Abri saying that they have "accepted Christ as Savior" but they are not even sure that God exists. They had never been confronted with the question of the existence of God. The acceptance of Christ as Savior was a thing abstracted. It had an insufficient content. It was just another kind of "trip."

The person who accepts Christ as his Savior must understand that, prior to the creation of the world, a personal God on the high level of trinity existed. Man has been made in the image of God and has value. Man's dilemma is not metaphysical simply because he is small, but it is moral because man revolted against God in an actual moment — the fall. If we "evangelize" by asking only for "acceptance of Christ as Savior" without an understanding of the content of Christianity, then all we have done is guarantee that a person will soon drift away and become harder to reach than ever. Of course, nobody knows everything; if we waited to be saved until we knew everything, nobody would ever be saved — but that is a very different thing from deliberately or thoughtlessly diminishing the content.

A Bible-believing Christian who stands against the liberal theologian who says there are no absolutes in the Bible can make the opposite mistake by adding other non-biblical elements as though they were equally absolute. That is, the liberal theologian can say, "After all, there is no such thing as an absolute, and specifically the Bible does not give absolutes," or the evangelical can reach over into middle-class standards and say, "These standards are equal to the absolutes of the Word of God." In other words, the absolutes of the Word of God can be destroyed in both directions.

● What are the more important facts about Christianity? Which of these facts or "contents" are vital to an understanding of salvation? What are the most important contents to tell a person who doesn't know Christ?

What other non-biblical absolutes have some Christians added to the Gospel? Have you added any? How can you avoid adding non-essentials to the Gospel?

●● How does Gospel message content affect salvation? What do you think are the most essential doctrines to be believed for salvation?

How can you teach these doctrines to the non-believers around you?

Give a few examples of how Christians sometimes add non-biblical content to the Gospel and then make it seem necessary for salvation. Why do they do this? How can you avoid making this mistake?

●●● What doctrines are a necessary part of the Gospel message? Must these all be believed, in order to be truly saved?

What is the danger in the "acceptance of Christ as Savior" without basic content understanding? How can this danger be avoided?

What non-biblical "absolutes" have evangelicals sometimes added to the Gospel? How can these be eliminated?

What exactly is the content of the Gospel message? Schaeffer has suggested several specific things. Michael Green, Anglican theologian and educator, Principal of St. John's College, Nottingham, England, offered the following observations on the content of the Gospel message among the first Christians.

Throughout the Gospel of Mark, Hebrews, the Pauline Letters, 1 Peter, and Acts, it is possible to discern the main bones of much early Christian preaching: The age of fulfillment has dawned. God has at last sent His Messiah, Jesus. He died in shame upon a cross. He rose again from the tomb and is even now Lord, seated at the Father's right hand. The proof of His vindication lies in the gift of the Holy Spirit. And He will come again to judge the world at the conclusion of human history. Therefore, repent, believe, and be baptized into Christ and joined to the church.

In particular, it was the death and resurrection (never the one without the other) of Jesus that formed the focus of their message. This Jesus, who had tasted death for every man, and Himself had taken responsibility for human wrongdoing, was alive indeed; He was enthroned in the universe. As such, He offered both pardon and power to those who committed themselves to Him. The long-awaited Spirit of God was His gift to believers.

The preaching demanded a response. This was not something shallow or emotional, but it touched the conscience, illuminated the understanding, brought the will into submission, and transformed the subsequent life. It was nothing less than a new birth.

17

What was the content of the Gospel message among the first Christians? Why do you think these particular facts were included? Are these facts still important for today's world? Re-read Schaeffer's comments. Notice what he said about the content of our message.

What should be the content of your Gospel message for your unsaved friends?

●●

What did the early church preach as the Gospel? Compare what Shaeffer said should be the content of our message with what Green said was the message of the early church. Why are there similarities and differences between these two?

What should determine the content of the Gospel message for non-believers today?

●●●

Compare the content of the Gospel message proclaimed by the early church with what Schaeffer said. What differences and similarities do you see? How do you account for these?

Draw up your own list of the necessary Gospel content for today's world. How would varying socio-cultural factors affect this list?

The comments of John R. W. Stott, Anglican rector of All Souls Church, London, provided another perspective on the meaning of salvation.

13 *Stott*

Salvation by faith in Christ crucified and risen is moral not material, a deliverance from *sin*, not from *harm*. The reason Jesus said, "Your faith has saved you" (see Mark 5:34, 10:52; Luke 17:19) is that His works of physical rescue, e.g., from disease, drowning and death (see also Matthew 8:25; Mark 15:30, 31) were intentional "signs" of His salvation and were understood by the early church to be such.

Humanization, development, wholeness, liberation, justice, etc., do not constitute the "salvation" which God is offering the world in and through Christ. To call socio-political liberation "salvation" is to mix what Scripture keeps distinct — God the Creator and God the Redeemer, justice and justification, common grace and saving grace, the reformation of society and the regeneration of man. If biblical "salvation" is neither psycho-physical wholeness nor socio-political liberation, it is a personal freedom from sin and its consequences which brings many wholesome consequences in terms both of health and of social responsibility. In many ways, "liberation" (personal, not economic or political) is a good modern word for "salvation" because it not only alludes to the rescue we sinners need, but it also hints at the "liberty" into which the liberated are brought.

Scripture lays its emphasis not on our rescue from wrath, from self, from decay, but on the freedom which this rescue will bring — freedom to approach God as our Father (Romans 8:14-17; Galatians 4:4-7), freedom to give ourselves in service (Romans 6:22; 2 Corinthians 4:5), and finally the "freedom of glory" (1 Thessalonians 5:8; cf. Romans 8:24), when, rid of all the limitations of our flesh-and-blood existence, we can devote ourselves without reserve to God and to each other.

C. René Padilla of Argentina, editor of *Certeza*, a university student-oriented magazine in Latin America, and Associate General Secretary for the International Fellowship of Evangelical Students in Latin America, had additional comments on the meaning of salvation. Notice the breadth of Padilla's view of the meaning of the Gospel, salvation, and evangelism.

The Gospel of Jesus Christ is a personal message — it reveals a God who calls each one of His own by name. But it is also a cosmic message — it reveals a God whose purpose includes the whole world. It is not addressed to the individual *per se*, but to the individual as a member of the old humanity in Adam, marked by sin and death. God calls him to be integrated into the new humanity in Christ, marked by righteousness and eternal life.

The lack of appreciation of the worldwide dimension of the Gospel leads inevitably to a misunderstanding of the mission of the church. The result is an evangelism that regards the individual as a self-contained unit — a Robinson Crusoe to whom God's call is addressed as on an island — whose salvation takes place exclusively in terms of a relationship to God. But the individual does not exist in isolation; consequently it is not possible to speak of salvation without reference to the world of which the individual is a part.

To evangelize, then, is not merely to offer an experience of freedom from the sense of guilt, as if Christ were a super-psychiatrist and His saving power separate from His Lordship. To evangelize is to proclaim Christ Jesus as Lord and Savior, by whose work man is delivered from both the guilt and the power of sin and integrated into God's plan to put all things under the rule of Christ. (See Colossians 1:13, 2:15; Ephesians 1:20-22; Philippians 2:9-11; 1 Peter 3:22.)

Without the proclamation of Jesus Christ as Lord of all, in the light of whose universal authority all values of the present age become relative, there is no true evangelism. To evangelize is to proclaim Jesus Christ as the One who is reigning today and who will continue to reign "until He has put all His enemies under His feet" (1 Corinthians 15:25).

The relation between the Gospel and repentance is such that preaching the Gospel is equivalent to preaching "repentance and forgiveness of sins" (Luke 24:47), or to testifying "of repentance to God and of faith in our Lord Jesus Christ" (Acts 20:21). Without this call to repentance there is no Gospel. And repentance is not merely a matter of a bad conscience — the "worldly grief" that produced death (2 Corinthians 7:10) — but a change of attitude, a restructuring of one's scale of values, and a reorientation of the whole personality.

This call to repentance throws into perspective the social dimension of the Gospel. It comes to man enslaved by sin in a specific social situation, not to a "sinner," in the abstract. It is a change of attitude that becomes concrete in history. It is a turning from sin to God, not only in the individual's subjective consciousness, but in the world.

If Jesus Christ is Lord, men must be confronted with His authority over the totality of life. Evangelism is not, and cannot be, a mere offer of benefits achieved by Jesus Christ. Christ's work is inseparable from His person; the Jesus who died for our sins is the Lord of the whole universe, and the announcement of forgiveness in His name is inseparable from the call to repentance, the call to return from "the rulers of this world" to the Lord of glory.

Salvation includes the whole man and cannot be reduced to the simple forgiveness of sins and assurance of unending life with God in heaven. Salvation is wholeness. Salvation is eternal *life* — the life of the Kingdom of God — life that begins here and now (and this is the meaning of the present tense of the verb *"has* eternal life" in the Gospel and the letters of John) and touches all aspects of man's being.

●

In what ways are the ideas of Padilla, Green, Schaeffer, and Stott different, and yet similar to each other?

Why is repentance a part of the Gospel? What does a person do to repent? How is he different because of his repentance?

What effects should salvation have on a life now?

How would you explain the Gospel to an unbeliever?

●●

What does it mean that the Gospel relates to the individual *and* to his whole world?

Why is liberation from the powers of darkness so vital to the Gospel? What makes liberation possible?

Why are repentance and the Lordship of Christ so important to the Gospel message?

How should repentance and Christ's Lordship affect your life?

What does Padilla add to what Green and Schaeffer have said?

●●●

What are salvation, the Gospel, and evangelism according to Padilla? How do his ideas compare with those of Green and Schaeffer?

What makes repentance and the Lordship of Christ vital to the Gospel?

Why has evangelicalism often been criticized for its individualism and lack of social concern? How does Padilla's view overcome this criticism?

What are the elements of the Gospel that you should proclaim?

You have studied the message of the Gospel. How is the Gospel affecting your world through you?

Do you know the essentials of what you believe? Can you share your belief verbally with others? Think through and discuss ways to relate your faith in Christ to those around you.

Nature

How much do we know of God apart from His special revelation in Scripture? Does God reveal Himself through nature? Do people everywhere know about God? How much can they know? Susumu Uda addressed himself to these questions at the International Congress on World Evangelization. He pointed out that nature has its limitations as a source of knowledge about God. But the "God of nature" is a point of contact between a Christian and a non-Christian.

Uda

The opening verses of the Epistle to the Hebrews inform us that it has pleased God to reveal Himself in "various ways." Throughout the history of the church, God's revelation has come to be commonly understood under two categories, namely, *general* and *special* revelation. Down through the centuries it has been an integral part of the teaching of the church that the Scripture teaches that God has revealed Himself in His works of creation. On the basis of the so-called "nature psalms" (Psalms 8, 19, 65, 104) as well as other passages such as John 1:3; Acts 14:17, 17:24; Romans 1:18-20, 2:14, the church has proclaimed that God always surrounds all of mankind 1) in human existence, 2) in the whole structure of nature, and 3) in God's providential government of human history. And this general revelation has long been taken as the basis of the church's assertion of the moral responsibility of all the human race, and also as the *point of contact* for the evangelistic call to repentance. However today, as we attempt to understand the exact *nature* and *meaning* of this general revelation, opinion differs and we find the situation is not so simple.

In Romans 1, general revelation is placed in a specific context. Sinful and fallen man is still surrounded by the light of general revelation, but this same man pollutes and misunderstands this light and suppresses it in unrighteousness (verse 18). This same man substitutes the image of a perishable man for the majesty of the eternal God (verse 23). And then he honors and worships the creature above the real Creator (verse 25).

Because of this, man stands under the wrath of God in the state of guilt (verse 18). Thus the context of Romans 1 shows that it is not permissible to separate natural man's knowledge of God from the dark aspect of his fickleness; and it is not right to talk about the value of general revelation without considering the anger of God, which condemns man's rejection of the truth and preference for unrighteousness. What Romans 1 makes clear is that the light of general revelation does not lead man to the knowledge of the true God; the kind of knowledge which the natural man has is a knowledge which, as a fatal consequence of sin, is transformed into the illusion of idolatry!

The natural man, allowing no authority to stand over him, thinks of himself as the ultimate judge of what can or cannot be. The facts of man's environment are not recognized as created or controlled by the providence of God. Instead, the universe is seen as controlled by chance. So as soon as there is any discussion between the Christian and the non-Christian about something which involves principle, the radical difference between them immediately appears. Any evangelistic effort which does not reckon with this decisive difference will be thwarted, and concessions to please the mind of the natural man can be no part of real Christian strategy.

In Romans 1 Paul makes clear that man, even in his sinful state, does not stand outside of any connection with the light of God's law and His ordinances for the preservation of human life.

In Romans 2:14 it is stated that the Gentiles are "without the law" and "have not the law" in the sense of specially revealed law (in other words, the Law of Moses). Nevertheless, 1) they are confronted by the law of God in their consciousness by reason of their nature, 2) they do things which this law prescribes, and 3) this doing is not by external constraint but by natural impulse. Verse 15 further states that not only does the doing of the things of the law prove that the work of the law is written in their hearts, but the witness of *conscience* also does. This conscience is certainly not to be viewed as an ever-changing something. Paul saw that even in the Gentile world people in one way or another are preserved from the full consequences of their alienation from God. In other words, there is still a witnessing of the law written in the hearts of men who neither know God nor serve Him. And man, being compelled to take note of this, cannot escape from the goodness of the preserving and ruling God and His holy law.

Today it seems to be a common thing to talk about the "death of God" and the subsequent disappearance of absolute moral standards. It must be noted that human life, even in its present radical estrangement from God, has not completely passed into meaninglessness and lawlessness. By God's preserving grace there are still standards for right and justice, for punishing evil and rewarding good (Romans 13:3-4). There is still appreciation for community, love, and social welfare. There is still a searching for a new humanism. In Japan the fact that new religious sects have mushroomed to a remarkable extent since the war strongly witnesses to the unrest of people's hearts. They are searching for a way to truer humanness and more dependable values. Their search will not end until they rest in God. Hence, in the midst of the ongoing secularism and pluralism in our society, the church must call attention to the doctrine of general revelation as a reminder that God, because of His love, still holds human life and does not abandon the world (John 3:16; Colossians 1:17).

If you have not done so already, read some of the Scripture that deals with natural revelation: Psalms 8, 19, 65, 104; John 1:3-9; Acts 14:15-17; Romans 1:18-32, 2:14-16. What does Scripture say can be known about God by God's general revelation to all men?

Why do people usually refuse to believe God's truth? Why does this rejection make witnessing more difficult?

What knowledge of God do the people have in your community? How have they distorted what they see? How can you best use their knowledge as a starting point for conversations about God?

Why do people usually reject the truth about God? How does this rejection of God's natural revelation make evangelism more difficult?

What are some predictable ways that people distort what they know about God?

How have people around you distorted their knowledge of God? What must be added to a person's limited knowledge of God as a starting point for your witness?

Why is general or natural revelation an insufficient source of the knowledge of God?

How do men today distort natural revelation? In what way can their limited and even distorted knowledge of God be a starting point for evangelism? Why is general revelation inadequate for evangelism?

Harold Lindsell, editor of *Christianity Today*, presented another viewpoint about the knowledge of God provided through natural revelation.

Lindsell

Scripture makes it clear that three lights provide guidance for men: the light of nature, the light of the law, the light of the Gospel (Romans 1-3). There are people who have heard the Gospel but rejected the Savior. There are those who are familiar with the ten commandments (the law), and have the light of nature or of human conscience. Yet they are lost if they have rejected the light. But what about those who know neither the law of God nor the Gospel?

First, let it be said that anyone who really wants to know God — even though he has no particular knowledge of the law or the Gospel — will be given the opportunity to hear of Christ and to receive Him as Savior. Unsaved people have welcomed the advent of missionaries with the Gospel message and indicated that they have been looking for them to come. One way or another God in His mercy will make known what the unsaved need to know if they really wish to know God.

Let us suppose for a moment that there are those who never received any knowledge of the Gospel or of the law of God, and they die this way. Are they then lost forever? The very least that anyone ever has by way of the knowledge of God is the light of nature or the law of conscience written in the hearts of all men. This indeed may be the light that lighteth every man that cometh into the world. In Romans 1, Paul argues that "what can be known about God is plain to them [Gentiles, i.e., people without the law] because God has shown it to them. Ever since the creation of the world His invisible nature, namely His eternal power and deity, has been clearly perceived in the things that have been made. So they are without excuse." "All who have sinned without the law will also perish without the law . . . When Gentiles who have not the law do by nature what the law requires, they are a law to themselves, even though they do not have the law. They show that the law is written on their hearts, while their conscience also bears witness and their conflicting thoughts accuse or perhaps excuse them . . . both Jews and Greeks, are under the power of sin . . . none is righteous, no, not one" (from Romans 2 and 3). Whatever may be the human situation, and however strongly we might wish that things were different, it appears clear that Scripture teaches that even people whose knowledge is limited to the light of nature or conscience are forever lost if they die without the saving knowledge of Jesus Christ.

●

What is the "light of nature"? How does it help people to know about God? Why is no one able to say, "I didn't know about God"?

● ●

On what basis does Lindsell teach that truth about God is available to all people?

What is your reaction when you think about people who are lost forever without Christ?

● ● ●

What differences do you see between what Uda and Lindsell said about natural revelation?

With which emphasis do you agree, and why?

Men everywhere tend to be religious even though they may not accept the one true God of Christianity. Uda cited Paul's address at Mars Hill (Acts 17:16-34) to call attention to man's religious nature.

At the beginning of his address, Paul's attention is focused upon the religious devotion of the Athenians, "I perceive that in every way you are very religious" (verse 22). His insight into their religiousness was mainly due to his view of the nature of man as the creature in the image of God and therefore made to respond to his Creator (Genesis 1:26-27). According to Paul's understanding, no matter how false or inadequate the Gentile religion might be as a consequence of sin, nevertheless its very existence was a confirmation of the fact that man still retained his fundamental character as a religiously responsible being. Man, even in his most extreme aberrations, does not release himself from the light of God's revelation. Man possesses an indelible "sense of deity," so that no man might shelter himself under the pretext of ignorance.

Paul evaluates the religion of the Athenians as one of *ignorance* (verse 23). He says, in effect, "That which you worship in open ignorance, I proclaim unto you in knowledge." In saying so he does not mean to complete what the Athenians already possess of true religion. On the contrary, what they acknowledge as ignorance about God has a far deeper meaning for Paul. He clearly makes contact with the Greek mind by way of the altar and the unknown God; his point of contact is the *ignorance* of the Greeks. He sees their ignorance more profoundly than they do. He calls them to repentance and conversion from this ignorance. Thus, Paul maintains a clear-cut distinction between the Christian Gospel and pagan idolatry (cf. his same consistent attitude at Lystra in Acts 14:14ff). Paul is neither accommodating his Gospel to Greek religiosity nor saying that the peculiarities of their religion are simply special forms of the common essence.

Paul proclaims God as one who is fundamentally unknown to them. Paul well knows that the tendency to create gods in man's own image, as had occurred in the idol worship of the Old Testament, lies in all of the so-called religions of men. And what man achieves by religion is never the true knowledge of God, but only a fiction that has nothing to do with reality. As man cannot, dare not, see himself as he is, he cannot and will not see God as He really is.

The declaration that God is "Lord of heaven and earth," and "does not live in shrines made by man" (verse 24) is a reflection of 1 Kings 8:27 and is the very point which Stephen affirmed (Acts 7:48). Being keenly aware of the Greek's view of the universe as basically one without a clear distinction between the Creator-God and the creature, Paul here witnesses to the important fact that only in the biblical outlook does the doctrine of the sovereign Creator and Ruler come to the fullest expression without any compromise.

●

Why do people everywhere believe in some sort of god?

Why do you think Paul talked about the "unknown God" to the people in Athens? Do you think Paul was suggesting that those people had found a little of God's truth?

Why do people tend to reject the truth about God that is in nature and in their own religious feelings? Why do people so easily worship false gods?

Why must Christians bring a special message about Christ to all people? What is your responsibility in this?

●●

What was the common point of contact between Christianity and the Greeks in Acts 17? How did Paul make use of this single point?

Did Paul mean that the Athenians possessed some truth about God? Why?

Why does man's religious nature make every person responsible for some knowledge of God? Why do most people reject that knowledge?

Why must Christians, like Paul, bring more detailed information of God's special revelation to all people?

●●●

Is there any commonality between Christianity and any other religion? If so, what is it? If not, why not?

Can you find a principle in Paul's "unknown God" approach that would facilitate Christian evangelism of non-Christian religions today?

What does Paul's appeal to special revelation in terms of his own experiences with Christ imply about natural revelation? How much of the Gospel can natural revelation communicate? Why is special revelation necessary?

People without special knowledge of God are lost. This is one of the driving forces behind evangelism — men without Christ are doomed. If you truly believe this, what are you doing about it? What should your peer group be doing?

Relevance

Sometimes we hear non-Christians complain that Christianity is irrelevant. They tell us that such an ancient book as the Bible has nothing to say to twentieth century people. They conclude that unscientific tribal people, nomads, and farmers from the dim past could not provide a book of great wisdom for our complex era. Is the Bible relevant for today?

At the International Congress on World Evangelization, N. P. Anderson, principal of the Melbourne Bible Institute in Australia, asked the important question, "Is Christianity relevant today?" Can Scripture speak as clearly to the needs of the present and the future as it did to the needs of the past? He answered by showing how the principles of biblical Christianity can be applied to all people in four areas of life.

The first area was worship. Here we see the need and meaning of worship as more important than the ways in which people express worship.

Anderson

Worship is a vital area of Christian life and experience and yet one in which the vitality of reality seems to have disappeared and "form" or "tradition" have taken control.

The people of God are not simply a collection of individuals, but a gathered people needing to meet together to fellowship and to pray. If this experience is to be real to the member and the outsider, somehow the expression of its "worth" must be clear. The experience must say what we know about the meaning of life and what we are trying to be because we are the people of God. The role of worship must be to reflect the believer's response to the truth of God — it must be vertical before it can be horizontal. Karl Marx wrote of man's alienation from man; the Scripture talks of man's alienation from God. Worship, irrespective of its pattern, must first and foremost give opportunity to express man's gratitude and joy that God has taken the initiative in the restoration of this relationship. It must be objective.

It must also give expression to the wonder of faith, i.e., the personal trust of the individual in God through Christ. It must be subjective.

Further, worship must be intimate enough to develop the "fellowship" of the Gospel in the way that bridges race, social status, education, and even language.

The form of a worship service will vary from culture to culture. So long as it helps the worshiper in the problem of values and meaning in life, and helps him to relate to the only source whereby these can be evaluated, form is functioning in its proper role.

In a study of the history of worship it is of interest to note the radical change from the Middle Ages to the Post-Reformation era. Changes in music in response to changing times have left the church with a vast heritage by which to praise God in worship. Popular music from the secular world today is having its influence on sacred music, not however without conflict and controversy. The question is raised, "What is wrong with it if it speaks to the modern man as older forms of music no longer do?" The confusion of thought here is intensified because frequently the champions of old versus new sit on either side of a generation gap. We have to recognize that the music of the early twentieth century church is very different from that of the church of 500 years ago. Is change in worship forms wrong, or does it merely represent changes in the culture as they are reflected in our emotional response to God? Does a change in architecture reflect anything about worship, or are we simply in the hand of the technician? Is the sermon-centered form of worship viable for our day, or is it a relic of an age now gone? These thoughts only begin to reflect the immensity of the question.

Our vertical relationship with God in worship must control our horizontal relationships with people. When this occurs, the form of the horizontal can change from group to group, age to age, and remain vital and relevant.

●

What is the purpose of worship? How does your church encourage worship?

Does a building or room affect how you feel about God? How does music affect your worship experience?

Why should the worship of God include people of other ages, races, social positions, educational levels, and languages?

What helps you to worship God more effectively? What could you do to help others worship more effectively?

● ●

Why do we worship God? What are some of the ways we worship God? Are there any absolutes (things that must be done, or must not be done) in the worship of God?

How do architecture and music affect worship?

How does the Holy Spirit help make worship meaningful?

Have you ever considered the *relevancy* of worship? What makes worship relevant to your needs?

● ● ●

Why have form and tradition become more emphasized than substance and vitality in so much of our worship? What is the role of the sermon in worship?

To what degree is worship culturally relative? What are the essential, supracultural elements of worship? What responsibility do church leaders, e.g., pastor, choir director, etc., have in making worship relevant to various segments of the congregation?

Anderson spoke next about ethical behavior — how we can know what is right and wrong.

He contrasted biblical ethics, based on principles of absolute right and wrong, with "situational ethics." Teachers of situational ethics say that right and wrong depend on each particular situation.

Joseph Fletcher's book *Situation Ethics* is a typical example of modern attempts to find an answer to behavior questions when the authority of God is removed. Nothing is universally right or wrong. Only one thing is intrinsically good — love — and love is defined as being the same thing as justice.

Biblical principles of ethics are a forceful part of revelation, and no amount of cultural relativity can be claimed in order to escape the implications of the revelation. Godliness is essential to ethics; this is the message of both Old Testament and New Testament. Biblical principles leave us no choice; we are absolutists.

Another issue remains to be considered. Are all the codes of behavior, dress, etc., always related to these absolutes? Once again we note a variety of answers from different cultural groups. Many different patterns of behavior are good. It is important to try to determine which matters are fundamental and which are cultural. Too often biblical truth is saddled with concepts which are purely social, and yet people cling to them with great eagerness.

The intrinsic value of the moral laws of Scripture needs to be made clear. The true nature of God must be proclaimed along with these great ethical themes.
1) The right to life (homicide, euthanasia, abortion, suicide).
2) Sex as God-given in marriage (homosexuality, adultery, pre-marital intercourse, prostitution, lust).
3) Freedom (racism, slavery, worship, expression of opinion).
4) Truth, honesty (stealing, false witness).
5) Envy, jealousy, hatred (the sins of the spirit and of motive).
6) The community responsibility, the strong help the weak, place no cause of stumbling.
7) Marriage, divorce.
It must be admitted that some of these are open to interpretation, but the basic norms are there. They relate to the Being of God and man's relationship to God.

●

What happens to our concepts of *right* and *wrong* if the authority of God is removed?

Why are evangelicals called "absolutists"? Does this mean that evangelicals teach that everyone should do things the same way?

Are codes of behavior, dress, etc., based on God's authority or society's?

How do you decide what is right or wrong? If God's Word does not specifically say that something is either right or wrong, how should you decide what to do?

● ●

Why is the authority of God so important to our ethical decisions?

What does it mean to be an "absolutist"?

Does this imply that everyone should behave as we do?

What is our authority for behavior and dress codes?

How do you decide ethical questions when the Bible does not give direct guidance one way or the other?

● ● ●

When biblical authority is removed what is substituted as the basis for ethical decision-making?

How can biblical ethics influence decision making on matters that the Bible does not explicitly declare to be either right or wrong?

How do biblical ethics relate to each of the seven areas listed?

Evangelism was the third area of Anderson's lecture. Note how he separated the *task* of evangelism, proclaiming God's absolute truth, from the various *methods* of evangelism.

Anderson

The vehicle which carries God's truth to man is evangelism — the proclamation of God's existence, of man's relationship to God, of man's destruction of that relationship, of God's initiative to deal with man's revolt, and of God's offer to man of His salvation.

Christ told His disciples that He was "truth"; He taught that the Holy Spirit was the "Spirit of Truth" and would lead His followers into truth. This is part of the Bible's testimony to God as the source of all truth. Today man is busy trying to forget that this is so. Some theologians have said that God is dead and truth is relative.

The meaning of words is twisted and warped. However, we have to use words for the message of evangelism; we must be able to convey truth, even ultimate truth about God. It is against this backdrop of worldwide confusion of the meaning of words and truth that evangelism must stand and declare God as the judge of culture and as ultimate truth.

Evangelism has power at its disposal — "but you shall receive power when the Holy Spirit comes upon you" — "the Gospel is God's power unto salvation" — "so that your faith might be built, not upon human wisdom, but on the power of God" (Acts 1:8; Romans 1:16; 1 Cor. 2:5).

But, in the methodology of evangelism, culture can and should play a part. Some time ago Bishop Chandu Ray of Singapore reported on the new life which was coming to evangelism in Asian countries when the concept of using Western patterns was no longer regarded as binding. Proclamation in some areas became a "family" matter, because the family was the basic unit of the community. The content of the Gospel message has an amazing capacity to be translated to different cultures. The methodology needs to recognize the cultural channels. When this is accepted, the timeless, God-given message begins to pulsate with life.

The Bible does not make any one culture or society a model for all others to follow. Why not? What does this suggest about evangelizing your peers?

Do you know people who require a special approach?

Why are *words* so important in evangelism? Do words always mean the same thing to all people? What does this imply for evangelism?

What people near you require a special approach if you are to win them to Christ? What kind of approach would be likely to win them?

The questions of epistemology, communication theory, and cultural relativity are crucial in Anderson's comments. Briefly, what are your own biblical views in those three areas? How are each of these areas related to evangelism?

How can we "up-date" the message of evangelism without losing its basic meaning?

Anderson's final comments centered on service to the world. He stated that personal salvation relates to responsible social action.

Anderson

Biblical theology shows that both individual conversion and social justice are indispensable. Personal holiness and social responsibility are closely linked.

The Bible reveals "a new man" who is committed to love of neighbor. The biblical doctrines of God having made man in His image and of God's ceaseless activity of redemption open up an area of responsibility which the early church accepted.

Problems of race, poverty, war, overpopulation, and ecology need an overall strategy. Giving "the cup of cold water" must be intensified to meet the needs of individuals at their moments of suffering. The greater strategy to help eradicate or reduce evil calls for vision and planning by those who are trained to see the need and capable of response. This must not be separated from the fact of man's greatest need. The vertical relationship must be proclaimed before the horizontal can be projected, "Thou shalt love the Lord thy God . . . and thy neighbor as thyself."

A Christian doctrine of service in the world must be God-centered; it reaches out to meet the total need of the total man. For all of this, it must be empowered by the Holy Spirit. It will then express true compassion — a compassion growing out of true understanding, out of outrage that sees wrong and evil as God sees it, and out of an identification fired by love — forceful, practical, effective.

30

●

"Saved to serve" might be a good summary phrase for what you have just read. Why does living a godly life imply helping other people?

Think of a particular social problem that is affecting some of the people that you know about. How can you find a way to be helpful in their need?

In what way is your action a natural part of evangelism?

● ●

Why should Christians be involved in helping others? Explain the relationship between "holy living" and social conscience.

What do you think is involved in "social responsibility"?

How can you and your group help people in need?

What can you do to alleviate social evil?

● ● ●

How are personal salvation and social justice related? Why should Christians be involved in more than simply proclaiming personal salvation? Why are so few involved in extensive evangelism?

As you see it, what are the more important tests of relevancy for the Gospel today?

In this section you have examined the question of how Christianity can be relevant and meaningful to people everywhere regardless of their age, sex, race, or culture. The Bible is relevant, biblical ethics are relevant, and evangelism is relevant. Through their everyday walk, the children of God demonstrate God's truth — by word and by action.

Universalism

Who will be saved? Will all men, regardless of what they believe about Jesus Christ, eventually be saved? *Universalism* teaches that a God of love would never condemn anyone to hell. They believe that even the concept of hell is ridiculous and immoral. Universalists claim that since Christ has already "completed His work," salvation and heaven will be enjoyed by everybody, Christians, Buddhists, Muslims, atheists, and agnostics, alike. All roads eventually lead to God. Christ is not the "One Way" to God. By this teaching, the distinctives of Christianity are lost in the diffused "broad-mindedness" of universalism.

The International Congress on World Evangelization dealt squarely with universalism. Several speakers presented the evangelical response to universalism. Dr. Donald McGavran gave this overview.

McGavran

Nothing affects world evangelism more than what the Bible teaches concerning the possibility of salvation of men through their adherence to various ideologies and religions. Today it has become popular in some sections of the church to affirm that men can be saved through sincere adherence to the best they know. God is at work, we are told, in the whole range of human experience. All that Christians need to do is to dialogue with people of other religions and move amiably forward in a joint search for God. Biblical evangelism holds that such a view is erroneous. The only salvation of which the apostles speak is that which comes through faith in Jesus Christ. To our own children, and to those of our Jewish, Buddhist, Marxist, Hindu, **Muslim, and** secularist friends alike, we declare that there is "no other Name." Christ alone is the Door. He alone is the Truth. He alone is Life. As ambassadors appointed by Christ, we beseech them all to be reconciled to God and become active members of the Body of Christ.

31

Billy Graham, in the opening meeting of the Lausanne Congress, also called attention to universalism and the biblical reply to it.

Graham

In some ecclesiastical circles, the postwar years have shown a steady trend toward universalism. Some have openly taught that there are many ways to God, that ultimately no one is lost. The vast permissiveness of our day has left its stain on the church. For these people, it is not "Christ the One Way," according to God's revelation, but many ways, according to one's culture and inclination. To all this evangelicals must return a resounding "No." Our Lord said, "No man comes to the Father but by me" (John 14:6). Scripture declares, "Neither is there salvation in any other: for there is none other name under heaven given among men, whereby we must be saved" (Acts 4:12).

Universalism begins with the Christian view that the Gospel offer is to all men — a universal message. So the universalist argues that since God wills that all be saved and since the Gospel is a universal proclamation, all will be saved regardless of their personal beliefs. C. René Padilla commented on this kind of thinking.

Obviously, God's salvation in Christ Jesus is universal in scope. But the universality of the Gospel must not be confused with the universalism of contemporary theologians who hold that, on the basis of the work of Christ, all men will receive eternal life, whatever their position about Christ. The benefits obtained by Christ are inseparable from the Gospel and, consequently, can only be received *in* and *through* the Gospel. To preach the Gospel is not only to proclaim an accomplished fact, but to proclaim the accomplished fact and, *simultaneously*, to make a call to faith. The proclamation of Jesus as "the Savior of the world" is not an affirmation that all men are automatically saved, but rather an invitation to all men to put their confidence in the One who gave His life for the sin of the world. "Christ does not save us apart from faith, faith does not restore us apart from Christ. He became one with us; we have to become one with Him. Without the affirmation of this double process of self-identification and of the results that follow it, there is no complete exposition of the Gospel." (Vincent Taylor, p. 273, *Forgiveness and Reconciliation,*" London, 1941)

●

What is universalism? Why do some people hold universalist beliefs? Why don't evangelicals accept universalism?

Why did the apostles preach the Gospel *and* invite people to respond to the Gospel? How did the actions of the apostles show that they did not believe that all men would eventually be saved?

●●

What are some arguments for universalism? On the basis of Scripture, what are the problems with universalism?

Why does Padilla say that preaching the Gospel requires both proclamation *and* a call to faith?

Are all men "in Christ" regardless of their beliefs?

What biblical evidence shows that Jesus Christ is the exclusive way to God?

●●●

What are some underlying premises of universalism regarding man's knowledge of God and the authority of Scripture?

What does the New Testament proclamation of the Gospel *and* the call to faith teach about universalism?

On what premise does Jesus claim to be the only way to God?

What happens to our theology if we deny Jesus' exclusive position? Is universalism Christian?

At the Congress, Harold Lindsell directed his whole paper to the subject of universalism.

There are no new heresies, just old ones dressed up in new garb. Universalism, the notion that ultimately all men will be saved and enjoy the eternal bliss of heaven, has antecedents that go back to Origen, who lived from 185-254 A.D. Origen theorized that all men and even fallen angels would be redeemed at last. His view received little acceptance in the church and was repudiated in the great creeds of the church and in the pronouncements of church councils. Traditionally, the Roman Catholic church, the Orthodox churches, and Protestantism have rejected universalism.

From Origen's time until the nineteenth century universalism was virtually dormant. It became a live option in the United States in New England. The Universalist churches that were formed went far beyond a renunciation of eternal punishment and of the doctrine of hell. Within a short time they denied many if not most of the major tenets of the orthodox faith including the Trinity, the deity of Jesus Christ, and the infallibility of the written Word of God.

Advocates of universalism, or those who refuse to cast a decisive vote against it, are to be found in almost every large denomination and among key leaders from all parts of the world. Universalism is not a Western idea nor is it limited to the churches of Western Christendom. It is to be found most widely in the modern ecumenical movement, and its presence, as we shall see, has altered the concept of mission and has wrought extensive damage to the missionary outreach of the church.

Many voices among Protestants have been raised in the propagation and defense of universalism. As a result of this neo-universalism there has been a radical shift in the definition of the mission of the church. Nowhere has this been more obvious than in the ecumenical movement, and particularly in the Commission on World Mission and Evangelism of the World Council of Churches. In the 1963 Mexico City meetings, and more recently in Bangkok in December of 1972, it was quite apparent that the central thrust of the conferences was based upon a commitment to changing the social, economic, and political structures of society. This was based, in turn, upon the underlying assumption that all men are now in Christ and only need to be informed of what is already true. Such being the case there is no reason why the mission of the church should not be redefined, personal evangelism neglected, and improving the temporal conditions of men made the focal point of reference. Both at Mexico City and Bangkok it was clear, however, that there are some within the World Council of Churches who still believe in a heaven and a hell, that men in their unbelief are not in Christ, and that those who do not experience the new birth are forever lost and undone.

How widespread is universalism? Where is it particularly strong? Do you think universalism has had a comeback? Why?

What Christian beliefs are challenged by universalists?

Where is universalism particularly making itself felt?

Why do you think universalism has revived?

What basic doctrines of Christianity are discarded by universalists?

What caused the revival of universalism in the nineteenth century? What theological issues does universalism seek to solve? What theological issues does universalism create?

Lindsell

There are only three possibilities with respect to the question of universalism. They are 1) nobody is saved; 2) everybody is saved; 3) some are saved and some are lost. Option one is obviously false and no further discussion of it is required. That leaves us with two options: all are saved, or only some are saved.

Several Bible passages throw light on the question of universalism. They help us decide if some people are eternally saved and others are eternally lost. Read each passage listed below to determine its relationship to universalism. Universalists cite these passages to support their beliefs. What do you understand from these texts?

John 12:32
Acts 3:21
Romans 5:18
1 Corinthians 15:24-28

2 Corinthians 5:19
1 Timothy 2:3-4
Titus 2:11
Hebrews 2:9

2 Peter 3:9
1 John 2:2

In contrast, many evangelicals point to the following verses as evidence against universalism.

Matthew 25:46	Luke 16:19-31	Romans 2:8-9
Matthew 28:19-20	John 3:16, 18, 36	1 John 5:11-12
Mark 9:47-48	John 5:24, 28, 29	Revelation 20:7-15
Luke 12:5	John 14:6	

Lindsell pointed out that accepting universalism leads to several conclusions. Assuming for a moment that universalists are right, then:

1) There is no hell, no lake of fire, and no eternal punishment.

2) There is no genuine freedom of choice. If all are saved there is no real power of contrary choice.

3) Whatever force is connected with the Great Commission is lost. If everyone is at last to be saved, then the urgency of the Great Commission is gone, and indeed the need for it is removed. All men are already in Christ whether they know it or not. They are going to be saved finally. There is no need for haste, since death without the knowledge of Christ will not keep them from heaven. Whether they stay in their own religions or not, or whether they have no religion at all, ceases to be important.

4) Why should the people of God suffer and sacrifice in going to the ends of the earth when the best they can hope for is to bring some people to a knowledge of the salvation they already have a little bit sooner? And what difference does a few years make in that regard in the light of the eternal ages?

5) Changing the mission of the church to the improvement of the temporal conditions of men is logical and compelling.

6) God forces men into the kingdom against their wills, and He thus becomes a capricious being and man is a virtual automaton.

On the other hand, accepting the evangelical position that some people are eternally lost and others are eternally saved also leads to several conclusions. Assuming that the evangelical position is right, then:

1) Universalism cannot be supported from Scripture and is a heresy.

2) The Scriptures do make a universal *offer* of salvation to all people.

3) God has ordained that people shall be saved through the proclamation of the Gospel. And they will not be saved if the Gospel is not preached. Therefore, it behooves the church of Jesus Christ to preach the Gospel to everyone everywhere so that they may have the opportunity to accept Christ.

4) Those who die without Christ are lost even if they do not know of the law or hear the Gospel.

Lindsell

Lindsell

35

How does each conclusion follow naturally from universalism or evangelicalism?

Which set of conclusions is based on the authority of Scripture?

Which set of conclusions do you accept?

If universalism is heresy and people will go to hell if they do not accept Jesus Christ, what should *you* be doing now to help people near you hear about Him?

Why does Lindsell emphasize the lack of freedom of choice in the universalist position?

In what way is the missionary task of the church related to the question of whether or not everyone is to be saved eventually?

Which set of conclusions (above) is based on accepting biblical authority?

Which conclusions do you accept? In what ways are you acting on your conclusions?

What additional conclusions can you add? Extend both lists if you can.

How is each point a logical outcome of the particular position? Discuss each one.

How do these conclusions affect evangelism? What direct personal effect do Lindsell's evangelical conclusions have on your Christian life?

In summary, John Stott suggests these definitions:

36

1. *Mission.* Mission is a wide term that covers everything God sends the church into the world to do. Christ's church is a servant church. Evangelism and social action are both authentic expressions of loving service.

2. *Evangelism.* Evangelism means "announcing the good news," no more, no less. This good news is Jesus, his death and resurrection as saving events, witnessed to by Scripture, and promising forgiveness and the Spirit to those who repent and believe.

3. *Dialogue.* We welcome dialogue which enables us humbly and sensitively to listen, to understand, and so to witness more meaningfully. But we must reject any dialogue that compromises Christ's uniqueness or our commitment.

4. *Salvation.* Biblical salvation is a personal freedom — rescue *from* judgment, selfcenteredness and death — freedom to give ourselves with joy and without reserve to both God and man. Salvation may lead toward or even motivate socio-political liberation, but salvation is the spiritual freedom that precedes these other consequences.

5. *Conversion.* Conversion is the necessary response to the Gospel, and includes repentance and faith. It involves a renunciation of evil, but not of all inherited culture, nor of the world, for Christ sends us back into it. Conversion is the beginning of an altogether new life, to be lived out in the world.

Contents -2

Acknowledgements

Authors and papers of the International Congress on World Evangelization used in this chapter are as follows:

Henri Blocher, "Our Unity According to the Bible";

Michael Green, "Methods and Strategy in the Evangelism of the Early Church";

C. René Padilla, "Evangelism and the World";

George W. Peters, "Contemporary Practices of Evangelism";

Howard A. Snyder, "The Church as God's Agent of Evangelism."

Church

What does it mean to go to church? You go to a building called a "church." But is this building the church? The church has existed since the First Century. What made those groups of people who met together the church? How did they as the church go about witnessing to the saving and transforming power of Christ? What principles can we learn from the Bible that will help the church today have more life and demonstrate that life in more effective and efficient programs, organization and relationships? How can the church best fulfill its God-given, Christ-directed, and Spirit-empowered work? How can you and your friends, a Sunday School class or groups of Christians *all together*, fit into Christ's plan for His church in today's society?

These questions and issues were a major emphasis of the International Congress on World Evangelization (ICOWE) held in Lausanne, Switzerland, July, 1974. International evangelical leaders gave insight to these and related concerns. As you read, discuss, and decide to act, you will have the benefit of teaching from important papers presented at the Congress.

The section below gives some idea of how important the church really is. As you read, ask yourself, "Why was the church this way and what helped it to be so?" Keep in mind your own experience in church; think about your Sunday School class, youth group, and other activities and responsibilities. How do these ideas relate to the needs in your own church situation?

Michael Green, Anglican theologian and educator, Principal of St. John's College, Nottingham, England, told the Congress . . .

41

Green

When a movement grows from a dozen peasants in an oppressed land, to become the official religion of the Roman Empire inside 300 years; when it is sufficiently independent of that civilization to survive its fall, and indeed the fall of every successive civilization since; when it is universal enough in its appeal to win millions of converts in all sectors of the globe among all types of men, belonging to every race, culture, and personality type — such a movement has something. That movement is Christianity! The church today is heir to the revolutionary forces which changed the face of the world in the decades following the death and resurrection of Jesus.

Read Acts 2:37–47. Here is an important description of the first church. Notice where they met, how often, what they did when they got together, and what others thought about them.

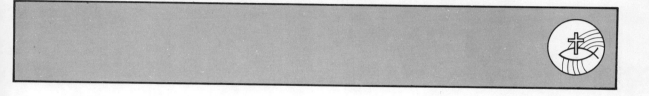

What made the church so great that millions of people have wanted to be part of it?

Are these the same reasons that your church is important to you?

As you think especially of your age group, why would a person want to join your church and your particular group in the church?

List what the church *did* in Acts 2 that made it so strong.

What might happen now if your group were involved in these same things?

On the basis of Acts 2, what would you expect people to do in the church?

What characteristics describe the apostolic church?

How do these define the role, nature and function of the church?

On the basis of this preliminary study, list and describe the elements you would include in a biblical definition of the church.

Some people criticize the church, but few take time to compare their church with a truly successful model. In order to know what a successful church is like, Green has listed several comparisons between the New Testament church and many churches today. As you read Green's ideas, keep looking for similarities to "the church" as you have experienced it.

The early church made evangelism its number one priority. Today for many it comes far down the list. The matter is not deemed sufficiently important.

The early church had a deep compassion for men without Christ. Many sections of the modern church are far from convinced that it much matters whether you have Christ or not. Other religions are nearly if not quite as good a way to God; humanists live blameless lives; and, in any case, it will all come right in the end — God is far too nice to damn anyone.

The early church was very open to the leading of the Holy Spirit; in every evangelistic advance recorded in Acts it is the Spirit who is the motivator and energizer. In much of the modern church of the West managerial skills, committee meetings and endless discussion are thought essential for evangelism; prayer and dependence on the Spirit are optional extras.

The early church was not unduly minister-conscious. Today, in many places everything centers around the minister. The paid servant of the church is expected to engage in God-talk; but no others.

In the early church every man was expected to be a witness to Christ. Today witness is often less valued than dialogue; and it is only expected of certain gifted clergy at best, not of run-of-the-mill Christians.

In the early church, buildings were unimportant; the early church did not have any during the period of their greatest advance. Today buildings are all important; their upkeep consumes the money and interests of the members, often plunges them into debt, and isolates them from those who do not go to church. Indeed, even the word has changed meaning. "Church" no longer means a company of people, as it did in New Testament times; these days it means a building.

In the early church evangelism was a natural, spontaneous sharing of good news; it was engaged in continuously by all types of Christians as a matter of course and of privilege. Today, it is spasmodic, heavily organized, and usually dependent on the skills and enthusiasm of the visiting specialist.

In the early church, the policy was to go out to where people were and make disciples of them. Today it is to invite people to churches, where they do not feel at home, and get them to hear the preaching of the Gospel. Today's church attempts inward invitation, "in-drag"; the early church practiced explosion, invasion, outreach.

In the early church, the Gospel was frequently argued about in the philosophical schools, discussed in the streets, talked over in the laundry. Today it is not discussed very much at all, and certainly not on "secular" ground. It belongs in church, on a Sunday, and a properly ordained minister should do all the talking.

In the early church, whole communities seem to have been converted at once. In the atomized church of the West, individualism has run riot, and evangelism, like much else, tends to come to its climax in a one-to-one encounter.

In the early church, the maximum impact was made by the changed lives and the quality of community among the Christians. Today, much Christian life-style is almost indistinguishable from that of non-Christians, and much church fellowship is conspicuous for its coolness.

●

Green examines evangelism, compassion, leading of the Holy Spirit, etc. How do these New Testament examples apply to your group? Is your group witnessing? Are your teachers, youth sponsors and officers doing all the work?

Do you go to church or do you see yourself as the church?

Decide: What can you do to make your group more like the church in Acts?

Do: How will you do this? Who will do it? When will it be done? How will you know when you have done it?

●●

What are your group's priorities? Compare your priorities with the priorities of the early church.

Consider especially evangelism, leadership, and relevance to people.

Decide: What changes should occur in your group's activities? How will you know if these changes are really making a difference in your group?

Do: Begin to make the changes necessary to help your group reflect the biblical picture of the church of Christ.

●●●

Note the elements of "church" that Green describes as important. Which of these are most important in your situation? What other factors can you add?

Decide: How are you helping others in your group or church to operate as the New Testament suggests?

Do: Add to your list other elements for a biblical definition of the church. In what ways would it help or hinder to specify goals, roles to be fulfilled, strategy to involve others, completion dates and measures to determine if goals are accomplished? Outline a plan to take these steps.

44

Community

You "go to church" on Sunday; the church must be a building. You say, "My church believes such and such"; the church must be its officers and leaders. You say, "We elected church officers"; the church must be an organization. You give money "to the church"; the church must be those who collect and spend the money.

Now, how can all of these be the church? Did Jesus have in mind buildings, officers, money collectors, and organizations when He told His disciples: ". . . I will build my church; and all the powers of hell shall not prevail against it" (Matthew 16:18)? How could Jesus be thinking of what we call the church today?

What is the church? Howard Snyder, Dean of the Free Methodist Seminary in São Paulo, Brazil, an American whose special interest and thinking have been in the area of the doctrine of the church, sought to answer this very important question at the International Congress on World Evangelization. Note Snyder's emphasis on "people" and "community" or "fellowship" in this selection. Your response may well determine what you will do for Christ and what the church will mean to you.

Snyder

The essential biblical figures of body and bride of Christ, household, temple, or vineyard of God, and so forth, give us the basic idea of the church. But these are metaphors and not a definition. I believe the most biblical definition is to say *the church is the community of God's people*. The two key elements here are the church as a *people*, a new race or humanity, and a *community* or fellowship.

"People" and "community" are two poles which together make up the biblical reality of the church (figure 1). On the one hand, the church is the people of God — a concept with rich Old Testament roots which underlines the objective fact of God's acting throughout history to call and prepare "a chosen race, a royal priesthood, a holy nation, God's own people" (1 Peter 2:9; cf. Exodus 19:5–6). The Greek word for "people" is *laos*, from which comes the Latin *laicus* and the

45

English "laity." This reminds us that the *whole* church is a "laity," a people. Here the emphasis is on the *universality* of the church — God's people scattered throughout the world in hundreds of specific denominations, movements, and other structures. *Seen in cosmic-historical perspective, the church is the people of God.*

Figure 1:

The Church as the Community of God's People

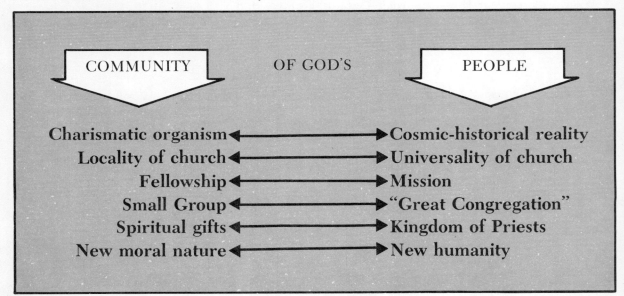

Snyder

On the other hand, the church is a community of *fellowship*. This New Testament emphasis grows directly out of the experience of Pentecost (Acts 2). If peoplehood underlines the continuity of God's plan from Old to New Testament, community calls attention to the "new covenant," the "new wine," "the new thing" God did in the resurrection of Jesus Christ and the Spirit's baptism at Pentecost. The emphasis here is on the *locality* of the church in its intense, interactive common life. *The church is the community of the Holy Spirit.*

The church, then, is the community of God's people. It is established by God as the agent of His cosmic plan for human history. It was to this church in its inconspicuous, unpromising beginnings that Jesus Christ entrusted the Great Commission.

What kind of *people* belong to the church? How does "fellowship" help God's people to be more like Him? Think of your own group: What is it that all of God's people have in common? Would we expect to be alike in all ways? What changes in your activities and meetings would help you to have a sense of "community," a oneness and sharing? How can you know that you are part of the universal people of God?

Analyze your own situation: How does your group demonstrate that you are God's people? How can you plan your meetings and activities to increase community (a oneness in Christ) and a sense of belonging together to God? Individuals and groups within the church should be constantly maturing under the Holy Spirit's direction. How should your group be "growing up" in Christ? What place do organizations, programs, buildings, and officers have in today's church? How much do organization, programs, buildings, and officers help or hinder the church in its tasks?

What constitutes the "people of God"? In what sense is the church a "charismatic organism"? How does the Holy Spirit enable "community" to develop among "people"? What does community suggest that "people" does not suggest? How does one show "community" in actual practice? What are some ways that "community" can be achieved? What might be done to bring the institutional church into better harmony with the biblical picture of the church? Now list additional items for a definition of the church.

No doubt you have heard people say that Christians are to be separate from the world. A common phrase puts it: "*In* the world but not *of* the world." How does one remain in close contact with the world without being a part of the world? Or, put another way, how does the church of our Lord Jesus Christ, the redeemed community, differ from every other community in the world?

The selection below by C. René Padilla of Argentina, Editor of *Certeza*, a university student-oriented magazine in Latin America, Associate General Secretary for Latin America for the International Fellowship of Evangelical Students and a leader of the Latin American Theological Fraternity, states that the Gospel shows conflict raging between God and Satan. This conflict is the reason for separation from the world. But, Padilla reminds us, separation from the world, i.e., not being "of the world," can be misunderstood. One extreme view is that there is no real separation between the church (Christians) and the world; the other extreme is that the church (the Christians) is totally separated from the world. Read what Padilla says.

Padilla

The Gospel does not come from man, but from God. Its entrance into the world necessarily leads to conflict, because it questions the absolute nature of "the desirable things" of the old era. Its presence alone means crisis, because it demands that man discern between God and the false gods, between light and darkness, between truth and error. Those who bear the Gospel, then, are "the aroma of Christ to God among those who are being saved and among those who are perishing, to one a fragrance from death to death, to the other a fragrance from life to life"

(2 Corinthians 2:15–16). The Gospel unites, but it also separates. And out of this separation created by the Gospel springs the church as a community called to be not *of* the world but to be *in* the world.

The concept of the church as an entity "separated" from the world lends itself to all kinds of false interpretations. At the one extreme is the position which holds that there is no real separation but only a simple difference regarding the amount of knowledge possessed: the church knows that it has been reconciled to God, while the world does not know — and that is all. At the other extreme is the position which holds that the separation is an impassable chasm between two cities that only communicate with each other as the one sets out on a crusade to conquer the other. Our concept of the nature of the separation between the church and the world inevitably influences our definition and our methods of evangelism. We urgently need to recover an evangelism that takes seriously the distinction between the church and the world, seen from the perspective of the Gospel.

What is the difference between the church and the world? How you answer this question could determine your outlook as a Christian.

By its calling, the church is not *of* the world in the sense that it has rejected the Great Lie implicit in materialism, with its complete acceptance of "the desirable things" that the world offers. Materialism makes absolute the present age in all it offers — consumer goods, money, political power, philosophy, science, social class, race, nationality, sex, religion, tradition — the "collective egoism" that conditions man to seek his realization in "the desirable things" of life, the Great Lie that man derives his meaning from "being like God," in independence from God. Though the old era is under the dominion of idols that have been set up as gods and lords, for the church there is only one God, the Father, and one Lord, Jesus Christ, the mediator of creation and of redemption (1 Corinthians 8:5–6).

In your own words, list some of the things that seem to you to be part of the "Great Lie." What is the danger in trying to be your own god? What do you lose when you are materialistic? In what ways should you and your group be different from the world (non-Christians)? How different really are you and your group from non-Christians? What could you change? Should you? How will you get the desire to change?

Separation is a matter of *doing* something different. (It's not enough that separated people don't do certain things.) What kinds of things should your group do that would show the world that you are *in* but not *of* the world?

How can you avoid the extremes associated with separation? How will your view of separation affect the kind of witnessing you do? How can you show the way to Christ *to* the world without becoming *like* the world?

How does a person's view of separation affect his practice and message of evangelism? If the Gospel, by its very nature, presents conflict, then the church is always in a state of battle. Is separation then to be understood as soldiers doing battle with the enemy? Why or why not? How does rejection of the "Great Lie" relate to separation?

What puts the church *in* but not *of* the world? How can you communicate this concept to your local church?

By now you should have a fairly good idea about the importance of the church and what the church is biblically. You should also have in mind the difference between Christians and the world of non-Christians. These are not mere classroom thoughts. They will make a difference in what you and your group do as witnesses to Jesus Christ. If you find your viewpoints shifting, you can expect a difference in your evangelism! Be sure that you spell out for yourselves what these ideas mean in your lives as Christ-followers.

Reconciliation

The church of Christ, the community of God's people, is very important to God. God demonstrated this by sending Jesus Christ to die to save us and to make us part of His Body, the church.

Read Ephesians 5:25–27 and Galatians 1:4. Notice how important the church is to God: He has more than just salvation in mind for the church. What are His purposes? How important to God is the group to which you belong?

The church is the very center of God's plan for the whole universe. The church is the agent or "doer" of God's work throughout time. As you read on, bear in mind that God's worldwide purpose includes a particular part for your church. Every group of believers shares in His activities — each member — you!

Snyder

Scripture places the church at the very center of God's cosmic purpose. This is seen most clearly in Paul's writings, and particularly in the book of Ephesians. Paul was concerned to speak of the church as the result of, and within the context of, the plan of God for His whole creation (Ephesians 1:9–10, 20–23; 3:10; 6:12).

What is this cosmic plan? According to Ephesians, it is *that God may glorify Himself by uniting all things in Christ through the church.* The key idea here is clearly *reconciliation* — not only the reconciliation of man to God, but the reconciliation of all things, "things in heaven and things on earth" (Ephesians 1:10). Central to this plan is the reconciliation of man to God through the blood of Jesus Christ. But the reconciliation Christ brings extends to all the alienations that resulted from the Fall — between man and himself, between man and man, and between man and his physical environment. As mind-boggling as the thought is, Scripture teaches that this reconciliation even includes the redemption of the physical universe from the effects of sin as everything is brought under proper headship in Jesus Christ.

Paul emphasizes *individual and corporate personal salvation* through Christ, and then goes on to place personal salvation in cosmic perspective (Ephesians 1:3–23; Colossians 1:3–20). The redemption of man is the center of God's plan, but it is not the *circumference* of that plan. Paul alternates between a close-up view and a long-distance view, for the most part focusing on the close-up of personal redemption, but periodically changing to a long-distance, wide-angle view that takes in "all things." — things visible and invisible; things past, present, and future; things in heaven and things on earth; all the principalities and powers — the whole historical-cosmic scene.

According to Ephesians 3:10, the church is the earthly *agent* of the cosmic reconciliation God wills. This means the church's mission is broader than evangelism. Evangelism is the *center* of the church's role as agent of reconciliation, and therefore is the *first priority* of the church's ministry in the world. But the mission of the church extends to reconciliation and "substantial healing" in other areas as well. To the extent the coming of the Kingdom of God takes place in space-time history before the return of Christ, God's plan is to be accomplished through the church.

Reconciliation means to have a friendship restored. In what ways are lost people not in a proper relationship with God? How did Christ help to reconcile (restore or bring back) people to God?

Why did Christ give the task of reconciliation to the church? Read 2 Corinthians 5:18–20 and answer: What is my personal task in the work of reconciliation (bringing people into proper relationship)? How can you and your group become more involved in the process of reconciliation?

How broad is God's activity of reconciliation? In what ways does reconciliation extend beyond lost people? In what ways is the church a central agent in reconciliation? What should be your group's task in reconciliation?

How can you become more involved in spreading the message of reconciliation?

What does reconciliation mean in the above context? In what way is the church the agent of reconciliation? Are individual Christians responsible for reconciliation (Read 2 Corinthians 5:18–20)? Why does Snyder say that reconciliation is broader than evangelism?

List any new elements you want to add to your definition of the church. You might want to subdivide your list into "attributes" and "actions."

According to what Snyder says, "evangelism is the first priority of the church's ministry in the world." For the church nothing is more important than evangelism. Evangelism is the key to God's whole plan of reconciliation. Evangelism is the "first priority" because it makes God's reconciling activities available to the world. Men and women are reconciled to God through faith. God's other reconciling activities can then be carried by them farther into the world.

Does evangelism have the highest priority in the church as you have seen it? What other activities or purposes tend to crowd out evangelism? Are there any other parts of reconciliation more important than evangelism? Why? What can happen when evangelism is the *only* activity of reconciliation by a church?

In the following section Snyder points out that the task of evangelism is not just to "witness" verbally to someone in hopes that the person hears and understands. Snyder puts the responsibility of communication on the Christian. Evangelism includes much more than "soul winning." Evangelism defined only as "witnessing" or "soul winning" will lead to problems in the church. The way that Snyder defines evangelism is important. He wants to overcome some of the problems caused by an inadequate definition.

In the text following, the special use of *presence*, *proclamation*, and *persuasion* are important. "Presence" emphasizes the Christian's influence through his life in general. "Proclamation" is the Christian's influence through what he *says* on behalf of Christ. "Persuasion" is what the Christian does when seeking to obtain a definite commitment to Christ by the hearer.

Just as all biblical figures for the church imply life, so do they suggest growth and reproduction. It is of the nature of the church to grow and reproduce, just as God's plan has always involved the charge, "Be fruitful and multiply" (Genesis 1:28). So when we discuss evangelism, we are really asking how the biblical church grows. Normal (that is, biblical) church life will properly produce church growth.

Biblical evangelism is church-centered evangelism. Evangelism should spark church growth, and the life and witness of the church should produce evangelism. In this sense the church is both the *agent* and the *goal* of evangelism.

Church-centered evangelism is evangelism which builds the church. It springs from the life and witness of the Christian community in an ongoing process.

C. Peter Wagner and others have rightly criticized views of evangelism which do not go far enough in the direction of church growth. Speaking of "presence" evangelism and "proclamation" evangelism, Wagner insists that neither is adequate, for the goal of evangelism must be persuasion. Christian *presence* must be the basis for Christian *proclamation*, which in turn must reach the goal of *persuading* men and women to come to Christ. In this view, the ultimate aim of evangelism is to make disciples. The line of reasoning is as follows:

Presence **Proclamation** **Persuasion**

But is it enough even to say the ultimate goal of evangelism is to make disciples? While making disciples certainly implies the formation and edification of the Christian community, this is only implicit, not explicit. To do justice to the biblical understanding of the church, we must go one step further and say *the goal of evangelism is the formation of the Christian community*. It is making disciples and, further, forming these disciples into living cells of the Body of Christ — new expressions of the community of God's people. Church-centered evangelism is concerned, then, with propagation (in the fundamental sense of reproduction by multiplication) as well as with persuasion:

Presence ➡ **Proclamation** ➡ **Persuasion** ➡ **Propagation**

In this process, propagation or reproduction feeds into a continuous cycle which, empowered by the Holy Spirit, makes the church a dynamic, living organism.

The goal of evangelism therefore is the formation of the Christian community, the fellowship of the Holy Spirit. There may be various legitimate motives for evangelism, but the goal must always be the formation of the biblical church. This is necessary in order to reach the ultimate goal of evangelism: the glorification of God.

What are the shortcomings of a definition of evangelism that limits it to "winning souls"? How does Snyder's definition overcome these? What are some new problems that develop from his approach? For example, what about the length of time between proclamation and propagation? How could an evangelist be responsible for such a long-range effect?

●

In what ways can the church grow other than through evangelism? Are these other ways *biblical*? Why or why not? How important is evangelism to the church? Why do you suppose Snyder makes evangelism such an important part of church life?

Describe in writing what *presence, proclamation, persuasion*, and *propagation* mean to you. List several ways that people in your group are examples of "presence." Do the same for each of the other three words.

● ●

What are several factors that lead to church growth? How can your group become involved in doing these things now? In what sense is it "normal" for Christians to do these things? In what way is presence, proclamation, persuasion, and propagation a cycle? Does propagation mean more *presence*?

What sort of church life best produces evangelism? How could this sort of church life affect your group?

● ● ●

Analyze Snyder's cycle (*presence, proclamation, persuasion*, and *propagation*) in the following ways:
1) How does "presence" vary with each different socio-cultural setting?
2) What is the minimum required in "presence"?
3) How does proclamation affect persuasion?
4) What does propagation mean to Snyder?
5) What kind of gap is there between persuasion and propagation?
6) How can we bridge that gap?
7) What kinds of organizations are best equipped to minister from presence to propagation?

Add to your definition of the church any new items this exercise has suggested to you.

53

One thing stands out clearly in this study of the church: the church of Jesus Christ, composed of those who are the community of God, *ought* to be evangelizing. But we find that not all of the church is active in evangelism. George W. Peters, Chairman of the Department of Missions of Dallas Theological Seminary, points this out in the following paragraph.

Evangelism as a way of life in some churches has practically disappeared. To an overwhelming degree evangelism has become the effort of "teams of specialists" and less the initiative and activity of the churches and the membership. This has made much of evangelism a grandstand experience with a few mighty giants of God facing the world and Satan in the arena and the multitude of Christians as the spectators in the comfortable and walled-off grandstand. It remains a fact that the main resources in manpower for evangelism have thus far not been tapped. Mobilization of all Christians for evangelism is heard as an occasional slogan but is not seen in general practice. A church of "we the people" is little believed and experienced. Evangelism as a groundswell and "people movement" is little known since the close of the third century.

What do you think of Peters' first sentence? Is evangelism a way of life in your community of God's people? What about your own group within that community? What about Christians in your school? Where you work? In your neighborhood? How can you and your group give evangelism first priority in your "ministry of reconciliation"? What resources do you have available that you can use to evangelize? As you think this through, try to avoid making evangelism someone else's job. Instead, emphasize the responsibility of each Christian as an evangelist!

We have looked at the church's ministry of reconciliation. Evangelism is the key to this reconciling ministry although there is more to reconciliation than evangelism. We have seen what evangelism means and how evangelism is related to church growth. We have noted that many churches do not take evangelism seriously. You have read and talked about many things. Now it is time to know what you are going to do — and prayerfully *do it*.

Growth

How does the church grow? What causes *normal* church growth? What principles can we follow to make sure that the Body of Christ increases in numbers and spiritual maturity?

The overriding dynamic force in all church growth is the Holy Spirit. The book of Acts shows that the Holy Spirit was the power behind all increase in the church. Read Acts 1:8; 2:47; 4:8; 8:29; 10:19–20, 44–48; and 11:19–24 to see how important the Holy Spirit was in the life and work of the church. How was the Holy Spirit responsible? What evangelism in Acts was done without the Holy Spirit's power? How much evangelism took place without preaching, teaching or witnessing?

Answering these questions reminds us that the Holy Spirit working through men and women is the biblical pattern. Snyder says four factors contribute to church growth: 1) direct evangelistic proclamation, 2) the multiplication of congregations, 3) the building of Christian community, and 4) the exercise of spiritual gifts. Here is what he said at Lausanne about each of these factors:

Snyder

1. *Direct Evangelistic Proclamation.* The evangelistic task of the church is to proclaim the good news of salvation in Jesus Christ throughout the world, making disciples and building the church (Read Matthew 28:19–20). Evangelism is the first priority of the church's ministry in the world for several reasons: the clear biblical mandate for evangelism; the centrality and necessity of personal conversion in God's plan; the reality of judgment; the fact that changed men are necessary to change society, and the fact that the Christian community exists and expands only as evangelism is carried out.

The church after Pentecost evangelized irrepressibly. The great concern and dynamic of the early church was to tell the Good News about Jesus and the resurrection, witnessing to what they had seen, heard, and experienced.

The church that fails to evangelize is both biblically unfaithful and strategically shortsighted.

55

●

Snyder says that the believers in Acts witnessed to what they had seen, heard, and experienced. Is this what you ordinarily do when you witness? How do you witness to what you have seen, heard and experienced?

●●

Why do you suppose the church in Acts was so active in evangelizing? What happens to the church that does not evangelize? What should be the major ideas in your witness to others?

●●●

What caused the church in Acts to evangelize so irrepressibly? Did they have ways to evangelize that are not available now? Do we have means today that weren't available then? How many ways are available for you and your group now? Which ones are you planning to use? When?

2. *Multiplying Christian Congregations.* Evangelistic proclamation is not an end in itself but must lead beyond itself to making disciples. The test of a healthy, growing church is the increase in the number of local churches, not mere numerical growth.

The ministry of Paul and other New Testament evangelists was a church-multiplying ministry. We know that converts in many cities quickly ran into the thousands; yet for nearly two hundred years no church buildings were erected. Such growth under such conditions can be explained only as the multiplication of small congregations. It is not surprising, therefore, that the New Testament often refers to "the church in your (or their) house." (See Romans 16:5; 1 Corinthians 16:19; Colossians 4:15; Philemon 2.)

Growth comes by the multiplication of *congregations of believers*, not necessarily by the multiplication of church buildings or institutional structures. If the church can grow only as fast as buildings are built, or pastors academically trained, or budgets expanded, then growth is limited to the resources available for these purposes. Church growth research would seem to suggest, however, that once a congregation has grown to a few hundred members the rate of growth will slow down unless new branch congregations are formed through growth-by-division. Where notable exceptions to this pattern are found, closer examination will usually reveal that the local "congregation" running into the thousands is in reality a whole collection of smaller "sub-congregations" in which growth-by-division is taking place as the normal pattern.

●

Why do you suppose church buildings came into existence? Do you think these help or hinder growth of the church? Does your church building help or hinder growth? Why? How can you apply "growth by division" to your Sunday School class, youth group, or church? How does this sort of outreach relate to your group's spiritual life?

●●

What implications does this section have for the place where you meet? Could you meet during the week for Bible study and prayer in a house rather than church buildings? How could this lead to multiplying congregations?

Do church buildings help or hinder church growth? How can you help your group get over any "hangups" about your church building?

●●●

Why is it that the New Testament pattern suggests the formation of a large number of congregations? What emotional blocks might some people have against multiplying congregations by dividing existing ones?

Snyder implies that "making disciples" is what multiplying congregations is all about. Do you agree with him?

3. *Building the Christian Community.* Even the multiplication of Christian congregations is not the final goal. Multiplication must lead to the edification of the Christian community in each particular case, for God's will is that all attain to "the unity of the faith and of the knowledge of the Son of God" (Ephesians 4:13).

Evangelism requires the existence of a witnessing community if church growth is to become a continuing process. The evangelistic message invites a person to become part of a new fellowship that differs from the rest of his society.

Protestantism has sometimes emphasized the individual over the community. Too often the church has been seen more as a collection of saved souls than as a community of interacting personalities. But the model of Christ with His disciples, the example of the early church, and the explicit teachings of Jesus and Paul should call us back to the importance of community. Authentic Christian living is life in Christian community. Individual and corporate edification go together and should not be separated.

Fellowship and community life are necessary in order to prepare Christians for witness and service. Every Christian is a witness in the world, but his effectiveness depends largely on his sharing the enabling common life of the Church. And this common life becomes truly enabling only as the community becomes, through the indwelling of Christ and the exercise of spiritual gifts, the fellowship of the Spirit.

●

According to Snyder, we need to be part of a group of Christians which will help us grow spiritually and help us in our witness. How important is your group to your spiritual life?

●●

How can you help your group become a "community of interacting personalities" rather than just a collection of individuals? Why is effectiveness of witness tied to community?

●●●

How are witness and Christian community related? Why are they related? How does a Christian community act? How can we develop the sort of community in Christ that will communicate evangelistically with the rest of society?

4. *Exercising Spiritual Gifts.* A primary function of Christian community is the awakening and nourishing of the gifts of the Spirit. The important discussions of spiritual gifts in Romans 12, 1 Corinthians 12–14, Ephesians 4, and 1 Peter 4, all place gifts in the context of the community life of the church.

Read Romans 12:4–8, 1 Corinthians 12:28, Ephesians 4:11–16, and 1 Peter 4:10–11. Some of these gifts are particularly needed for leadership in the church. Classify each of the gifts listed as a "leadership gift" or a "general gift." Then continue to read what Snyder says.

There are, first of all, the leadership gifts: apostle, prophet, evangelist, pastor, and teacher. The Spirit gives these basic leadership gifts primarily for instruction, order, and equipping.

But these are not the only gifts. An undetermined number of other gifts are bestowed by the Spirit. These gifts are also given "for the saints' work of ministry" and include "workers of miracles, healers, helpers, administrators," tongues-speakers, and many others.

All spiritual gifts are relevant for evangelism in one way or another. Although not all Christians are called or gifted to be evangelists, spiritual gifts contribute to evangelism in at least five ways. First, several of the God-appointed leaders — particularly apostles, prophets, and evangelists — do evangelistic work in the world. Secondly, many individual believers use their gifts for evangelism as they are equipped spiritually to do so by the equipping ministers. Thirdly, those who exercise the more "inward" [primarily benefiting fellow Christians] gifts of teaching, encouragements, contributions, etc., provide the continuing spiritual support (and sometimes even economic support) for those who carry on evangelism in the world. Fourthly, those who exercise their gifts within the community to sustain its inward life contribute to evangelism through the training and integration of new converts into the church. Finally, this harmonious over-all functioning of the Christian community is itself a demonstration of the truth of the Gospel and thus a witness in and to the world, preparing the way for evangelism.

According to Scripture, "God has given each of you some special abilities; be sure to use them to help each other, passing on to others God's many kinds of blessings" (1 Peter 4:10). Snyder has been saying that the community of God, the church, is composed of people who have been given special gifts and abilities by God. Each person is responsible to use his abilities and Spirit-given gifts to upbuild the church and to evangelize the lost.

What gifts or abilities do you have that should be used in the Christian community? What gifts or abilities does your group, congregation, class, school, or family (as a whole) have that should be used for the benefit of the Christian community?

●

How do leadership gifts help to build up your Christian life? How well do your leaders help you grow? In what ways could they help you more?

How are you using your spiritual abilities to help Christians in your group grow in their spiritual life? What different "ministries" does your group have as Christians? What help do you need to aid you in your work or ministry?

●●

What kind of spiritual abilities are necessary for evangelism? Why is the following statement wrong? "I do not witness because I have not been given the spiritual gift of being an evangelist." In addition to the spiritual gifts listed in the text, are there other gifts that God gives to the church today? Are these equal to those listed in the New Testament? Why?

●●●

Make a list of the spiritual abilities that you think are necessary for your local church to function as the community of God. How successfully are these necessary spiritual abilities being exercised?

How can you help others discover and use their spiritual gifts? Are the biblical lists of spiritual gifts meant to be exhaustive? Why? What other gifts might have been included? Why weren't they?

The ministry of the Holy Spirit is the force that makes all four factors come alive. Worship is the Christian's response to the ministry of the Holy Spirit through the Word of God. The relationship between God and the church is the vertical dimension of the dynamic church. The Holy Spirit works in our lives to give us power to help the church grow. In turn we do our work here on earth, and also direct our worship and prayer to God. Thus the entire process is complete. Snyder displays a diagram, Figure 1, to show this more clearly.

Figure 1.

Normal Church Life

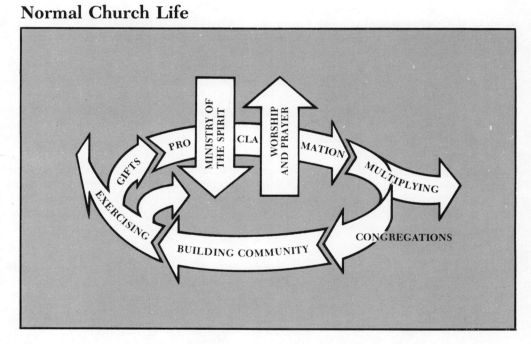

You have probably thought of several things that you and your group should do to help the church grow in accordance with the biblical principles in this study. As you relate your ideas and plans to the diagram, does it suggest anything else that you should be doing? What is *your* next step?

Organization

A very practical question arises out of the previous study: How should the church be organized and structured? Suppose you were invited to organize the body of Christ, the church, in your area. How would you go about it? What would you do? Would you turn to the Bible for help?

How would you structure your small group as a part of the church? Would you use small groups? Large groups? Are both necessary? Would you have Sunday Schools? Youth groups? Adult groups? How often would these groups meet? On what basis?

What would you do about denominations? Would you have mission boards? What about Christian publishers, schools, hospitals, and all of the other Christian groups and agencies that help local churches?

Where would your church gather for worship and fellowship? Would you meet in houses, rented offices, an auditorium or theater, or would you erect a building? What kind of people would emerge as leaders?

Do you need help in answering these questions? Read what Snyder says about church structure.

Snyder

The Bible gives very little specific guidance regarding church structure. It presents a clear picture of what the church is intended to be and gives the early history of the church in two cultural contexts: Palestinian Jewish society and first-century Graeco-Roman society.

We must look for general principles or insights which seem to be implied by the biblical description of the church. A church structured in harmony with the biblical understanding of the church will, by definition, be an evangelistic church.

60

No one is going to find in the Bible a detailed description of how to organize or structure a church. What we find in Scripture are principles or general guidelines for church structure. Snyder suggests three basic scriptural principles. First, Snyder sees a clear distinction between the church as Christians (the body of Christ, the church) and organizations composed of Christians. He calls these other organizations "para-church structures." By this he means organizations that are similar to or a variation of the church — but not the church itself.

Snyder

When we look at the contemporary church, we see not only the community of God's people; we find also a proliferation of denominations, institutions, agencies, associations, and so forth. Such structures obviously have no explicit biblical basis. How should we view them?

A helpful option is to view all such structures as *para-church structures* which exist alongside of and parallel to the community of God's people, but are not themselves the church. They are useful to the extent they aid the church in its mission, but they are man-made and culturally determined. Whereas the church itself is part of the "new wine" of the Gospel, all para-church structures are "wineskins" — useful, at times indispensable, but also subject to wear and decay.

In dealing with the whole question of church structure, then, we should make a very clear distinction between *the church* as the community of God's people and all *para-church structures*, whether denominational organizations, mission agencies, evangelistic organizations, educational institutions, or other ecclesiastical forms. It is critically important — especially when we are dealing with a worldwide, multi-cultural situation — to emphasize that the church is *people*, not an organization; it is a *community*, not an institution.

● Why should all Christian organizations be thought of as "para-church" structures? In what category would you place your group — church or para-church?

If your group dissolved, would that end part of the community of God's people? Why or why not? What sort of structure or organization does your group need? What can your group do to eliminate any activities or organizations that do not meet the needs of the group? How could this help the needs of the group members?

● ● Why should all organized Christian structures be considered as para-church? Is your local church "para-church" or "church"? Why?

How can you distinguish between the church as the community of God's people and any other organization of those people? Should your group be considered church or para-church? Why?

Do you ever feel that some of what your group does may once have been useful but is now worn and decaying? What can you do to change that?

● ● ● Is the local church "para-church" or "church"? In New Testament times was each local church an organization?

How can there be a local body of Christ without some organization?

What guidelines might help distinguish between church and para-church structures?

What is meant by "structures"? How important is the distinction between church and para-church in cross-cultural evangelism?

In an attempt to clarify the difference between church and para-church structures, Snyder presents the following chart (Figure 2). As you look at it, keep in mind your group's structure.

61

Figure 2.

Differences Between the Church and Para-Church Structures

The Church
1. God's creation
2. A spiritual fact
3. Cross-culturally valid
4. Biblically understood and evaluated
5. Validity determined by spiritual qualities and fidelity to Scriptures
6. God's agent of evangelism and reconciliation
7. Essential
8. Eternal
9. A divine revelation
10. Purpose: to glorify God

Para-Church Structures
1. Man's creation
2. A sociological fact
3. Culturally bound
4. Sociologically understood and evaluated
5. Validity determined by function in relation to mission of the church
6. Man's agents for evangelism
7. Expendable
8. Temporal and temporary
9. A human tradition
10. Purpose: to assist the church in glorifying God

●

Would you expect a group of Christians in a foreign country to do things the same way that you do? What about Christians in a different size city in our own country? Why or why not?

Talk about each of the elements in Figure 2. What do they mean for your group's existence and work?

● ●

How would you determine if your group's structure is worthwhile? Would it be unbiblical to change something in a para-church structure? What would you modify in your group now? Why?

If "structure" means organization (officers and membership) and program (meetings, activities, and study materials), how would you determine which structures are best for your group?

● ● ●

How do socio-cultural factors affect para-church structures? What do these factors do when the church (community of God's people) goes across socio-cultural borders?

Where does Christ, the head of the church, exert His leadership in the para-church structure? In Snyder's list, which are absolute elements and which are only relative? What additional items would you add to your list of descriptive and defining characteristics of the church?

In addition to the distinction between church and Christian organizations, Snyder suggested a second biblical principle in church structure:

Snyder

Leadership should be based on the exercise of spiritual *gifts*. No forms of church government or organizational patterns must be permitted to obscure or overwhelm the basic biblical pattern of charismatic (that is Spirit-appointed and endowed) leadership.

In the New Testament, leadership was at first provided by the original eleven apostles, and later by Paul and an expanding group of other apostles, prophets, evangelists, pastors, teachers, bishops, deacons, and elders (Acts 20:28, 21:8; 1 Timothy 4:14). It is clear that, in the New Testament, leadership was based on the exercise of spiritual leadership gifts which were recognized (either formally or informally) by the church.

All spiritual gifts should be emphasized, not just the leadership gifts. But these gifts are especially crucial, for their function biblically is precisely to awaken and prepare the other gifts (Ephesians 4:11–12). Thus not only leadership, but the entire life of the church is based on spiritual gifts.

We must be careful not to think that those who have leadership gifts in the church are somehow better or greater than those who have other spiritual gifts. Neither should we think that leadership gifts are for ministers and pastors (clergy) whereas other gifts are given to the rest of the people (laity). Snyder warns about this. You might want to refer to the earlier discussion in this chapter on spiritual gifts.

Snyder

We have here merely a *functional distinction* between leadership gifts and the remaining gifts of ministry. We must be careful not to read the modern clergy/laity division into these passages. Prophet, teacher, evangelist, and pastor were non-technical and non-professional terms in the New Testament. There is no basis in the New Testament for any division of the Christian community into "clergy" and "laity," since all Christians are the people of God and all have some "work of ministry."

The contemporary church needs the spiritual gifts of apostle, prophet, evangelist, pastor and teacher — and God has promised to give them. These gifts are necessary in order for the church to function biblically as the community of God's people.

●

Do groups like yours need people who have spiritual gifts of leadership? Should *all* groups within a local church have leaders with the spiritual gifts of leadership?

Is it correct to think that a youth group president, adult sponsor, or Sunday School teacher — as well as a pastor — should have gifts of leadership from God? Why? How can a group be sure that they have leaders who have spiritual gifts of leadership?

● ●

Why is it important to recognize that the New Testament does not set up two rigid groups in the church — the professional people like pastors or evangelists and the regular members of the community of God's people?

How could a group decide what kind of leadership it needs? Ultimately the Holy Spirit gives gifts of leadership, but how can your group determine those gifts and appoint leaders?

● ● ●

If the difference between Christians with leadership gifts and Christians with the other gifts is functional, why do local churches and ecclesiastical bodies seem to have a rigid dichotomy between the clergy and laity; that is, between professional and non-professional? Is today's "clergy" — "laity" dichotomy a valid expression of para-church structure?

Is this dichotomy unbiblical?

Snyder suggests a third basic guideline for church structure or organization:

Snyder

The life and ministry of the church should be built on viable large-group and small-group structures. The early church's common life of worship, fellowship, nurture, and witness reveals a dual emphasis: "in the temple and at home" (Acts 5:42). While the community life of the church centered primarily in the home, worship and nurture took place both in the temple and in small house gatherings (Acts 2:42, 2:46–47; 4:34–35; 5:42). Both large-and-small-group gatherings seem to have characterized the life of the early church throughout the Mediterranean World.

These were the two foci of early church life: the large congregation and the small group. This was also the pattern the disciples had followed with Jesus. For two or three years Christ's disciples spent much of their time either among outdoor crowds, in the temple, or in private small-group conferences with the Master. There was always this small-group — large-group rhythm, the small group providing the intense community life which gave depth to the large-group gatherings.

Theologically, large and small-group gatherings are the structural implications of the church as the people of God and the fellowship of the Holy Spirit. Peoplehood implies the necessity of large-group gatherings while fellowship or community requires small-group structures.

Church history reveals a recurrent tendency to absolutize and institutionalize the large group, wedding it to a specific building and form, while at the same time neglecting or even condemning the small group. Virtually every major movement of spiritual renewal in the Christian church has been accompanied by a return to the small group and the proliferation of such groups of some kind in private homes for Bible study, prayer, and the discussion of the faith.

Whatever other structures may be found useful, therefore, large-group and small-group structures should be fundamental. Although the specific form of such structures may vary according to culture and circumstances, both are necessary to sustain community and witness. No other structure or form should be allowed to subvert or replace the large corporate group or the small fellowship group.

64

●

What could you do in small groups to help your spiritual life? What could a large group do to help your spiritual life? How could you use the small-group — large-group rhythm in your church situation?

●●

Why does the church as *peoplehood*, i.e., the people of God, imply *many* people?

Why does the church, the *community* of God's people, imply small groups?

Does your group have both large and small-group gatherings? How is each used? What is a good balance between large and small-group experiences?

●●●

Why are large groups and small groups ". . . the structural implications of the church as the people of God and the fellowship of the Holy Spirit"?

What other structures could there be for the church besides small or large groups?

How do Christians decide what the program should be for small and large groups?

How are "witness" and evangelism related to both the large and small groups?

We have seen that the church of Christ is not to be equated with the different organizations called "church." Neither is it to be equated with any other kind of Christian organization that is involved in Christian work. The church is people — God's people — in different places worldwide. How God's people organize and structure themselves depends on who they are and where they are. Whatever way the people of God organize themselves, they must have leadership based on the use of the spiritual gifts of leadership. They must also use both small groups and large groups.

You have been thinking about the three guidelines of church structure, and what they mean to you, your group and your church. Now it is up to you and your group to apply them as you have opportunity.

Unity

Jesus prayed, ". . . that they may be one, even as we are one." And Paul said, "There is one body and one Spirit, . . . one hope . . . one faith, one baptism, one God and Father of us all." In Scripture the unity of Christians stands out.

Yet, even in a small town you will see two or three different churches on the same street. Or, you notice the advertisements on the church page of the newspaper listing Baptist, Episcopal, Methodist, Disciples of Christ, Presbyterian, etc.

All of these church denominations claim to be a part of the total people of God in this world and a true representation of what Christ wants for His church. How can they *all* be correct? Is this Christian unity? Or, to look at the other side, some denominations are getting together through mergers. By merging they feel they can be truly unified. Is this really Christian unity?

In this section, we will try to determine what unity means to the organized church and to the community of God's people today.

At the International Congress on World Evangelization, Henri Blocher, Free Theological faculty at Vaux, near Paris, focused his presentation on the biblical view of our unity as Christians. Blocher gave the following overview of two main ideas regarding the meaning of Christian unity:

Blocher

Very roughly outlined, today's two main conceptions of Christian unity are in opposition to each other:

1. Unity is *lost*, and it must be found or built again. According to common opinion, the dominant feeling is that there is an *absence* of the unity that is sought for. It will take the shape of a *visible* unity, institutionalized and administrative. Many in the ecumenical movement (the movement to restore visible unity) deplore the fact the Jesus' request in His prayer (John 17:11) is not being fulfilled among us. They greet as steps toward true unity the mergers that gather varied communities into the same organization. In order to avoid producing the spectre of the super-church, others do not insist so much on administrative unity. Instead, they leave the image of the desired unity more fuzzy. As a general fact, however, the emphasis remains on unity of the visible institutions as a proposed goal for their efforts.

2. A majority of evangelical Christians turn toward a very different vision. They believe unity is given, and they stress it; it is *invisible* and "spiritual." No one can destroy the link which joins all the true believers, the answer to Jesus' request, a request the Father could do nothing but fulfill because He always grants His Son's requests. The existence of varied denominations has nothing to do with this certain unity, definitely obtained in the "Spirit."

What sort of unity do you have with Christians of other local churches? Is it visible or invisible? Do you have Christian friends who are not members of your church?

Which kind of unity, visible or invisible, do you think would most likely influence a non-Christian? — Why?

When does organized unity between church denominations show Christian unity?

How can invisible unity show non-Christians that we are part of the community of God's people?

Do you think these two views on Christian unity are antithetical? Is there any way to draw both views together? How?

Christian unity is a very practical matter. Find and read the Scripture references as you study the teachings of Blocher.

Blocher

The Bible establishes a link between the unity of the church and its growth through the addition of new members. The book of Acts suggests a relation between the outstanding unity among the first believers and the adding by the Lord to their community of all those who came to salvation (Acts 2:44–47). Several of the following passages give the same sound (Acts 4:32–33; 5:12, 14; 9:31). In the prayer about Christian unity, Jesus asks His disciples to be one so that the world may believe that the Father sent Him (John 17:21, 23). In the powerful synthesis brought to us by the epistle to the Ephesians on the same subject, the unity of the tightly bound body is accomplished through a constant edification, inseparable from evangelism (Ephesians 4:1–16).

With your group think about Christian unity and how it is related to evangelism. How does the Scripture cited by Blocher help answer this question? What happens to evangelism if there is disunity during a special evangelistic emphasis? What happens to Christian witness if the people in a local church are feuding with each other? How important is Christian unity to evangelism?

Ephesians 4:1–16 is the basic Scripture passage on Christian unity. Blocher emphasizes key words in it. Before you read what Blocher says, read Ephesians 4:1–16. Note the words and ideas that are repeated.

Blocher

One Spirit. The Scriptural presentation very strongly shows that we are one in the Spirit. This way, Christian unity is the gift of God rather than the fruit of our works. The unification of all believers belongs to the real mission of the Holy Spirit. "One body" first depends on "one Spirit." Paul proclaims to the Corinthians, "For by one Spirit are we all baptized into one body" (1 Corinthians 12:13). In the development of the theme in Ephesians, Paul sees the parts of the body serving the unity in the ministries which he elsewhere calls the gifts of the Holy Spirit (Ephesians

66

4:11–16; 1 Corinthians 12:4,5). Most certainly, unity is of the Spirit. And Christian experience echoes in witness. We know our unity when we feel in the other believer the presence of the same Spirit that lives in us.

One Hope. Our unity also is "in hope," the unity of walking together, the unity of the pilgrim people moving toward a unity at last perfectly expressed which would take in everything. We are united to struggle and pray so that "the total unity will some day be restored."

One Lord. The Spirit leads to Jesus Christ. He does not speak about Himself, but glorifies the Son (John 16:13,14). The Holy Spirit unites us to the Head so that all His grace flows over the members of the Body. The Holy Spirit works by and with the Word. Thus the subjective experience of salvation is always grounded in objective truth.

One Faith. "One faith" refers to the great structure of truth which the apostles, evangelists, pastors, and teachers must communicate in order to assure unity in the teaching (Ephesians 4:11–14). It is "the faith which was once delivered to the saints" (Jude 3), the truth which should "sanctify" the believers, setting them apart so that they may be one according to Jesus' prayer (John 17:17–19). No experience of unity, no matter how dynamic or exciting, can replace the unity of the faith. If the biblical authors agree on one point, it is on their warnings against false teachers (Romans 16:17–18; Galatians 1:6; 2 Corinthians 11:4; 2 Peter 2:1; 1 John 4:1–3; and 2 John 9–11.) No unity is possible outside the one faith. Jesus Himself said, "He that is not with me is against me; and he that gathereth not with me scattereth abroad."

One Baptism. The apostle is referring here to the Christian water baptism, a public commitment to the Lord's service joined to a confession of faith (Romans 10:9–10). Baptism is to be understood as the doorway to the visible church. It represents the whole of the organized church. Our subjective experience of the Spirit is linked to the life of a definite "society," a society of exercising discipline.

One God and Father. In the unity of God, all unity gets its roots. From the sovereign grace of God proceed all the positives of salvation, objective and subjective. For the glory of God, the Spirit's working operates in us, as does the Lord Christ's work avail for us.

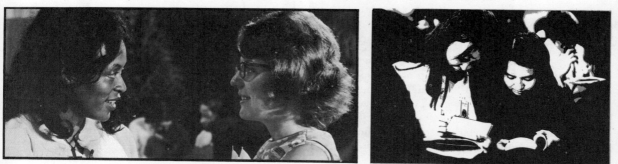

Fill in the table below so that it represents what Blocher emphasizes and Ephesians 4:4–6 suggests to you. In the middle column write briefly in your own words what you believe each biblical word means. In the third column jot down the consequences of these key words for you and your group.

Biblical Word	My Understanding	Consequences For Me and My Group
One Spirit		
One Hope		
One Lord		
One Faith		
One Baptism		
One God and Father		

It is easy to have Christian unity when everyone believes the same thing, but there is no such total agreement among Christians. Blocher examines this problem and suggests four major guidelines for handling it:

Blocher

1. *The possibilities of expressing Christian unity are proportional to the doctrinal agreement reached.* The fellowship and cooperation which express unity have various stages and forms. They can be institutional, permanent, frequent, occasional, exceptional; in worship, evangelism, teaching, social work. Two ministers can feed the same flock, or join on the same platform to protest against pornography. I suggest that we draw several concentric circles on a paper. The inside circle would be one of almost complete agreement; other circles would correspond to a less complete agreement that would permit only looser associations.

68

2. *Five criteria make it possible to evaluate the relative importance of a doctrinal question under discussion.*

a. *Biblical criterion.* The place given to a subject in the Bible, especially in the New Testament, is an indication of the importance Jesus and the apostles attributed to it.

b. *Theological criterion.* The clearer the consequences, and the more they relate to the very center of evangelical truth, the more this point is of importance. There are strategic doctrines: if you touch one of them, everything falls. Others are on the periphery and one difference will leave the rest of the "building" standing.

c. *Practical criterion.* It is also necessary to analyze the consequences on a practical basis. What are the implications for the organization of the church, spiritual life, the methods, and the message of evangelism?

d. *Historical criterion.* In order to escape from the narrowness of our personal horizons, we need to be helped by our brothers and fathers in the faith. They have not been infallible, but we must respect and appreciate the wisdom God gave them and profit from it.

e. *Contemporary criterion.* God has given such clarity to His Word that the essentials of the message cannot be hidden to the respectful and wise reader. When we find competent men of God, who profess to be obedient to the Scriptures, equally numbered on the two sides of a discussion, we can conclude that the object of the discussion does not belong to the vital heart of Christianity.

3. *The Christians ought to consider as abnormal their differences in the matter of the faith, even secondary ones.* We comfort ourselves with a "spiritual" notion of unity which is a far cry from the New Testament pattern.

Let us not forget that invisible unity must be expressed in a visible way. Alas, a very evident contradiction can show up: some believers — who are *one*, and will always be — betray in their conduct that spiritual reality which sustains them. With the help of all the various ministries, we must move with all our energies toward unity of faith and of knowledge, to the maturity of the full stature of Jesus Christ (Ephesians 4:13).

4. *Let us not mistake customs, language, or style of presentation with faith.* The Bible sometimes demands separation for doctrinal reasons. It forbids it for any other. But we too often let social and cultural differences deprive us of the expression of unity. We all tend to give to the expression of faith the value of faith itself. The Bible is very little concerned — so little we are amazed to realize it — with the external form of prayer and with the emotional flavor of Christian experience. It does not seem interested in the rigidity or the freedom of liturgical order (even though it condemns disorder, 1 Corinthians 14:40). Preferences in this realm are legitimate. As persons we have personal sensitivities. It is only natural that our preferences play a role in the liberty of expressions of Christian unity, but true unity is supernatural! It is evident that we all need to learn the price of diversity.

69

●

Do you think Christian unity is something that all people should see? What do Christians do when they are living in unity with each other? Does unity mean that all differences between what Christians believe are erased?

Customs, language, and ways of worshipping and learning are different between various groups within a local church (e.g., the elderly and young); what can you do to show Christian unity with people in your church who prefer to do things differently?

●●

How can we show Christian unity in actual behavior?

How are doctrinal differences between true Christians best settled? If all Christians lived in unity, would this automatically erase all doctrinal differences?

Is Christian unity a visible thing that all can notice or is it a spiritual thing that only Christians realize?

How well does your group demonstrate unity with other Christians in your area; with other Christians in your local church?

How are Christian unity and evangelism related? How would unity help your local churches in evangelism?

●●●

How do you know when Christians are living in biblical Christian unity? Try to evaluate a few disputed doctrines using Blocher's five criteria: i.e., the mode of baptism, eternal security of believers, the virgin birth of Christ, the lostness of man, and form of church government. Are Blocher's criteria helpful in distinguishing the important from the unimportant doctrines?

How is evangelism related to Christian unity?

How can there be true Christian unity and still be individual and socio-cultural differences? Add additional criteria to your definition of the church, as suggested by your responses to this question.

You have been studying the theme "Reaching All" by being "all together." To help you summarize your thoughts, review the following questions:

●

If someone asked you, "What is the church?" what would you say? Who within the church has the task of evangelizing the world?

What should you and your group be doing to reach people around the world with the Gospel? What should you and your group be doing to reach those nearby with the Gospel?

●●

What is the church? What are the church's responsibilities to the world? How can you know if the church is living up to its responsibilities toward the world?

What should you and your group do to evangelize those in your own age group? What do you plan to do about sharing in the evangelization of the world?

●●●

From your definition of the church, write a brief summary of the nature, function, and role of the church as you see it.

What is the church's relationship and responsibility to the world? How can you know when the church is functioning as God intends?

What could be done to help your church and the subgroups within it evangelize those they contact?

How can your local church become more aware of the need to reach out to the world in evangelization?

What is *your* personal role?

Contents ~3

Acknowledgements

Authors and papers of the International Congress on World Evangelization used in this chapter are as follows:

Michael Cassidy, "Evangelization Among College and University Students";

Lit-sen Chang, "Evangelization Among Buddhists and Confucianists";

Joseph K. Cho, "Rural Evangelism in Asia";

Billy Graham, "Before Winter Comes";

Roger S. Greenway, "Urban Evangelism";

Os Guinness, "Evangelism Among Thinking People";

Marge Alcola Isidro, "Teaching Families to Witness in the Community";

Byang H. Kato, "Evangelism Opportunities and Obstacles in Africa";

Okgill Kim, "Christian Higher Education and the Evangelization of the Third World";

J. V. Manogarom, "Evangelism Among Secondary School Students";

Donald McGavran, "Ten Dimensions of World Evangelism";

K. N. Nambudripad, "Evangelism Among Hindus";

Bruce J. Nicholls, "Theological Education and Evangelization";

R. Keith Parks, "The Great Commission";

Pablo Peréz, "Biblical Theology and Cultural Identity in Latin America";

Patrick Sookhdeo, "Evangelization Among Minority Racial Groups";

Herman H. ter Welle, "Evangelization of Children";

F. S. Khair Ullah, "Evangelism among Muslims";

Ralph D. Winter, "Seeing the Task Graphically";

James Y. K. Wong, "A Strategy of Evangelism in High-Rise Housing Apartments."

The Task

People of all nations, tribes, and tongues are the focus of evangelization. Missionary songs and hymns emphasize this. As children, many of us sang ". . . red and yellow, black and white; they are precious in His sight . . ." In the Great Commission our Lord Jesus Christ said, "Go therefore, and make disciples of all nations . . ." (Matthew 28:19). Proclamation of the Gospel pictured in Revelation 14:6 is to *all people* on the earth.

Participants in the International Congress on World Evangelization grappled with the issues confronting modern-day evangelism: the meaning of the Great Commission today, the identity of unevangelized people of the world, the place of missionaries in today's world, and the communication of the unchanging Gospel to people in different cultural settings. This study will look at these issues and problems.

Dr. Donald McGavran, professor at the School of World Mission and Institute of Church Growth, Fuller Theological Seminary, Pasadena, California, pointed out the task that faces world evangelization.

McGavran

The huge numbers of the unevangelized constitute a most important human dimension of world evangelism. More than two-thirds of mankind have not yet heard of Jesus Christ. C. Peter Wagner calls this two-thirds the "Third World." A small part of the Third World is in Europe and North America, where some ninety million have never really heard the words "Jesus Christ," and consequently have never thought of accepting Him as Savior and Lord. The overwhelming majority of the Third World, however, lives in Latin America, Africa and Asia. Although the missionary movement of the last two hundred years has established many churches there, still in these vast areas all of the baptized put together, both real and nominal Christians, are only a tiny minority of the total population. Often only one in 100 is Christian; in some places less than one in 1,000.

Furthermore, while the Gospel has been widely proclaimed, it has not been widely received. A few population groups have become Christian but most have not. As a result, congregations in Latin America, Africa, and Asia are usually made up of Christians from one or two tribes, castes, or levels of economic or educational advancement. For example, in South India, where there are hundreds of castes, most Christians come from only five castes: the Nadar, Pariah, Mala, Madiga, and Syrian. In Bolivia, most evangelical Christians come from *one* ethnic unit — the

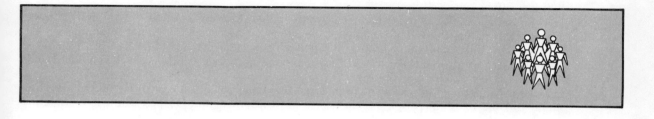

Aymara people. In Fiji, ninety-eight percent of the church comes from the aboriginal tribes and less than two percent from the 200,000 East Indian immigrants. These "pockets" of Christians have difficulty evangelizing beyond their linguistic and ethnic boundaries. Outside their own ethnic units, the evangelizing power of churches is usually minimal.

Let us think of these little clusters of churches as ethnic "islands," surrounded by "oceans" of men and women who have never heard of Jesus Christ, have never seen a Bible, and have never listened to a Christian. This is the basic evangelistic problem faced by the world church. This is the hard fact confronting world evangelism.

A policy advocated by some — that each cluster of congregations evangelize where it is, and the world church de-emphasize sending evangelists from one land to another — is no solution. If carried out, it would deny the Gospel to huge populations, which are growing larger every year.

The right way is for the whole church in the whole world to undertake the whole task as commanded by the Lord Himself. The Christians on the "islands" will do their part in the evangelization of the "oceans," but these tremendous reaches of humanity (which the "islands" of Christians are not able to evangelize alone) must be evangelized. God will send obedient servants from elsewhere. Christians on the "islands" will welcome these helpers as comrades in the urgent task of carrying the bread of life to the hungry multitudes.

Two billion fellow human beings are living and dying with no allegiance to, and usually no knowledge of, the Savior of the world who "offered for all time one sacrifice for sins and took His seat at the right hand of God" (Hebrews 10:12). The church must not overlook this two billion.

McGavran also called attention to the people who *are* responding to the Gospel. He stated that today there is ". . . unprecedented receptivity to the Christian religion."

Taiwan in 1946 had only 33,000 Christians. Twenty-five years later, in 1971, it had 650,000. Perhaps 50,000 of these were Christians who in 1948 came over with Generalissimo Chiang Kai-shek from the mainland, but the vast majority were converts won in Taiwan. In these twenty-five years the church in Taiwan multiplied twenty times.

In the newly created Indian states of Meghalaya and Nagaland, Christians are now either in the majority or soon will be.

In 1952, Africa south of the Sahara had twenty million Christians. In 1968, sixteen years later, a second calculation showed fifty million. In less than twenty years, the Christian population had increased by thirty million. Nothing like it has been seen in Christian history. The church continues to grow apace, especially in Korea, Indonesia, Brazil, Chile, and a dozen other lands where there are notable ingatherings.

Responsive populations are so huge in these areas that we are not yet adequately harvesting them. But the resistant peoples of the world must also hear the Gospel. The Bible straightly charges us to preach to *all* the world, resistant as well as receptive. We should obey that command; but we should also answer all who call, "Come over and help us." And we should baptize all who respond to Christ so that none holds out his hands in vain.

We must beware of pessimistic generalizations suggesting that evangelism is out-of-date, missionaries are not wanted, modern man demands bread not God, and a pluralistic world simply cannot conceive of one way to God and one revelation of His will. Some of these gloomy generalizations are the fruit of the guilt of neglect. Others are caused by decades of defeat within resistant populations. This defeat is set forth as universal truth concerning world evangelism. Negativism is the outcome of eroded faith, non-biblical presuppositions, and heretical opinions phrased in seemingly objective judgments about "the modern mind" and "current trends." We must reject sub-Christian philosophies and theologies masquerading as scientific assessment of the situation.

The facts support a far different assessment — unprecedented receptivity! Facts call for evangelism on a greater scale. Churches from more nations than ever before must thrust out ambassadors of Christ. Churches in regions where earlier missionaries have evangelized are beginning to send out significant numbers. They must be helped to send still more and counseled so that their missionaries and evangelists may take advantage of two hundred years' experience gained while most world evangelization was still in the hands of Europeans and North Americans. The church in all six continents must surge forward in evangelism.

Receptivity is a human dimension based on responsive persons. But it has also a divine dimension. God has spoken to these multitudes. The Holy Spirit has made them receptive. They hear the voice of the Great Shepherd and seek to follow Him. Christ's church in all six continents must look to her Master and follow His lead in proclaiming the Good News of salvation, incorporating believers in multiplying thousands of Christian cells, churches of Christ, congregations of the redeemed.

List the reasons why the task of world evangelization is so great. Which reason do you think is most important? Why?

Why does "unprecedented receptivity," the unusual willingness to accept Jesus as Savior and Lord, make the task easier? How does this receptivity make evangelization more urgent?

Why are missionaries necessary? How do these facts affect the planning of your own life?

Why is the task of world evangelization so great? Why cannot the "islands" of Christians evangelize the "oceans" of non-Christians? Why is missionary activity still very necessary?

How does "unprecedented receptivity" make the task easier? In what way does it make it more urgent?

What implications do you see in all of this for your own life?

What factors make the task of world evangelization so great? Why can't the "island" Christians greatly affect the "ocean" of non-Christians?

How would you answer someone who said that missionary activity is passé, no longer a necessity in today's world?

How do you reconcile McGavran's statements that the Gospel has not been widely received yet there are huge populations that are receptive?

What role are you considering for yourself in all of this?

The motive for evangelization and missionary activity is based on the Great Commission of Jesus to His disciples as found in Matthew 28:18–20; Mark 16:15–16; Luke 24:46–49; John 20:21–23; and Acts 1:8. Why was the Great Commission given? What is the basis for this command? R. Keith Parks, secretary for Southeast Asia of the Foreign Mission Board of the Southern Baptist Convention, said there are three bases for the Great Commission:

Parks

1. The origin of the Great Commission is in the nature of God Himself. Since God is the one true God, all created things are His possession and are under His dominion. Thus the worldwide scope included in the Great Commission is consistent with His essential nature. The essence of His being is love. That love is defined in simple grandeur in John 3:16 where its object is the world. In John 1:29 Jesus is heralded as "the Lamb of God who takes away the world's sin" (See also 2 Corinthians 5:19; 1 John 2:2; Ephesians 1:8–11, 3:4–13; Colossians 1:27–29; and Acts 17:26–32).

2. The Great Commission is also based on the authority of Jesus Christ. This authority centers on His human experience, in which as fully God and fully man He Himself went forth to make disciples. Then, through His sacrificial death and resurrection, He demonstrated His eligibility for full authority. It was this Jesus who in quiet, supreme confidence stood on the mount in Galilee and said to those gathered there, and to all who would come to Him throughout human

history, "I have been given all authority in heaven and earth" (Matthew 28:18). In a unique sense Jesus has the authority to commission His people to disciple all peoples.

3. The Great Commission is rooted also in the condition of mankind. According to the revelation of God, every human being is separated from God. He is cut off from the only source of life. He is in the grip of death, being contaminated by sin, being hopelessly, helplessly dominated by Satan.

●

What does the Great Commission tell us about what God is like? Where did Jesus get His authority to command His followers to disciple all nations? Man's sin makes the Great Commission necessary.

Is it reasonable to expect that the need for evangelization and missions might soon be over?

●●

In your own words, explain why God's nature produced the Great Commission. Why could Jesus give His followers such a command?

Why does humanity's condition require the Great Commission?

●●●

What in God's nature is the basis of the Great Commission? How does the authority of Jesus relate to the nature of God? What are the bases of Jesus' authority?

Why does mankind's condition require the Great Commission?

31

The Great Commission

Unfortunately some people have misunderstood the meaning of the Great Commission. Parks explained several of these misunderstandings.

Parks

Considerable emphasis has been given to the teaching that in Matthew 28:19 the word "go" is in fact the participle "going." Some conclude that Jesus has never commanded us to deliberately go to evangelize the world. They suggest that Jesus meant that if we happen to be going for some other reason, we ought to disciple the nations wherever we go. Without arguing about the particular verse in question, it would be wise to analyze the total biblical teaching and the experience of the early church.

An analysis of John 20:21 shows Jesus sending each of us on the same mission that His Father sent Him. In Acts 1:8 the final statement, given immediately before His ascension, about the empowering of the Holy Spirit is for the purpose of sending Christians to the ends of the earth. The very fact that the early followers were called the "sent forth ones" (apostles) indicates that Jesus was committing His followers to a worldwide task. The whole emphasis of the book of Acts describes the early gathered community of Christians as a going-forth, discipling community — rather than a community that just happened to go somewhere and disciple the nations. The early experience at Antioch indicates that under the leadership of the Holy Spirit, Paul and Barnabas were set apart and sent forth. The command to go to the ends of the earth is basic in the Christian experience and the teachings of Jesus Christ.

Various versions of the Great Commission also emphasize that every Christian is under this clear command. It is a dangerous error to say that only a specified few, called "missionaries," are sent to the ends of the earth. It is clear in the statements of the Great Commission that every Christian, wherever he is, is commanded to disciple others. We are to be involved in discipling wherever we are when we commit ourselves to Christ. We are to continue discipling every place He leads us. This is the privilege and obligation of each Christian and every gathered body of Christians who desire to be obedient to Jesus Christ. It is not just for foreign missionaries or for ordained pastors or deacons. The Great Commission is the expression of Christ's will for every Christian and every group of Christians.

Did Jesus teach that the Christians should fully meet the spiritual needs and fully disciple those in Jerusalem before they moved to Judea, and culminate that task before they moved to Samaria, and finish that work before they moved to the ends of the earth? It is remarkable that a number of Christians justify their involvement locally and their neglect of the rest of the world on the basis that their "Jerusalem" has great need and so they can't spare personnel or resources for the rest of the world. They must first do a better job at home.

Peter, called to work primarily among his own people, the Jews, was still sent to Cornelius, a Gentile. Paul became known as the apostle to the Gentiles, but wherever he went he communicated in the synagogue with the Jewish people before he moved on into a Gentile community.

The Great Commission means that Christians are to be engaged in discipling every kind of person living in every area of the world in each generation.

The purpose of sending Christians is the salvation of the lost world. Implicit in Matthew's Gospel is that they are first to turn from sin, become followers of Jesus, and publicly identify themselves as Christians. In Mark's statement the purpose is that they might believe and be saved. The sobering alternative is that not to believe is to stand before God condemned. In Luke's Gospel again the emphasis is that repentance and remission of sin should be preached in Jesus' name beginning at Jerusalem and going out among all other nations. It was the witness to this truth that was laid upon the new Christian community.

A simple proclamation of the Gospel and an initial yes or no to Jesus Christ was not all that was included in the Great Commission. There is mentioned in both Matthew and Mark the command to baptize. Baptism was related to a public acknowledgement of Jesus in the context of a Christian community. It seems that Jesus was emphasizing that His sending forth was not just to announce the Gospel in passing, but was also to minister to the new converts in such a way as to identify them with other Christians in their locality.

It appears that the charge of Jesus Christ is more inclusive than simply bearing a brief witness and moving on. Obviously, the command to the whole body of Christians requires more than a seed-sowing ministry to fulfill the intention of the Lord's command. Of course the further emphasis in Matthew 28, urging the teaching of those discipled to observe all things that Jesus had commanded, certainly lays upon the followers of Christ a significant and heavy responsibility that will never be fully completed before the Lord does return.

There are many who mistakenly believe that a Christian community which is still young and without many material resources should not be expected to be involved in witness to the uttermost parts of the earth. This is a contemporary distortion of the Gospel.

The clear teaching of the New Testament is that from the initial gathering of a group into a fellowship, each group was reaching out into its own Jerusalem, further to its own Judea, past its own Samaria to the uttermost parts of the earth. Through the prayers recorded in the New Testament, through the going forth of the early Christians, through the setting apart of those to go out, and their support in prayer and finances, it is without question a fact that from the first the New Testament church felt a divine obligation to be obedient to the Great Commission of our Lord Jesus Christ.

For anyone today to teach that new Christian communities need not enter into the clear privilege and responsibility of a worldwide ministry is to rob them of a part of their inheritance in Jesus Christ. Every Christian community is, at its inception, to be involved in obedience to the Great Commission.

Some Christian groups today are saying that since there are growing bands of Christians in certain countries, the missionaries can, or should, be removed. This would be contrary to the teaching of the New Testament. The Great Commission of our Lord Jesus Christ has not been revoked or withdrawn. Even if one percent or even ten percent of the population becomes Christian, there is no Scriptural base for a Christian community to withdraw from that area to wait for an invitation from the emerging church. Certainly courtesy and spiritual wisdom must be exercised. Cooperation and joint planning between missionaries and the growing national or local church have great advantage, but the command to disciple the nations is still addressed to all Christians. The total Christian community must continue to be aggressively involved in worldwide mission until the Lord returns.

●

How are our tasks as Christians similar to Jesus' tasks? Why is being *sent* more definite than just *going*?

Why is no Christian omitted from the command to go and make disciples? Where and to whom are Christians to go to make disciples?

What is a disciple? Where are you likely to help make disciples?

● ●

What are some ways that the Great Commission has been misunderstood? How would you answer each?

What is the difference between a person sent to disciple others and a person who is discipling as he happens to go somewhere? Which does the Great Commission present to Christians?

What does the command to baptize suggest about the depth of the work of evangelism?

● ● ●

Why do misunderstandings of the Great Commission occur?

Define the minimum to be included in the fulfillment of the Great Commission. How can you know if you are fulfilling the Great Commission? How does it demand more than proclamation?

When does a convert to Christianity become a disciple of Christ?

Why should every community of believers be actively involved in evangelism?

Parks stated that the Great Commission was to be part of the task of the church until the Lord returns. Why is this so? Will it ever be completed? Why or why not? How can you help to fulfill the Great Commission in your own particular area and with your own group?

The Great Commission is a command to all of us. Many people of the world are willing to respond to the Gospel. What then should be the response of the church of the Lord Jesus Christ? Billy Graham stated:

Graham

> We have one task — to seek and save those who are lost. Whether in the high-rise apartments of Singapore, the skyscrapers of Brazil or Berlin, whether in the forest of Amazonia, the steppes of Russia, or the jungles of Kalimantan, whether in the rice fields of India, the palm groves of the Philippines, or the cornfields of Iowa— we are going to proclaim Jesus Christ in the power of the Holy Spirit, that men may come to put their trust in Him as their Savior and serve Him as their King in the fellowship of His church. Evangelization holds the center of the stage.
>
> Churches of every land, therefore, must deliberately send out evangelists and missionaries to master other languages, learn other cultures, be willing to live in them for life, and thus evangelize multitudes. Crossing salt water is not the first consideration. For example who will send the many thousands of missionaries and evangelists to reach the billion-and-a-half in Asia? Who will reach the Turks in Germany? The Algerians in France? The Muslim world? The nominal Christian West?
>
> World evangelism means the continued and increased sending of missionaries and evangelists from every church in every land to the unreached two billion.

McGavran stated the need for increasing the number of evangelists and missionaries. He used some new phrases to describe different kinds of evangelism: "E-1 evangelism is carried out with people in one's own language and culture." "E-2 evangelism" is done with people of a *similar* language and culture. "E-3 evangelism" is done with people who come from totally different language and culture groups. For example, a middle-class American who witnesses to his next-door-neighbor is doing "E-1 evangelism." This same Christian who witnesses to a sub-cultural group of Chicano migrant workers is doing "E-2 evangelism." If that same Christian went to India, or even to the Navajos, he would be doing "E-3 evangelism."

Mc Gavran

> Global evangelism in the modern world means multiplying evangelists. Multiplying E-1 evangelists means promoting spontaneous evangelism, mobilizing churches for outreach, and equipping lay Christians to multiply churches in their own cultures. Significant extension in each piece of the mosaic where the church is now strong has become abundantly possible today and must be pressed.
>
> Many kinds of evangelism are required. Most people know of pieces in the mosaic of mankind: language groups, religion groups, castes, tribes, classes, occupational groups, fishermen, peasants, elite, students, etc. Some, however, have *not* realized that each piece of the mosaic

demands an evangelism specially suited to itself. *Many kinds* of evangelism are required. Each must be tailored to suit one particular piece of the mosaic.

God is calling for thousands of evangelists. The responsive masses of the world can be discipled only as churches from every land send their best people to carry the Gospel across cultural frontiers. The task is international in scope. "Sending churches" are now everywhere. Christ calls messengers across cultural barriers to hundreds of thousands of villages, towns, and cities where tremendous numbers have not heard the Gospel. He says, "Find and feed my sheep."

Multiplying evangelists is costly. We must resist the shoddy idea that world evangelism can be achieved cheaply without sending missionaries. Sacrifice is demanded. Life must be poured out. But, if that is done, never in the history of the world have the prospects been brighter for the Water of Life to flow freely to thirsty people. Let there be no failure of nerve, no faltering of faith. These are years when, with the apostle John on Patmos, we must see "every creature in heaven and on earth and under the earth and in the sea crying:

Praise and honor and glory and power to him who sits on the throne and to the Lamb for ever and ever" (Revelation 5:13).

How do you answer the apostle Paul's questions: "How shall they ask Him to save them unless they believe in Him? And how can they believe in Him if they have never heard about Him? And how can they hear about Him unless someone tells them? And how will anyone go and tell them unless someone sends him?" (Romans 10:14-15). What is *your* personal responsibility to help others hear and believe in Christ? What could you do with your life to keep on increasing local and world evangelization?

Urbanization

People, people, people! Thousands of millions of people! Almost four billion people are on earth, and the population is still increasing. How can we grasp this number? How can we begin to see with God's eyes the vast multitude of unreached people who have not had a meaningful hearing of the Good News about the Lord Jesus Christ? We could classify them by color: yellow, black, white, or red. We could think of them by nationalities or cultures. We might look at where they live: urban or rural. We could think of them by their religious background. Or we could classify people according to their needs. In this unit and the next we will be looking at people who could be classified as having new needs or new problems. By this we mean that they, their situations, and their needs have recently been recognized or understood in a new way.

One of these new needs results from movements of large numbers of people from rural areas to further increase the size of the cities of the world. James Y. K. Wong, director of Church Growth Study Center of Evangelism International, Singapore, made the following comments about the importance of the city in the apostle Paul's evangelization.

It is generally agreed that in Paul's missionary journeys the city presented a special challenge to him. In his strategy he focused the evangelistic thrust on the cities. There were two reasons for doing this. First, as centers of commerce and government, cities exercised a vital function — with their concentration of people — to get the Gospel spread out to the surrounding countryside. Second, Paul found that the urban dwellers within the synagogue community were receptive to the Gospel. These two advantages, a concentration of people and their spiritual receptivity, are also found in many of our twentieth century urban communities.

Contemporary United Nations population studies indicate that the trend toward a greater concentration of people in cities will increase. In 1920 the total population in the world was 1.9 billion. By 1970 the population increased to 3.5 billion. Projecting a modest growth rate, it is estimated that by 2000 A.D., the world population will exceed 6.1 billion. And most of this growth will be in the cities!

In 1920 approximately 250 million people were classified as urban dwellers. By 1960 this increased three times, to 750 million. During this period the rate of urban growth was found to be more rapid in the Third World countries than in the developed nations. For example, between 1920 and 1960 the urban population increased by *five times* in Latin America and Africa, more than *four times* in South Asia, and nearly four times in East Asia. By contrast, the urban population in Europe hardly changed.

Another fact indicated by this U.N. study is that larger cities (population exceeding 2.5 million) increased 4.8 times from 1920 to 1960, whereas smaller towns (population less than 100,000) increased only 2.3 times over the same period.

As we think through a strategy of evangelism to penetrate the world with the Gospel, we need to give greater attention to urban evangelism — particularly in areas where there are large concentrations of people, as in the vast housing developments with high-rise apartments.

Roger S. Greenway, Latin American Director of the Board of Foreign Mission of the Christian Reformed Church, summarized the data on growth rate of cities.

Greenway

The astonishing growth of city populations is one of the most awesome characteristics of modern life. Urban populations in developing countries are doubling every fifteen years and are expected to total more than one billion by the end of this century. The problems generated by such large concentrations of people boggle the mind. Demographers predict that within twenty-five years, five-sixths of the population of the United States will be living on one-sixth of the nation's land, and that half of all Americans will live in two huge megalopolises — one extending from Chicago to Washington and Boston, and the other along the California coast from San Francisco to San Diego.

But what about trends in the church's investment? At least in America, awareness of the city as the dominant reality of need has not yet been widely recognized, either for overseas missions or for local concern.

88

Greenway

Protestant Christianity, it seems, prefers the suburbs. Churches in Western countries have fled the cities along with their members. Old and stately church edifices now stand with broken windows and dreary facades like deserted "white elephants" in the inner city ruins. Around them are the poor, the unchurched, and the masses in turmoil. The congenial neighborhoods which these churches formerly served have changed. The former parishioners now worship God in the new churches they have built in suburbia, where "decent people live."

●

Why were cities important to the apostle Paul? In what ways are cities still the same today as they were in Paul's day?

What causes cities to grow?

● ●

How did the apostle Paul demonstrate that he thought cities were important? Why are cities so strategic for evangelization?

What facts about worldwide urban growth strike you?

● ● ●

What general principles about the importance of the city does the apostle Paul's ministry suggest?

What facts about urban growth impress you as being important for evangelization?

Wong and Greenway were both concerned about problems found in cities of the world.

Wong

The population of some high-rise apartment complexes in Singapore, for example, ranges from 20,000 to 200,000 residents. With so many people living in such close proximity, a variety of social and community problems are bound to arise. When thousands of urban slum dwellers and rural squatters are uprooted from familiar surroundings and brought together suddenly, tremendous problems of adjustment exist.

Greenway

Crime, poverty, congestion, pollution, noise, racial polarity — these are the familiar problems of city life. Why is the city plagued with such a disproportionate number of problems? The basic reason is also the most obvious: too many people, with all their needs, sinful inclinations, and diverse characteristics, are pressed together in the city. The problems seem endless as the number of babies born each year keeps rising and rural-urban migration increases. Despite all the money that is spent on research and experimental programs, there is no plan in sight which will effectively ease the problems of the city or provide the social services, job opportunities, and adequate housing which the masses require.

Urban problems, like urban sprawl, take somewhat different forms around the world. Yet the overall picture is the same. Rubens Vaz da Costa, president of the National Housing Bank of Brazil, informs us that today over sixty percent of Brazilians live in cities and that in 1980 two out of every three will be a city dweller. While on the one hand he applauds urbanization as a hallmark of development, he says also, "Our cities are growing too fast . . . over five million homes are classed as unfit for human inhabitation . . . 500,000 units must be built annually just to keep up with present demand . . . only about 26 out of 54 million inhabitants were served in 1970 by water mains . . . only thirteen million city dwellers have public sewage disposal. There is no way the 80 million people who will live in cities in 1980 can have such service . . . We must learn to slow the rate of population growth so that our cities will not be inundated with people to the point where we can no longer adjust . . . no longer progress . . . no longer survive."

"The Lot of the Poor: A Struggle in Life and Death," was the title of a full-page article in *The Washington Post*. The "poor" referred to were city poor. About five million people, or one-fourth of all persons over 65 in the United States, have no relatives, says the article. It is no surprise, therefore, that many live alone in bare rooms with little contact with other people. They live alone because they are poor, public transportation is not available or is difficult for them to reach, and the fear of crime prevents them from venturing far from their own residence. Since many of them are without telephones or anyone close by, there are no lifelines between them and the world outside. If they get sick in the night, they cannot call for help. They simply die.

89

"Urban anguish" is an expression used to describe the mental suffering, emotional insecurity, and utter loneliness of millions of city people around the world. Many of them are new migrants from rural areas, and they do not feel at home in the urban setting. Others are simply the poor, the jobless, and those who are ignorant of the basic services which even crowded, impersonal cities make available. Where but in the city are suicides so numerous and space, even cemetery space, so scarce?

Right now in almost every part of the world, social orders are changing, vast movements of people are taking place, and problem-filled urban centers are mushrooming. By the end of the twentieth century ours will be an urban world. Some predict gloomily that Christianity will be lost in the city, and they point to the church's poor urban record as evidence for what they say. Others cling valiantly to the hope that the same Spirit who led the church out of the doldrums in the past will renew her again for urban mission in this hour.

"Arise, go to Nineveh, that great city, and proclaim to it the proclamation which I am going to tell you." That is what God said to Jonah, and He is saying it again to churches today.

There lies the city . . . and our mission. The city needs the church and the church needs the city.

Is it possible that the Gospel can get into the city and help to change it? Again, both Wong's and Greenway's statements are direct and positive answers and challenges to the church. They said the cities are filled with opportunities to evangelize if it is properly done.

Wong

When people experience rapid social change they are also more open to religious change. Several case studies have been carried out in Singapore among the residents of high-rise housing estates. In a 1972 community survey of the "religious orientation" of the people living in high-rise apartments I found that the residents were most responsive to the presentation of the Gospel message during the initial period of settling into a new housing development. If churches are planted early enough in new housing they will have considerable opportunities to exercise an effective service and witness role among the residents. Evangelization and church planting will be more successful when it is being carried out in these spiritually responsive housing apartment blocks and when it is initiated right from the beginning as the residents move into the area, rather than waiting until the people have firmly settled themselves in the neighborhood.

Greenway

The city needs the church because city life cannot endure, or be endured, without spiritual and moral dimensions. At the same time, the church needs the city because she has been commissioned by her Lord to preach the Gospel to all people. The cities are where people are. Behind every social problem threatening city life, there lies a religious issue to which the Word of God speaks. Fundamentally, the crisis of the city is religious. Cities without God are beyond human endurance. Therefore, churches which proclaim the Word of God and the Lordship of Christ over city life hold the key to any real and lasting urban renewal.

Simply stated, the church's urban mission is to proclaim Christ as Savior and Lord and to call city people to repentance, faith, and discipleship. "What is the city but the people?" To evangelize the city means to bring the Gospel to the people, rich people and poor, powerful and weak. It means to reach all races and social classes, all ethnic communities and tribal communities that live in the city. The city has gods such as money, power, drugs, and sex, which influence urban life for evil at every stage. In opposition to the demonic forces at work in the city, the church proclaims the Saviorhood and Lordship of Jesus Christ. The result is the moral equivalent of war. Christ's Gospel challenges the vain philosophies of the pseudo-intellectuals and exposes the mass idolatry of men on the street. The church calls men to repent of sin and become new creatures in Christ Jesus. In order to do this, the church must be present in the city, it must be in contact with city people, and it must proclaim its message in ways which people will understand. Mission to the city forces churches to make hard decisions and to reach out to people to whom they would not ordinarily minister.

Why do you think it is difficult for the church to minister in the city?

To what problems of the city does the Gospel have an answer?

Why do we call the city a "new need" when cities have been in existence for thousands of years?

Why does the city need the church?

Why do you think evangelization in the city is difficult? Why have some Christians not seen the city as Paul did?

Which problems of the city impress you as being severe?

Why do we call the city a "new need" when cities have existed for thousands of years?

Why do the city and church need each other?

Why is urban evangelization difficult?

Why has the city not been a more prominent concern of evangelical groups? What do you think should be done to reverse this?

Why is rapid social change actually a help to evangelization? What does this suggest for evangelization priorities?

Urbanization causes problems. But the movement to large cities enables people to be contacted with the Gospel. As you consider the recent growth of urban areas how do you see yourself fitting into an effective presentation of the Gospel to some of these millions of people with such great spiritual needs? How should we pray for the cities of the world?

Self-Identity

Nationalism and cultural awareness are an important reality in today's world. Since the end of World War II dozens of new nations have come into existence, gaining independence from colonial European powers. The attitudes and feelings of nationalism and cultural awareness in relation to world evangelization were raised by many participants at the International Congress on World Evangelization. Evangelical leaders from Asia, Africa, and Latin America expressed the desires of many of the peoples from their parts of the world for: 1) a sense of national identity apart from dependence on European and North American powers, and 2) a reliance on their own decisions to administer their own spiritual welfare and to plan evangelization and church growth.

Since the major world powers are sometimes considered the "communist world" and the "non-communist world," the unaligned nations have been called the "Third World." Okgill Kim, president of Ewha Women's University in Seoul, Korea, shared the displeasure of many non-Westerners with the use of the term "Third World." She also explained some of the main ideas involved in nationalism and cultural awareness.

Kim

"The Third World" is a name used in international politics. It seems to mean all those nations in Asia, Africa, and Latin America which have been variously called "underdeveloped" or "developing" nations, or the "have nots" of the world.

One thing seems to be clear: the people in the Third World want to get out of the Third World category. The people in these nations are in the process of discovering their identity as non-dependent nations. We Koreans want to get out of the state of economic underdevelopment, and at the same time we do not want to identify ourselves with either West or East. We want to know exactly what *Korean* means when we say that we try to make Koreans more Korean and not Western. We call these efforts "nationalism."

Os Guinness, a Britisher, formerly with L'Abri Fellowship and presently a free-lance writer living in Switzerland, was quite excited over the rise of nationalism in developing countries of the world.

Guinness

It would be difficult to express adequately the excitement of the present moment for anyone who loves God's truth and seeks to relate it to our time. Five hundred years of virtual European dominance in the world have ended, and with them is disappearing a whole complex of accepted ideas and traditions. It is the challenge of new, emerging civilization, as yet only sensed, which makes this a unique moment. New values, new principles, new patterns of thought are in demand. Our generation is in a shopping mood for answers.

What is nationalism? Why is it so important to the people of the developing nations?

If your country had recently received its independence from direct Western control, how would you feel about your new country? How do you think those in Western nations might look upon your new country?

What are some of the main feelings expressed in nationalism?

How will the outlook of the West affect evangelization? Why do you think Guinness is so excited by the end of European dominance of the world?

What do you think he means by, "Our generation is in a shopping mood for answers"? How is this related to nationalism? How is it related to evangelization?

How could nationalism be a help to the evangelization of new nations?

What parts of the world have been most affected by the end of dominance by Western powers?

Have only the people of developing countries been affected, or also the people of Western countries?

Cultural awareness is an emphasis within a country upon its own culture and its own history. It is also a de-emphasis on foreign cultures and a determined drive to discard many foreign influences in the country. A number of participants at the Congress made specific statements about cultural awareness in relation to the worldwide task of evangelization. Keep in mind that these are committed followers of Christ and leaders from various parts of the world. They are trying to help all of us get a glimpse of how non-Westerners think and feel. What they say applies to world evangelization. How?

Byang H. Kato, general secretary of the Association of Evangelicals of Africa and Madagascar, gave the following insights into how some governments now react to outside religious influence.

Kato

Some African governments are so sold on cultural revolution that to stand for the uniqueness of Christian faith is considered illegal. Missionaries are constantly attacked for "destroying our culture." The freedom of individual Christian bodies to evangelize in the way they once did is drastically curtailed in Zaire. (Zaire, pronounced Zie-EAR, is the independent nation replacing the former Belgian Congo.) It is alleged that at least seventeen pastors have been jailed, churches reduced to ashes, and missionaries ousted in the Republic of Chad because the Christian leaders refused to undergo ritualistic practices in the name of cultural revolution. In other African countries there is more emphasis on traditional dancing, some of which either have pagan religious connotations, or immoral tendencies, and usually both.

While contextualization (expressing in a relevant way the unchanging message of the Gospel in the ever-changing cultures of the world) which is compatible with the Christian witness should be encouraged, the call of separation for Christians must be maintained (2 Corinthians 6:17–18). Christianity must judge every culture, whether European, Asian, or African. It is not going to get easy for the African Christian, but our Lord did not promise us an easy road. While a prisoner, Paul warned, "Indeed, all who desire to live a godly life in Christ Jesus will be persecuted, while evil men and imposters will go on from bad to worse, deceivers and deceived" (2 Timothy 3:12–13). May the Lord give grace to God's children in Africa who may have to suffer for being Christians (1 Peter 4:16).

Christianity has always had relevance for any given group of people. True Christianity is always more than a local way of life. When Christianity enters a culture, changes must come. This, of course, causes conflict with those who do not want anything to change their culture. Such people want to preserve as much as possible the "original" and "pure" life-style of their culture. But in Christ *all* things become new!

Pablo Peréz, a pastor and teacher in the National Presbyterian Church of Mexico, pointed out just what Christianity does when it enters a culture. He used first century Christianity as an example.

We have almost forgotten the counter-cultural spirit of early Christianity. While it acknowledged that peoples and tribes had a particular life-style expressed in their cultures, the Spirit of Christ had a corrective effect upon them. It brought with itself divine judgment against their negative points as well as encouragement of the positive aspects. The apostles and their followers did not hesitate to condemn idolatry, every type of immorality, and the philosophical doctrines which kept people's minds ensnared.

No doubt this was one of the aspects which contributed to the success of the preaching of the Gospel and the early church. It was the simple condemnation of sin and a call to repentance leading to forgiveness and the transforming power which could drive its possessor to a new life. "Repent," said the Lord in His first public message; "Let men repent," reiterated Paul before the Athenians.

Those who listened to the Gospel message were confronted with the fact that there were some negative elements in their culture from which they should turn away. At the same time, they were exhorted to take a new stance which would let them establish trends pleasing to God, even if this meant that such a trend would run contrary to the existing order. It can thus be noticed that the door would then be opened for divine intervention in any given culture, obviously governed by biblical directives toward the goal which the Lord Himself set.

Bruce J. Nicholls, a New Zealander, and the International Coordinator of the Theological Assistance Program of the World Evangelical Fellowship, stated that the Gospel must be related to individual cultures but that it must also judge and renew each culture according to biblical principles.

The Gospel is never proclaimed to people living in a vacuum. All people are conditioned by their culture, and hear the Gospel through their conditioned minds. All have a philosophy of life even if they have never consciously articulated it. All have grown to accept some assumptions about the nature and existence of God, His relationship to the world and to man, the nature of suffering and evil, and about life after death and how to achieve it. All have adopted a personal and social ethic.

Every person, though made in the image of God, is in rebellion against God and His law. As systems, all religions and ways of life suppress the truth and create a god in their own image, projecting their own form of idolatrous worship. Religion and culture have developed through interaction. The Gospel judges all cultures and fulfills only those elements that are consistent with biblical revelation.

The Gospel, therefore, cannot be equated with any one culture, for all cultures transmit human sinfulness. Where the Gospel has taken root some elements of culture will be rejected, others renewed, and new patterns of culture will emerge. John F. Robinson of Zaire, writing in *Theological News*, July, 1973, says, "The Christian in Africa should be, in his particular culture, the embodiment of those African values which are consonant with the will of God, and he should express them in a distinctively Christian way. Only then will the Body of Christ in Africa have become the incarnation of the Gospel that God intended it to be."

And Kato added:

Christianity stands to judge every culture, destroying elements that are incompatible with the Word of God, employing compatible modes of expression for its advance, and bringing new life to its adherents — the qualitative life that begins at the moment of conversion, and is fulfilled in the return and reign of our Lord Jesus Christ.

Is Christianity a threat to people's life-style? Why or why not?

What culturally different people are near you? Consider inner city people, people of different races, different ethnic or religious backgrounds, different age groups, different social and economic groups, etc. What kinds of approaches are necessary to reach them effectively?

What causes a culture or a people to reject outside influence and to try to "go it alone"? Why is missionary influence a seeming threat to non-Christian governments?

When Christianity enters a culture, new things begin to take place. What are some of the things that happen? Why should they be expected to happen?

How will understanding a group's culture help to evangelize that group more effectively?

What is the counter-cultural spirit of early Christianity?

How does early Christianity demonstrate the relationship of a Christian to his culture?

National Christian leaders are speaking to mission leaders in the West. Kato's comments serve as an example of ideas expressed along these lines. What these participants are saying is that national Christian leaders want to, and must, participate in the total missionary plans in their own countries.

Kato

Christian organizations working in Africa can be an instrument for evangelism or a hindrance to evangelism. One sad thing with some Christian organizations working in Africa is that they act like they know too much. We appreciate the fact that organizations with leadership in London and New York are in a position to have a wider view of the whole continent of Africa than an African in a Timbuktu ghetto. It does not always follow, however, that the people with the money know "where it itches"; overseas bodies sometimes want to dictate to African leadership. The time is long overdue for Christians overseas to listen to African voices in order to be able to meet real needs.

Why do you think people in developing nations are saying things like this? How will increased leadership from national Christians help to evangelize the world?

Nationalism among non-Westerners is part of the overall challenge facing evangelization today. The spirit of nationalism, however, is not limited to non-Westerners. European and North American countries have also demonstrated feelings of nationalism. Consider your own feelings of national pride. Would you be willing, if necessary, to give up your nationality to help spread the Gospel? Is your national way of life the same as what you understand the Christian way of life to be? Can you tell which is which? What can you do to make sure that your faith is firmly established in Jesus Christ and not in any kind of national religion or political or religious leader?

In the rush toward nationalism and the movement of people to the cities, certain segments of people are emerging with a new need. These people are the minority groups, the people who are culturally different from the majority of those around them. Until recently, many minorities have not had much opportunity to find their voices and engage in direct contact with those who form the majority people in their nations. Today this is changing.

Patrick Sookhdeo, a staff member of the Evangelical Alliance in Great Britain with special responsibility for those from overseas, presented the following report to the Congress on minority groups and the church.

Sookhdeo

Minority groups are a neglected and forgotten element in our world. As Christians we need to develop a new awareness and concern for those caught in the dilemma of not belonging. A "minority" is a group of similar people speaking a common language, claiming a common ancestry, and living in a particular geographical area where they are less numerous than one or more other groups. All minorities are involved to varying degrees in the happenings of our age: rapid change, mobility, nationalism, modernization, education, changes of values, and industrialization.

Minority groups can be classified within the following categories:

1) Tribal Minorities — for example Amerindians in South America, Aborigines in Australia, Konds in India, etc.

2) Refugees — the results of war, political and religious oppressions, famine, etc. They are to be found in most countries of the world and their numbers are increasing. Examples are the Biharis in Bangladesh, Eastern Europeans exiled throughout the world, Asians from Uganda, etc.

3) Migrant Workers — have come into being through:

a) The Pull Factor: countries with greater economic, demographic, and social developments in need of manpower have a drawing effect on those outside of its borders.

b) The Push Factor: peoples living in conditions of high unemployment and poverty leave these areas in search of economic betterment.

4) Historical Racial Minority Groups — as for example blacks in Brazil, blacks in the U.S.A., gypsies in Western Europe, etc.

Minority groups should be important to the whole church, both nationally and internationally. None of us can escape the challenge of minority groups.

What minority groups are near your church? How could you become involved in bringing the Gospel to them?

What makes minority groups different from many of those involved in urbanization and nationalism?

Why does the church have a responsibility to evangelize minority groups?

Why are minority groups considered part of the new need among the people of the world?

How are minority groups related to the new needs associated with urbanization and nationalism?

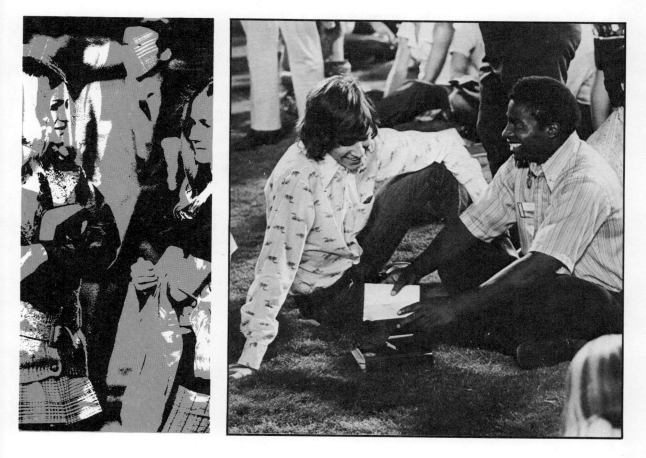

Youth

The emergence of new needs, as noted in the last two units, demands our attention, but we must continue to be concerned about needs of which there has been an awareness for centuries. Certain "old" needs have become increasingly important. They have been around so long that they seem to have been accepted as a way of life, but they are still important!

One continuing need, child evangelism, was emphasized at Lausanne by Herman H. ter Welle, founder-director of a national children's ministry in the Netherlands.

With nearly four billion people on earth already, the world's population is growing at an alarming rate of approximately eighty million children annually. The great burden of our hearts is that this newest generation will be effectively reached with the saving Gospel of the Lord Jesus Christ.

Although the first task of teaching the children belongs to the parents, the second agent in evangelizing the children is the church. The church has the commission to disciple all nations and to teach all believers (Matthew 28:19-20). One-third of the world population is children and they should be led to know Christ. The task of the church to educate the people of God means men, women, and also children (Deuteronomy 31:12).

On the whole, one can notice within the church a sense of inferiority when it comes to the field of evangelization of children. In some of the most prestigious theological colleges and seminaries, there is little emphasis on training future church leaders in procedures for children's evangelism.

It is impossible to overestimate the importance of spiritual education for children. The emphasis of the church must not be solely on adults. It is often difficult to convince some sectors of the church that they are neglecting to pass on the great heritage of Christ to the younger generation.

It is our responsibility to make sure that all children hear the message and receive knowledge of Him who gives them glory and virtue. Every child may receive Jesus as his Savior, for Jesus says, "Let the children come unto Me, for the Kingdom of God belongs to such as they" (Mark 10:14).

Why would anyone neglect the evangelization of children? Consider your own church or group. Is evangelization of children going on? What could you do to encourage more outreach to children through your church or group? Should you be thinking about how your own personal ministry can reach children more effectively?

Another continuing need is the family. Marge Alcala Isidro, chairman of the Christian education department of the Febias College of the Bible in Manila, Philippines, emphasized that families should be evangelized and Christian families should be witnessing units.

The family is strategic in witness. The family is here to stay. Institutions come and go, people come and go, ideas come and go, but the family remains basic in the midst of change.

Writing in "The Christian Family in Today's World" (*Adult Education in the Local Church*, Roy B. Zuck and Gene A. Getz, eds., Chicago: Moody Press, 1970), Oscar Feucht made a cogent observation. "The home is the school of Christian living, the most fundamental institution in the world, the nursery of every generation, the college of life, and the training ground of the child. The families are launching pads for their children . . . parents are not all authors of books, but they are all writing the lives of their children . . . parents can enrich life or they can mar or scar a life, depending on the type of nurture the give or the lack of it."

Many families today are destitute of good relationships. When they reach out for help they hear only the noisy static of harried, busy lives. In an era of supermarkets, super-stars, superjets, and super-everything, it seems like people are trying to cover the emptiness within. People are almost afraid to be left alone lest they be confronted with the impoverished state of their own lives. So super-fences have been built around homes and personalities. Psychologically, the more elite, monied, and sophisticated families have built walls of complacence, nonchalance, and smugness. The poor have also built walls of an 'I-couldn't-care-less' attitude. Walls of anger, apathy, resignation, and even shirking of responsibility have been erected. The emerging middle class has built walls of competition, drudgery, and busy-ness. Hence there is no time for the family, no time for God, no time for the church. These are formidable walls that need to be broken down or penetrated by family witness. It is to families like these that we have been commissioned to communicate the Gospel.

On the other hand, criticism has been hurled at the Christian community because they have organized walls around themselves also by creating Christian ghettos. Bible classes have degenerated into a comfortable fellowship of the same Christian people. These activities are good, but they often sap the vitality of Christians who spend all their time together, thus robbing themselves of the opportunities to make an aggressive witness. Some Christians in walled compounds hardly reach out to people outside their fences. This unity is more like "glued-togetherness." We have not been called to a cloister or to build a city of the redeemed here on earth. Would to God that Christians in the Christian community would take the initiative to reach out to other families!

What makes families so crucial in evangelism? What are some of the barriers that have been raised to communicating Christ to other families? How can these barriers be overcome?

How successful has your family been in communicating the Gospel to other families? What can your church or group do to help its Christian families witness effectively to non-Christian families?

Evangelization of high school and college age youth is another persistent need for the church. J. V. Manogarom of Madras, India, the Central Asia area Director of Youth for Christ, International, had this to say about this need:

No one can deny that laying a spiritual foundation in the lives of young people while they are going through secondary education is of utmost importance. To a large extent, many of the problems we are facing among university students would be solved if proper and effective evangelization were being carried out at the secondary school level.

In many nations, evangelization among secondary schools is greatly diminished due to the secularization of governments which eventually prohibit religious teaching and activities in the schools as part of the curriculum. While fantastic strides have been taken to meet the physical, mental and social needs of the students, the spiritual need has been greatly neglected, and in the majority of cases totally neglected. But in the midst of this situation there has never been a generation of kids more open to first-century Christianity than this present questioning generation. "The rugged Christ of the first century who says, 'Follow me' is more attractive to youth than He has ever been," said Jay Kesler, President of Youth for Christ, International, U.S.A. If this had not been true, many of us who have been working among them would have been wiped off the scene by the overwhelming changes that are occurring today.

Today's teens constitute a large proportion of the world's population. They are not only an increasing generation but also a changing generation. They are becoming taller in height, bigger in size, and even faster in movement. Besides this, they learn more, buy more, travel more, and see more than we did twenty to twenty-five years ago.

What are students in the eyes of the world? What are they in your eyes?

"just children"—to the parents
"a menace"—to the police
"weapons to be used to an end"—to the Communist
"a market"—to the businessman
"the unreachable"—to the church
But to themselves, they are "*ADULTS.*"

Manogarom used Indian teenagers as an example of what is happening with youth in both the Western and Eastern countries.

In India, right now, 79 million students study in secondary schools. Writing about the situation of education in India, one author said, "What India is trying today is to harmonize her old values with the values of the modern world. The old values are spirituality, tolerances, and universalism under vague concepts like "Dharma" and under more specific concepts like the family, marriage, religion, and caste practices. And when they try to harmonize these old values with the values of the modern world, they create a great confusion in the minds of the young people. The average teenager today in the East is terribly confused by the old values of his own culture and traditions, and the values of the modern world that are sweeping all over the world."

Michael Cassidy, director of African Enterprise, said:

Challenges, opportunities, and needs exist on the modern campus. With over half the world's population under 21, the high school and university campus becomes an increasingly critical focus of Christian concern. In the U.S.A. there are over seven million students on 3,000 campuses. Asia, which previously lagged in its university facilities, suddenly has over four million students. Tokyo alone has over 500,000. Numerous Third World countries did not even have a university twenty years ago. Now no country is without one. Twenty years ago, no one had heard of "student power." Now it is a cliché.

This phenomenon represents not only an incredible opportunity for strategic evangelism but an immense area of human need. As such it is important that those who would evangelize the student should not simply think of him strategically — as a key person, a potential leader, a future opinion-maker — but as a young human being, often with deep if not desperate needs. The Christian therefore has a special incarnational responsibility to be *on* the campus. This is particularly true when the local church is failing to make the desired impact. Carl F. H. Henry wrote of one campus he visited: "The local churches were reaching less than ten percent of the entire student body of 6,500."

Bill Bright has said: "Students represent the major source of manpower to help change the course of history. They need to be reached for Christ." The challenge is that simple, that difficult, and that glorious.

Why are university and secondary school age youth so crucial in the overall plan for evangelizing the world? What is it about young people that makes them open to the Gospel? What is it about the Gospel that makes it acceptable to young people?

How many secondary and university age youth are within reach of your church or group? What can you do to communicate Christ to them?

How could evangelism of children, youth, and families be integrated into a unified thrust in your area? What resources of personnel, program, and finances would be needed to have such a unified evangelistic thrust? Would a unified action be more effective than several programs "doing their own thing"?

Cultural Religion

Several very large cultural and religious groups of people living mainly in Asia and Africa represent long-standing needs. Missionary work has been done among these people for many years. In fact, tradition says that the apostle Thomas came as a missionary to India in the first century. However, these people whose culture and religion are so intertwined have been relatively difficult to reach with the Gospel. Thus they are a persistent, continuing need.

Joseph K. Cho, a professor at Tokyo Christian College and pastor of a Korean church in Tokyo, Japan, called attention to certain rural people.

Cho

The farming villages of Asia politically, economically, and especially evangelistically were for a long time forgotten and passed by. We know that the population of Asia as of 1971 was 2.1 billion. Of these, 1.4 billion, or 67 percent, were farmers. We must pay attention to these 1.4 billion people who live in a cultural valley and, without ever hearing the Gospel, pass from this earth like a wide river of lost souls.

Christian evangelism in farming villages meets many obstacles. In Korea most of the pastors live in the cities. Although several hundred students graduate from theological seminaries every year, still there is only one pastor for every two to three farming village churches. This is one of the better rural situations because most of the villages of Southeast Asia still have not even heard the Gospel.

In 1971 I took fourteen students from my college and did research on conditions in the farming villages of Japan. It was a farming area that could be reached within two hours by train from Tokyo. In five days we contacted 700 farm houses. We were very surprised to discover that 97 percent of those farmers had never heard the Gospel since the day they were born. The other three percent had heard the Gospel through radio or by receiving a tract when they had been in the city. The nearest church to that farming village was about one hour walking distance, and it was a weak church of about twenty members. Hardly any of those village children had ever heard the familiar song "Jesus Loves Me."

For the farm villages where the harvest is great, the Lord is seeking specialized workers. Up until now missionaries, pastors, denominations, and theological seminaries have not been very interested in farm village evangelism. But we cannot forget the salvation of 1.4 billion farm people in Asia. Someone must bring the Gospel to them.

The farm village evangelist must be a Gospel worker and at the same time a leader of the farm people in other ways. First, he must know the Lord's pain of heart for these souls. Then he must be a true friend of the farm people and pray for them. He must be qualified to be a leader of the farmers technically, socially, and evangelistically.

Why do you suppose rural people are neglected? What special problems are often associated with rural evangelism? Why must the farm village evangelist be more than just a preacher of the Gospel? How does being a "good friend," a capable farmer, and a social leader relate to the work of this kind of evangelism?

Ralph D. Winter, professor at the School of World Mission, Fuller Theological Seminary, Pasadena, California, presented a graphic description of three continuing cultural-religious needs. He showed the growing number in these three groups.

The task of winning non-Christian Asians and Africans is often referred to as reaching the two billion who have never heard the name of Christ. In Figure I we break down these groups of people into cultural categories. Immediately three groups loom large. Most missionaries and most mission boards may hope that someone else will worry about the special problem of winning Muslims, Hindus, and Chinese, since these have historically been the most resistant to the Gospel. But let's face it — these groups are by far the larger part of the task we face.

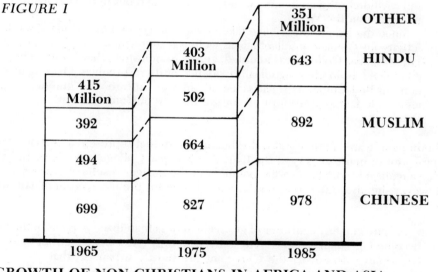

FIGURE I

	OTHER
351 Million	
403 Million / 643	HINDU
415 Million / 502 / 892	MUSLIM
392 / 664	
494	
699 / 827 / 978	CHINESE
1965 1975 1985	

GROWTH OF NON-CHRISTIANS IN AFRICA AND ASIA

Lit-Sen Chang, a Chinese, former Buddhist, and now a special lecturer in missions strategy at Gordon-Conwell Theological Seminary in South Hamilton, Massachusetts, provided a glimpse of the Buddhist and Confucianist world.

Buddhism and Confucianism are two major world religions. It is generally estimated that there are more than 400 million Buddhists and about 300 million Confucianists in the world. Geographically, they occupy Asia and total about one-fourth of the entire world population. Ideologically, they have manifested for over twenty-five centuries their toughness in their way of thinking. Spiritually, these religions are strongholds erected by Satan to impede the spread of the light of the glorious Gospel of Christ. Strategically, they are formidable rivals which should not be ignored by any missionary strategist concerned about the tremendous task of world evangelization.

With the great upheaval resulting from World War II, there has been a great resurgence of Buddhism. Buddhism was sometimes considered as a hobby of elderly retired people, but now it has caught the hearts and minds of the young people. Young Buddhists are taking the initiative in outreach. They even look down upon Christianity and consider its supernaturalism as unscientific and as a naive religion for the child of superstition. Buddhism is no longer a quiet and secluded religion in a monastery; it has turned out to be very aggressive and has even made an impact on the West.

Since the Communists have taken over mainland China, Hong Kong has become a center of activity for Chinese intellectuals as well as a center of a resurgent movement of Confucianism. The New Asia College was founded, and a "Manifesto to the World on behalf of Chinese culture" was issued as another significant evidence of its resurgence. Over against the "cultural revolution" in Red China, a "renaissance of Chinese Culture" movement was promoted. This movement is in fact another form of the resurgence of Confucianism.

The Hindu people are another cultural-religious group that represent a persistent need. K. N. Nambudripad, a professor of neurosurgery at the Christian Medical College in Vellore, India, and president of the Union of Evangelical Students of India, pointed out the meager results of evangelism among the Hindus in India. However, he also stated that now is a good time for the evangelism of Hindus.

In spite of many centuries of evangelism, less than three percent of the population of India had become Christian by 1971. These lived in only a few states. Other states are virtually without Christians. Moreover, the Christians are mostly urban, so that the villages remain virtually untouched.

Evangelization of the Hindu is urgent business because about 540 million of them are unconverted. Hindus are more approachable with the Gospel today than perhaps at any other time in history. They are fast losing faith in almost everything Indian. There is a vacuum in their experience of life, and they are hungering for reality. Only Christ can fill the vacuum. Above all, Christian compassion demands that we help them in their hour of spiritual need.

The third cultural-religious group is the Muslim people. Khair Ullah, director of the Creative Writing Project of the Christian Publishing House in Lahore, Pakistan, pointed out one of the major problems in the evangelization of Muslims: religion and culture are very intertwined. Muslims usually assume that they must leave their cultural and family background to become Christians.

We must realize that Islam, the Muslim religion, is more than a religion — it is a complete way of life. Unless we appreciate the social and cultural complex within which Muslims exist, we cannot effectively communicate the Gospel to them. A Muslim is not simply one individual but a member of a close-knit society, and within it a member of an even closer-knit family. This is an idea that people from the West may not be able to imagine. A Muslim on hearing the call of our Lord is subjected to many conflicting loyalties — those of family, society, and the state, besides the personal inner conflicts. The Muslim in the Arab world thinks of the Christian Church as a separate *millet* [any non-Muslim religious group] perhaps with different language, certainly with a different "ethos" [guiding belief] and different cohesion. What is a renunciation of sin looks to one's kin as the denunciation of all that makes one "belong."

I think the message for the twentieth century evangelist among the Muslims is perhaps best given in these words [quoted from James T. Addison, *The Christian Approach to the Moslem* (New York: Columbia University Press, 1942), p. 294]:

> In place of a frontal attack launched on the intellectual level, the best of modern missionaries to Islam pursue the method of intimate personal fellowship, of loving service, of sympathetic testimony, and of united prayer. Believing that the essence of conversion is direct experience of the saving power of Christ, they seek to lead the Moslem to that experience. In counting upon Christ Himself, and not theories about Him, to exert the drawing power, they are aided by the fact that the character of Christ does attract the Mohammedan. . . . The most hopeful note in the Islamic world today is the . . . irresistible attraction of the Person of Jesus Christ. To make the Moslem feel that attraction through deepening friendship, through a guided study of the New Testament, through leisurely conference, and through that prayer together which confesses God's Spirit alone can convert — this is the primary aim on which all else depends.

What impresses you about these three very large groups of people? Why do you think they have remained so resistant to the Gospel? Why is there good hope that their resistances might be changing? Why is it that Muslims seem to be more effectively reached through a warm, personal contact rather than through preaching and evangelistic campaigns? Why are these three cultural-religious groups so important to worldwide evangelization?

We have considered in these studies the new and the old, the rising and continuing needs associated with various groups of people: children, youth, families, rural and urban people, nationalistic feelings in people, cultural and religious groups, and minority groups. The issue is whether or not the church will relate effectively to these unreached peoples of the world. But an even more important issue is for you to decide — what you will do about these new and old needs. What responsibility does your church or group have? What more should you do collectively? What should you do individually? How will you respond to the peoples of the world who have not yet responded to the Gospel?

We have seen throughout the six units of this study that billions of people throughout the world are without Christ. If you look around you, you will find some of those billions. How will you seek to reach them?

The overwhelming numbers of people must be reached by someone going to them across cultural and language borders. Missionaries are needed and wanted from all parts of the world. What part can *you* have in worldwide evangelization?

The Great Commission says, "Go and make disciples of all the nations, baptizing them in the name of the Father and of the Son and of the Holy Spirit, and then teach these new disciples to obey all the commands I have given you; and be sure of this — that I am with you always, even to the end of the world" (Matthew 28:19–20). What does this require of you?

Contents ~ 4

Acknowledgements

Authors and papers of the International Congress on World Evangelization used in this chapter are as follows:

Peter Beyerhaus, "Evangelism and the Kingdom of God";

Samuel Escobar, "Evangelism and Man's Search for Freedom, Justice and Fulfillment";

Carl F. H. Henry, "Evangelism and Personal and Social Ethics";

Donald McGavran, "Ten Dimensions of World Evangelism";

René Padilla, "Evangelism and the World";

George W. Peters, "Contemporary Practices of Evangelism";

Francis A. Schaeffer, "Form and Freedom in the Church."

Realities

Jesus Christ is always Good News for mankind. Today, people need to *hear* this Good News and *see* it put into practice worldwide. No matter how different their economic, social and spiritual needs, all people can find salvation in Christ. These realities were discussed by church leaders at the International Congress on World Evangelization in Lausanne, Switzerland. In this study we shall take a brief look at how the Gospel of Jesus Christ affects the spiritual and social needs of mankind.

Samuel Escobar, who is a writer, lecturer on Latin American social, political, economic and religious affairs — and is presently General Director of Inter-Varsity Christian Fellowship in Canada — began his presentation to the Congress with a quotation:

Imagine that all the population of the world was condensed to the size of one village of one hundred people. In this village 67 of that 100 people would be poor; the other 33 would be in varying degrees well-off. Of the total population only 7 would be North Americans. The other 93 people would watch the 7 North Americans spend one-half of all the money, eat one-seventh of all the food and use one-half of all the bathtubs. These seven people would have ten times more doctors than the other 93. Meanwhile the seven would continue to get more and more and the 93 less and less. [from Clifford Christians, et al., eds., Who In The World (**Grand Rapids, Michigan: Wm. B. Eerdmans Publishing Co., 1972), p. 125.**]

This dramatic account of the disparity of wealth in the world becomes more significant for Christians today because it can be said that Christianity at the moment is concentrated in that part of the world where the privileged 33 percent live. Moreover, the average annual income in the developed world is about $2,400, while the average for the underdeveloped world is $180. This gap is widening, and it is expected that in the next ten years another $1,100 will be added to the difference. What are the consequences for Christians in the developed countries — North America, for example — who have an evangelistic concern?

As part of the wealthy seven we are trying to reach as many of the other 93 for Christ as we can. We tell them about Jesus and they watch us throw away more food than they ever hope to

eat. We are busy building beautiful church buildings, and they scrounge to find shelter for their families. We have money in the bank and they do not have enough to buy food for their children. All the while we tell them that our Master was the Servant of men, the Savior who gave His all for us and bids us give all for Him . . . We are the rich minority in the world. We may be able to forget about that or consider it unimportant. The question is, can the 93 forget? [Christians, p. 125]

As we think of evangelism in a world dimension we cannot forget the facts that surround our task these days — the reality that overpopulation, hunger, oppression, war, torture, violence, pollution, and the extreme forms of wealth and poverty are not disappearing but rather growing at an astonishing pace.

Man's sinfulness is evident in the totality of his life as an individual and as a member of the human race. Evil is a reality in the intellectual as well as in the physical and social dimension of man's life and human structures.

C. René Padilla, theological secretary for the International Fellowship of Evangelical Students, added:

Man's problem in the world is not simply that he commits isolated sins or gives in to the temptation to particular vices. It is, rather, that he is imprisoned within a closed system of rebellion against God that conditions him to absolutize the relative and to relativize the absolute, a system whose mechanism of self-sufficiency deprives him of eternal life and subjects him to the judgment of God.

How do man's social, political, and economic situations affect his personal morality? Worldwide, is man's situation getting any better?

Padilla says that people absolutize the relative and relativize the absolute. By this he means that people make important what is not really very important and make of little or no value what *should be* very important. In other words, God, the Absolute One, is considered to have little or no value to much of mankind.

For example, people make material things or pleasures, their gods. What examples of this do you see in the people around you? What unimportant things do they make important?

How does man's sinfulness affect all areas of his life? Are just the personal areas of his life affected by sin? How are the social, political, economic, and religious areas affected by sin? What are his gods?

How do social problems like poverty, oppression, and pollution, as well as personal problems, affect evangelization?

Are there areas near you affected by pressing social needs? How does evangelism respond?

How does sin affect the social, political, economic, personal, and religious areas of people's lives?

Why is it impossible to separate the individual from corporate society?

What implications for Christianity do you see in the disparity between those who "have" and those who "have not"?

What are some ways that man absolutizes the relative and relativizes the absolute?

Would a poor person's preoccupation with seeking food, clothing, shelter and basic medical care be what is meant by absolutizing the relative?

How do social ills affect the hearers' response to the Gospel? Begin now to list reasons why evangelization implies social responsibility and action.

115

Several authors of Congress papers claim that the Gospel message is relevant to people's needs in all situations. In his paper, Escobar quoted George B. Duncan:

> *Evangelism has been defined as the offering of a whole Christ for the whole man by the whole church to the whole world. If this is indeed evangelism then it will require the three channels of communication . . . there must be the declaration; there must be the illustration of the Gospel; and finally the products of the Gospel must be able to stand the closest examination.* [(*Carl F. Henry and Stanley W. Mooneyham, eds., One Race, One Gospel, One Task (Minneapolis: World Wide Publications, 1967), Vol. I, pp. 60, 62.*]

George W. Peters, Chairman of the Department of Missions of Dallas Theological Seminary, emphasized our responsibility to relate the Gospel to specific situations:

There is a peculiar note of emphasis in the various messages of the apostles in the book of Acts, an emphasis that relates that message uniquely to that particular people and that situation. *It is a relevant message that did not miss the mark.* It won a hearing and it hit the target because it met man in his struggle with sin.

There is an emphasis of the Gospel that is peculiarly relevant to the different generations, the different peoples, the different cultural molds, the different situations. *The effectiveness of evangelism depends to a great extent upon our ability to make the Gospel message relevant to the religious needs and hopes, the aspirations and anticipations, the yearnings and strivings, the fears and frustrations of the people.* Only then will we win a hearing. Here is our initial and effective point of contact and departure to the deeper and full needs of the spiritual nature of man in his sin and guilt, bondage, and lostness. Man will hear when he can expect that a need will be met, a hope will be fulfilled, an anticipation will be realized.

What are the various needs in the world? In what way is Christ "good news" for these needs? List some of the needs of society and individuals that you think Christ is capable of meeting. As you think this through consider the following: *economics* (poverty, use of money, food, shelter, clothing, transportation, consumer goods, etc.), *politics* (government, individual freedom, peace, war, etc.), *race* (segregation, discrimination, prejudice), *sex* (exploitation, discrimination, dating, pornography, marriage, family), *values* (ethics or how to tell right from wrong, value of a human life, the use of technology such as television or newspaper to control men), *religion* (sense of God, desire to worship something or someone, guilt, etc.), *psychology* (fears, guilt, joy, sorrow, etc.), *social* (status, caste), and *environment* (pollution, use of natural resources, conservation, etc.). Feel free to add categories as you continue this study.

There are dangers in talking about the Gospel and the social needs of people. In the recent past organized Christianity has been split by what has been called liberalism's "social gospel," that is, preaching social improvement apart from personal salvation in Christ. In reaction to this message, many evangelicals have stressed only the personal salvation in Christ. Both approaches were examined at the Congress. Peter

Beyerhaus, a Lutheran theologian from Germany, Samuel Escobar, and René Padilla made pertinent comments about these two approaches. Note carefully the major criticisms of the liberal and the evangelical approaches to salvation.

Beyerhaus

One of the fatal errors in mission work is the idea that it is our task in this present age to Christianize the world and thereby to establish the messianic kingdom by our own power. Such mistaken Christians are directed by the utopian vision of a unified mankind in which perfect peace and justice have already become a universal reality. They are, however, frustrated by the fact that a great part of mankind simply refuses to accept the Gospel and to live according to the new law of Christ's Kingdom. Therefore, they place no confidence in purely spiritual means, such as evangelistic methods that rely wholly on the challenging impression of the Word of God on the human conscience.

A mistaken alternative is offered by other Christians who substitute for the messianic kingdom a human vision to be realized by political means. They repeat the error of the Zealots at the time of Jesus who wanted to force the Kingdom of God to come by ejecting the Romans by the sword. The physical resources of the Christian churches are not sufficient, of course, to remove all forces of oppression. Therefore, some people even suggest alliances between the church and the liberation movements within non-Christian religions and ideologies. This new concept of "mission" is today's greatest menace to the worldwide church. I must call it the Mission of Barabbas; it has no promise of the Lord. A worldwide kingdom which is achieved by the combined spirits, concepts and methods of the dynamic movements of this age would be a kingdom without Christ. It would be the anti-Christian kingdom.

117

Escobar

Liberalism presented the social gospel of a wrathless God who was going to save a sinless man through a crossless Christ. The ethical demands of Christ were presented as separate from the saving power of His Cross and resurrection. He was presented as a model to be followed, but there was no transforming power that would help men to follow in His steps.

The temptation for evangelicals today is to reduce the Gospel, to mutilate it, to eliminate any demands for the fruit of repentance and any aspect that would make it unpalatable to a nominally Christian society. The church must, by all means, keep constantly alert to the needs of the millions who have not heard the Gospel. But with equal zeal it must stress the need for the whole Gospel of Jesus Christ as Savior and Lord whose demands cannot be cheapened.

The danger of evangelicalism is that it will present the Gospel as a spiritual message that has nothing to say about social problems. The task of evangelism and missions is to snatch up souls from perdition and hell. Though not always expressed, the implication is that the social behavior of the convert is not vitally and visibly affected by the message.

In the light of the biblical teaching there is no place for an unconcerned "otherworldliness." Biblical Christianity results in the Christian's commitment to his neighbor, rooted in the Gospel. There is no place for statistics on "how many souls die without Christ every minute," if they do not take into account how many of those die victims of hunger. There is no place for evangelism that sees the man who was assaulted by thieves on the road from Jerusalem to Jericho as only a soul to be saved — ignoring the person. "What does it profit, my brethren, if a man says he has faith but has not works? Can his faith save him? If a brother or sister is ill-clad and in lack of daily food, and one of you says to them, 'Go in peace, be warmed and filled,' without giving them the things needed for the body, what does it profit? So faith by itself, if it has no works, is dead" (James 2:14–17).

●

What are some major reasons that liberalism's approach to salvation is not sufficient? How did evangelicals react to the "social gospel"? Examine your own witness. Have there been times when you witnessed without caring about the person's other needs? Do you pray for the conversion of people in school or at work with you? How can you show care and concern for them as "whole persons"?

●●

In your own words, write out the approaches to salvation of liberalism and evangelicalism. What are the criticisms of each approach? In what ways have you neglected the whole person when witnessing or praying for their salvation? How would you change this approach to demonstrate care for the whole person?

How can your church show concern for more than just "souls"?

●●●

In your own words, write out the approaches to salvation of liberalism and evangelicalism. What are the criticisms of each approach? Why did liberals develop the "social gospel"? Why did evangelicalism react so strongly against the "social gospel"? How does your witness demonstrate concern for the whole person?

How can evangelistic campaigns communicate more than just personal salvation? Should they?

Whole

The question has been raised: What *is* the relationship of the Gospel to social responsibility and action? In order to see what the Bible emphasizes, individually read and classify the Scriptures listed below, placing each text in one of the three major classifications: 1) personal salvation only with no relation to daily living; 2) ethical living only for individuals and/or society with no direct comment on personal salvation; 3) personal salvation that is related to the life situation of the individual and/or society.

Isaiah 59:1–16, 20–21
Amos 5:10–15, 24
Micah 6:8
Matthew 5:13–16
Matthew 11:2–6
Matthew 25:31–46
Luke 4:16–21
Luke 19:1–10
John 3:3, 16, 17

John 4:1–29, 39–42
Romans 12:1–3, 9–17
Ephesians 2:8–10
Colossians 3:1–17
Titus 2:11–14
Titus 3:1–8
James 1:27
James 2:1–10, 14–26
1 Peter 2:9

Share your conclusions about this task with the rest of your study group. Then consider this question: If *sin* makes each individual a sinner and all of society shows man's sinfulness, what will be the impact on society when someone becomes a "new creation in Christ"? Will his conversion and Christ-like new nature also affect his society?

Escobar

God's salvation transforms man in the totality of his life and in that way affects man's life and human structures. To give only a spiritual content to God's action in man, or to give only a social and physical dimension to God's salvation are both unbiblical heresies, and as such evangelicals should reject them.

God's call to His people to be a different people, salt, light, a holy nation (Matthew 5:13–16; 1 Peter 2:9), was given in a world that was like ours, an imperfect world torn apart by sin and its consequences. God's call to witness and to the proclamation of His name demands immediate obedience. There is no indication that God's people have to wait until the world becomes better in order to obey His call and demands. For those who have heard the call of the Lord and live under His Lordship, obedience is unavoidable, whatever the circumstances.

Concern with the quality of the new life in Christ is precisely relevant to the discussion of the relation between evangelism and social evils. The sinfulness of man is visible in the way every dimension of his life has been distorted from the original design of the Creator. Oppression and injustice, as they become visible in the structures of community life and nations, are the results of disobedience to God and idolatry. When men turn to God and are transformed by the Spirit, their individual lives as well as the structures in which they live are affected. This is evident in the book of Acts where the end of idolatry is a danger for the business structure of a city (Acts 19), where the spiritual liberation of a girl also affects the social and financial life of a group of people and brings political accusations against the apostles (Acts 16:16–23). The individual and the world in which he lives cannot be the same after the Gospel has entered in (2 Corinthians 5:17). Christ creates a new man within reality (the social, political, and material areas of life), and through the new man transforms reality. God had a purpose in creation and when men turn to Christ a process begins in them by which they grow in the fulfillment of the original purpose of God. This fulfillment involves every area of life through which man can love God. It has to do with his whole being: heart, soul, strength, and mind (Luke 10:27).

If a man is really renewed in Christ, this renewal will start internally in him. If this new spiritual life develops in a healthy way, it will make itself felt in all spheres of a man's life and social involvement. Truly regenerated Christians are better citizens. Their Christian life generates in them a new spontaneity and creativity in moral action, a new responsibility in public positions entrusted to them, and the desire to bring about reconciliation, solidarity, and mutual participation.

●

Why does a person's salvation change his life? Why will a Christian's life have some effects on people around him?

What kind of influence for Christ do you have on your friends? What kinds of influence do the Christians in your group have on the people around you?

● ●

How much of your life should salvation affect? Why hasn't salvation affected every area of our lives equally?

Will a person's conversion affect his society? How? What should happen when several people become converted within a relatively small group? How is *your* conversion affecting your society?

● ● ●

Does a person's individual sin affect his society? What, then, is a sinful society?

Does a person's salvation in Christ affect society? If so, how much? How is individual salvation connected to changes in society?

What kind of life and social changes can we expect from one individual conversion?

How is *your* salvation in Christ demonstrated in social action?

The extent of our social involvement as a result of our salvation has no boundaries. Earlier, Samuel Escobar referred to the Christians in society as lights in the world, reminding us what Jesus said (Matthew 5:14–16). Jesus taught that Christians are witnesses to the grace of God among the people of the world who live in darkness. Escobar also referred to Christians as salt (Matthew 5:13). This passage means that just as ancient peoples used salt to keep meat from spoiling, Christians are to be a preservative in society. Christians help to keep society from being totally sinful. Escobar gave examples of Christians who are active in society.

The missionary work of proclamation of the Gospel has always been accompanied by results that affected social and political structures. Many of those who fought for independence in the anti-colonial movements that followed the Second World War were people who had been educated and motivated in their love for freedom by the missionary schools established during the last century and the first part of this century in Asia and Africa. In Latin America, the presence of evangelical missionaries in countries like Mexico, Peru, Argentina, Guatemala, and Ecuador was welcomed by those who were fighting for freedom and justice in society. Pablo Besson, a Swiss Baptist missionary in Argentina, was a fighter for religious and civil freedom in Peru. In several Latin American countries, evangelicals have been champions of the rights of the Indian majorities enslaved by centuries of white domination.

It might be well to point out that the intention of these evangelicals was basically evangelistic and their missionary zeal had a deep spiritual dimension, but the evils of society were such that their Christian calling compelled them to become involved in the fight for social change. What the Finnish evangelical Paavo Kortekangas said in Amsterdam then is true: "Part of the tragedy of our time is that evangelical Christians are avoiding the revolution that they themselves caused (by their earlier biblical social witness), and so others have stepped in."

●

What influence does your belonging to Christ have on your school? your work? your city? What is your influence on the student government or city government? What is the relationship between you and your teacher, or your supervisor at work? What kind of effects *should* the Gospel have on your activities?

●●

Consider the social and political situation in your school, your city, or relationships between employer and employees. What effect should the Gospel have on these structures?

How can you begin to help the Gospel influence at least one of these areas?

Why will this improve evangelism?

●●●

Why hasn't much missionary work been involved in social and political areas? Is there time to do more than "preach the Gospel" for personal salvation? What might happen if all Christians got involved in applying their oneness with Christ to the structure of society and politics?

What can you do to influence the social and political structures around you?

The life and ministry of the Lord Jesus Christ is *the* pattern for individual living and for the life of the church — the community of God's people. Read John 20:21. What was commanded? What did Jesus say was fulfilled in Himself? Is this evangelization? Please reread Luke 4:16–21.

As you read what Escobar and Padilla say about this, consider the way that Christ's life entered into the early church and how His life can enter into yours.

Jesus Christ, our model missionary, was not only the carrier of a message, but He Himself was the message by His way of being among men, by the qualities of His character, and by His compassion and His readiness to come close to men in their need. The New Testament is clear in the demand for the Christian and the church to be a living expression of the message — to be a "living letter," as Paul puts it in 2 Corinthians 3:1–3.

The primitive church was not perfect, but evidently it was a community that caught the attention of men because of the qualitative difference of its life. The message was not only heard from them, it was also seen in the way they lived. Consequently, in the evangelistic and missionary process as we see it in the Bible there is a reality to be seen and experienced by men, as well as a Gospel that is proclaimed. If we read the epistles we see that the emphasis is not so much on exhortations to evangelize as on the qualities of the new life in Christ. Christ has commissioned us to be His messengers by word and deed, by a way of being and by a way of speaking.

The message of salvation is not only heard in verbal propositions but also visible in a group of people who live by it and are ready to die for it. The church, the community of those called by God, shows what God can do with man as an individual and as a member of the human race.

The church is the community patterned after the Servant-King, in which each member gives according to his means and receives according to his needs, since "it is more blessed to give than to receive" (Acts 2:45; 4:34–35; 20:35). It is a community of reconciliation with God and reconciliation among men (Ephesians 2:11–22). And it is a community, finally, that serves as a base for the resistance against the conditioning by "the present evil age" and makes it possible for Jesus' disciples to live *in* the world without being *of* the world.

Francis Schaeffer, speaker, writer and founder of L'Abri Fellowship in Switzerland, provides a sketch of the community of God's people in action. As you read this selection, try to determine if these things could happen in your local church.

Schaeffer

My favorite church in Acts and, I guess, in all of history is the church at Antioch. It was a place where something new happened. The great, proud Jews who despised the Gentiles came to a breakthrough. They could not be silent. They told their Gentile neighbors about the Gospel, and suddenly, on the basis of the blood of Christ and the truth of the Word of God, the racial thing was solved. There were Jewish Christians and Gentile Christians and they were one!

More than that, there was a total span of the social spectrum. We are not told specifically that there were slaves in the church of Antioch, but we know there were in other places. There is no reason to think they were not in Antioch. We know by the record in Acts that there was no less a person in that church than Herod's foster brother. The man at the very peak of the social pile and the man at the bottom met together in the church of the Lord Jesus Christ and they were one in a beauty of human relationships.

There was a man called Niger (meaning black) in that church. More than likely he was a black man. The church at Antioch, on the basis of the blood of Christ, encompassed the whole. There was a beauty that the Greek and the Roman world did not know — and the world looked. And then there was the preaching of the Gospel. In one generation the church spread from Asia to Spain. If we want to touch our generation, we must be no less than this.

I would emphasize again that community reached all the way down into the realm of material possessions. There is no *communism*, as we today know the word *communism*, in the book of Acts. Peter made very plain to Ananias and Sapphira that their land was their own and when they

123

had sold their land they were masters of what they did with the money. No state or church law, no legalism, bound them. There was a love in the early church that was so overwhelming that they could not imagine having one man hungry and one man rich in the church of the Lord Jesus.

The church cared for one another's material needs. Read James 2. James asks, "What are you doing preaching the Gospel to a man and trying to have good relationship to him spiritually if he needs shoes and you do not give him shoes?" It has been considered spiritual to give for missions but not equally spiritual to give when my brother needs shoes. That is never found in the Word of God. Of course, the early church gave to missions; at times they gave money so Paul did not have to make tents. But Paul makes no distinction between collections for missions and collections for material needs, as if one were spiritual and the other not. For the most part, when Paul speaks of financial matters, he does so because there was a group of Christians somewhere who had a material need and Paul then calls upon other churches to help.

Moreover, it was not only in the local church that Christians cared for each other's needs; they did so at great distances. When the church of Macedonia, which was made up of Gentile Christians, heard that the Jewish Christians — the Jews whom they would have previously despised — had material need they took an offering and sent it with care hundreds of miles in order that the Jewish Christians might eat.

How did the Gospel affect the social life of the people of God in the church in Acts? Situations change and needs are different in different periods of history and in various countries. Can you suggest any effect of the Gospel that should happen in your church in today's world?

Schaeffer makes a bold statement in the selection following. As you read it, think how you would answer it from your experience as a part of God's community.

Have we exhibited this community in our evangelical churches? I want to say no, by and large, no. Our churches have often been two things — preaching points and activity generators. When a person really has desperate needs in the area of race, or economic matters, or psychological matters, does he expect to find a supporting community in our evangelical churches? We must say with tears, many times no!

What more can you do to practice the Gospel in your church and community? How can your life show concern for the spiritual as well as other needs of people? Remember, if the church does not act as light and salt in society, then Christ has no effect on society.

Masses

How does the Gospel apply to our society? How does it apply within social relationships? Can a Christian change the economic approach to supply and demand of his country to a Christian approach? Since we as Christians have a responsibility to feed the poor, clothe the naked, and give a cup of cold water to the thirsty, how can we begin to do it?

In the studies that follow, we will examine the statements of several Congress papers on how the Gospel relates to certain major areas of society.

Dr. Donald Mc Gavran, former missionary, author, and professor at the School of World Mission of Fuller Theological Seminary, Pasadena, California, explains the importance of the masses of the world, and Christianity's importance to them.

The day of the common man has dawned. An irreversible tide is sweeping the voiceless multitudes to positions of tremendous power. Illiterate peasants, country serfs, factory laborers, poverty stricken miners, cannon fodder, the poor, the hewers of wood and drawers of water have been given the vote in nation after nation. They are the court of last appeal. This is the fruit partly of Christian conviction and partly of western democracy, fertilized of late by Russian and Chinese Communism.

There have always been enormous numbers of common people; but today they have become aware of their importance, and their power. They are demanding equal pay, equal educational opportunity, equal leisure, — in short, they demand social justice.

The awakening multitudes are often basically receptive to the Gospel. The huge majority of those accepting Jesus Christ and becoming Christians always have been common people. The masses have a built-in receptivity to the Good News. Oppressed and ground down, they, like ancient Israel, are "looking for a Saviour." Their ears are attuned to Him who cries, "Come unto me all you who labor and are heavy laden."

The Christian church has good news for the awakening masses — that God the Father Almighty is just and intends to have a just world. The revolutionary impact of this simple statement should be grasped. It affirms that the very structure of the universe favors the common man. It proclaims that God intends an order of society in which each man can and will receive justice. This meets the deepest needs of the proletariat. Contrary to paternalistic thinking, the greatest need of the masses is neither aid nor kindness. Their greatest need is neither handouts nor social action, but a religion which gives them bedrock on which to stand as they battle for justice.

The highly valuable gifts of the Christian religion are God the Father Almighty who hates injustice, God the Son who died for each man of the masses, and the Bible which demands justice for the common man. The Christian religion endows every human being with infinite value. "Making people Christian," along with other things, means giving them a world view and a Bible which irresistibly, though often slowly, create equality of opportunity and undergird all strivings against entrenched privilege. With this wealth in hand, the masses can conquer secondary poverties.

●

What kind of people make up the world's masses? How far from where you live do you find people like this?

The Gospel can meet the needs felt by the masses. What are their needs? How can you show people near you — especially the poor — that the Gospel is for them?

●●

Who are the masses? Who are the masses near you?

What makes the Gospel attractive to the masses? In what ways is the Gospel "Good News" to them?

To what kinds of social or religious movements might the masses turn if Christ is not proclaimed to them?

How does Christianity do what McGavran says in his last two sentences above?

How can you present the Gospel to the masses around you so that they can see that Christ is interested in them?

How can you avoid making the Gospel seem like an escape from reality for the masses?

●●●

How important is it to reach the masses of the world with the Gospel? In what ways is the Gospel "Good News" to the masses?

In what sense does Christianity set the masses free and provide justice for them?

Do you agree with McGavran's last two sentences above?

McGavran suggests responsibilities that lie beyond preaching the Gospel to the masses. Do you know Christians who are ready and able to do this?

Marx called religion "the opiate of the people." How can we prevent the message of the Gospel from being misunderstood as an escape from reality by the masses?

Carl F. H. Henry, theologian, writer, and lecturer-at-large for World Vision, provides another view regarding the Gospel and the masses.

Henry

From the very first, the Christian message has emphasized the need of totally new selfhood, has called men to love of God and fellowman, and has stressed concern for public no less than private righteousness. For untold multitudes the problem of human meaning and worth turns upon their dire poverty and their powerlessness to change their destiny. Their existence revolves around the search for food and shelter to survive another day. When Christians fail to emphasize that it is morally wicked for human creatures to starve and suffer like animals, and that insensitivity by the rich to the physical needs of those around them is ethically wrong, they yield to Marxists the privilege of formulating social criticism. They also nourish the propaganda that only communism or socialism can guarantee a just society. In some places like Latin America with its vast areas of poverty, the burden of the status quo is so heavy that all existing social structures are deplored as oppressive. Consequently, the underprivileged and victimized reach for radical alternatives that retrieve hope from some remote future and insert it into the immediate present and its problems. Roman Catholicism, by far the dominant religion in Latin America, has done little across four hundred years to insert hope into the economic plight of the masses. Evangelical Protestantism, while bringing vital personal religion, has similarly done little to cope with the problem of poverty. To stress that the total human predicament will be solved only when people are personally converted to Christ lacks assurance because even a phenomenal church growth rate of more than five percent in a single decade would still miss the vast majority. It also lacks credibility when one notes the limited reversal of poverty even among people in evangelical churches. The longing for material fulfillment in the face of poverty is widespread among the masses. The relentless Marxist attack on capitalism promotes socialism as the utopian alternative and revolutionary violence as the way to achieve it.

Henry suggests several things that Christians should do to remedy these problems. In which of these will you be involved?

1. Christians must indict the moral wrongs of human destitution, suffering, affliction, and oppression.
2. Christian proclamation must not speak only of personal spiritual conversion nor ignore social criticism attuned to biblical justice. It must elaborate a persuasive alternative to a forced redistribution of wealth.
3. Christians must contrast socialist uncertainty about the identity of the ideal man and the express nature of the new society with Christian certainty about the Second Adam and the regenerate society as a beachhead in history for the coming Kingdom.
4. Christians must emphasize that Marxist proposals for utopia do not really, as claimed, overcome human alienation, but in fact perpetuate that alienation by substituting one preferred class for another, and deepen it by ignoring man's fundamental spiritual relationships to the living God.

What additional points come to your mind that should be added to this list? What definite actions do these items suggest to you? How reasonable is it to expect poverty and other problems of the masses to disappear because the Gospel is preached? What should Christians do to help overcome the problems of the masses?

Power

What about money? How does a Christian view wealth in money or property? What should be a Christian's response to the poor? Carl F. H. Henry presented the following thoughts at the Lausanne Congress:

The Protestant emphasis has been that accumulated wealth should be invested to produce additional wealth, although the allurements of wealth were to be resisted and the rich, no less than the poor, were to live frugally. The deceitfulness of riches is a recurring New Testament theme. Since all we possess is held as a divine stewardship, the apostles emphasize that one who has more than others has greater opportunity to bless those who have less. No true Christian can be rich and use wealth merely for self-gratification.

Yet distribution to others was voluntary. There were times when, for a specific objective, believers voluntarily pooled possessions, but this procedure is never declared to be a Christian moral imperative; private property is not scripturally viewed as evil in itself, and a case can even be made biblically that some property is universally necessary to personal fulfillment. The eighth commandment establishes the principle of ownership, "Thou shalt not steal" (Exodus 20:15). Scripture sanctions the acquisition of property by legitimate means, whether it be by work, purchase, or inheritance.

The Bible's main focus is on the use of possessions and reflects a consistent concern for the poor. Possessions enable one to support and advance evangelical witness in the world, to minister to the needs of the household of faith, neighbors, and others in need (James 2:16; Galatians 6:10).

Illegal acquisition of profit, whether by deceit, false weights, oppression, or high interest is sharply condemned. The Bible repeatedly contrasts the principle of greed with that of gratitude. While it considers fair profit legitimate, the Bible's concern is that riches not corrupt their possessor by indulgence, misuse, or indifference to the needs of others. A most familiar text is Jesus' classic question: "What does it profit a man, if he gain the whole world, and lose his own soul?" (Mark 8:36).

The Old Testament prophets and New Testament writers as well thrust the problem of poverty upon the conscience of God's people. While the concern of Scripture is with spiritual and moral need, it does not gloss over material need. Jesus launched His public ministry with Isaiah's prophecy of good news to the poor, and the Gospel must therefore reach people in need as a message of hope in their total predicament. Jesus unobtrusively gave to the poor (John 13:29), and Paul took up collections for the poor. Distribution to those in need is viewed biblically as evidence of love for God (Matthew 19:21). The first charitable work of the early Christians took the form of gifts to impoverished widows. The classic reminder that "Christ became poor that we might be rich" (2 Corinthians 8:9) utterly disarms anyone clinging to possessions in the face of need.

Sensitive Christian conscience should support programs responding to needs of the aged, blind, lame, and dying; supplying food for the starving, job-training for adults, and non-discriminatory educational opportunities. The blind, lame, and aged poor can hardly escape their poverty by hard work; the poorly educated often face unrewarding jobs, and race and sex discrimination have impeded opportunities for still others.

Believers should set an example by providing for their own kin and those of the fellowship of faith. Healthy adults should in any event contribute to the well-being of the community to be temporarily out of work is no necessary mandate for state support. The Bible places restraints on consumer aspirations. It emphasizes the responsibility of all men (even those who have less) in respect to neighbors in need. God has an eye for the poor, and divine blessing is promised those who are charitable toward them (Psalm 41:1), and who advance justice in their behalf.

Samuel Escobar makes a forceful statement on the Christian and social responsibilities:

Spirituality without discipleship in the daily social, economic and political aspects of life is religiosity and not Christianity. The love of God and His plan for the life of a man who is exploiting others and swindling them is not only that he should become an active member of a church giving good offerings to the cause. It is also that he should repent and show the signs of a new life in his business (Luke 19:1–10).

●

Are there wrong ways to become wealthy? When is it wrong to be wealthy? Is it better always to be giving most of your money and other wealth away than to save it?

How can wealth be used for the spread of the Gospel?

How do you act as a good steward with whatever God has given you?

What can you and your group do to help the poor near you? How could your help be a means of evangelism?

●●

When is wealth dangerous? What is the proper use for wealth? Is it better to give away most of what you have or save it?

How does being a Christian "steward" enter into the question of wealth?

Why are the poor, widows, orphans and sick singled out in Scripture to be helped by Christians?

How could the stewardship of whatever you possess be used for the advancement of the Gospel?

What can you and your group do to help the needy in your area?

How is helping the poor a means of evangelism?

●●●

Why is discipleship linked to stewardship of wealth and care for the poor?

When should a person stop saving his money and start helping others?

Is it morally wrong as a Christian to accumulate great wealth?

What is the proper way to help the poor?

Are you a good steward of what you have? How can you aid the poor in your geographic area?

Under what circumstances can you call "social action" evangelism?

130

Politics surrounds the Christian on local, regional and national levels. How does a Christian respond to politics? Carl F. H. Henry has these ideas:

Henry

The call for Christian participation in political life is grounded not simply in the moral and spiritual chaos of the modern nations, but in a biblical mandate as well. Christians should be politically active, where they have citizenship, to the limit of their ability and competence. The penalty for failure to lead and to be vocal is that others who misuse and exploit political power for objectionable ends and by objectionable means take over. But Christian witness regarding government also has a transcendent dimension. Christians pray for rulers (1 Timothy 2:1–2), knowing that Christ is King of kings. Civil government will pass away, while the rule and reign of Christ in the Kingdom of God remains. The church is to witness to the world of the supremacy of love in the life of the fellowship that endures.

When the Christian church has been strong in society she has had no less an interest in law and jurisprudence [the science or philosophy of law] than in grace and theology. That fact does not by any means demand a Christian political party, but it does demand Christian political responsibility. In the absence of a will to do the good, no law, however desirable, can assuredly achieve its public objectives. Evangelism can bring to multitudes the good will and moral dynamic necessary to make good laws work.

Henry stresses that Christians should be involved in politics. C. René Padilla tells why this is so and what Christians can bring to politics. Think of the difference that it would make if Christians would act in politics as Padilla suggests!

Padilla

Jesus' kingdom is not of this world, not in the sense that it has nothing to do with the world but in the sense that it does not adapt itself to human politics. It is a kingdom with its own politics, marked by sacrifice. Jesus is a king who "came not to be served but to serve, and to give his life as a ransom for many" (Mark 10:45). This service to the point of sacrifice belongs to the very essence of His mission. And this must be the distinctive sign of the community that acknowledges Him as king. According to the politics of man, "those who are supposed to rule over the Gentiles lord it over them, and their great men exercise authority over them"; in the politics of the Kingdom of God, he who wants to be great "must be slave of all" (Mark 10:43–44). Thus Jesus confronts the power structures by denouncing their deep-seated ambition to rule, and by proclaiming another alternative based on love, service, self-dedication to others. He does not take refuge in "religion" or "spiritual things," as if His kingdom had nothing to do with political and social life, but He presents Himself as the Servant-King, the creator and model of a community that submits to Him as Lord and commits itself to live as He lived.

●

How are politics and evangelism related?

Are there good reasons for a Christian to be in politics? In what ways should a Christian politician be different? How can you be more involved in the politics of your own special interest groups?

●●

How active should a Christian be in politics? Why is the church interested in politics?

How can you be involved in local and national politics?

●●●

Why should a Christian's social responsibility include political involvement? How can this responsibility be worked out in local or national politics?

How can a Christian's political activities help or hinder evangelism?

You have considered questions about the masses, wealth, and politics. These are all related to the needs of man worldwide and thus to the task of evangelism. In what way is evangelism related to the masses? How can wealth be used for the proclamation of the Gospel? Why is politics important to evangelism? And what are *you* going to do that will make even a small difference to the *masses* with whatever *wealth* you have and through your engagement in *political* activities?

Worth

Many prominent secular scholars, theologians, and Christian leaders have spoken about the Western world's preoccupation with sex. In what way is the Good News of the Gospel related to sex? In the following selection, Carl F. H. Henry sketches a biblical view of sex, some ways that people have warped sex, and how the Gospel can make a difference in matters of sex.

Henry

Because of the wholeness of human personality, what one thinks and does sexually has consequences for the entire self in this life and the next. For Christians, sex involves considerate gratitude, personal devotion, and welcome responsibility under God. Modern society increasingly views sex solely in terms of biological gratification and in a context of license and irresponsibility.

The human need of man and woman for each other springs from an original relationship grounded in God's creative act (Genesis 2:18–25). The family is a basic natural order of creation. Parents find new life together in union; children are divinely given as a sacred trust. The origin and norm of all genuine love is God's love for man, a love offered to undeserving sinners. The biblical revelation of man and woman as one flesh through covenant-responsibility calls for steadfast fidelity of one man and one woman to each other in lifelong relationships that death alone can sever.

Many regard the marriage contract as only temporary. This absence of lasting commitment conditions the relationship in psychically adverse ways. The New Testament does not correlate marital intercourse solely with procreation, but rather with the total personality needs of the marital partners (1 Corinthians 7:3–5). The Gospel summons marriage partners to Christ's love for the church as an analogy for the marital relationship (Ephesians 5:22–23).

The soaring divorce rate in many lands is often turned into a plea for relaxation of New Testament principles in the name of "love" as a superior criterion. But this overlooks the importance of permanent interpersonal commitments at the heart of true marriage. The psychological damage done by broken homes to the personalities of parents and children alike is incalculable. No member of the family can ever again be what he or she alone was before the divorce. Nor are the consequences for society to be minimized. The Gospel does not require two persons whose love has died to live in marital hell. It offers new life and new love that none can scorn in good conscience.

Modern notions of liberation often nurture promiscuous sexual attitudes. The availability of scientific contraceptive techniques and of "abortion on demand" have fostered a sex-centered generation preoccupied with genitals. Jesus directed burning indictments against sexual immorality (Matthew 5:27–28); the New Testament catalogues of sin repeatedly reproach sexual deviations (Galatians 5:19; Ephesians 5:3, 5). Many young people themselves confess that as sex has become free and easy, love has become elusive.

Promiscuity denies the basic Christian concepts of sex as a God-given entrustment requiring respectful responsibility and of sexual misconduct as sin against God. In a sex-saturated age the Gospel can break the power of temptation and equip the human spirit with new motivation and dynamic. Christ-given freedom liberates sexuality for true enjoyment as creative and renewing, rather than weakening and destructive.

A tide of pornographic materials floods much of the modern world. Christians should publicize their views of the moral wrong of degrading sex into a cheap animal commodity. Strangely enough, socially-active churches were so preoccupied with politico-economic issues and evangelical churches with changing persons that neither did much to stem the tide of pornography.

Christians should enter the arena of public persuasion, emphasizing not only the adverse effects of pornography on the morals of youth but also its offense to God. The full answer to the problem lies both in an evangelical changing of unregenerate engrossments and in the production of a creative literature of love. The church has *agapē* to combat *eros*. The preaching of the Gospel would summon sinners not only to experience *agapē*, but also so compellingly to publish it to the world that *eros* will seek the altar rail.

●   ●●   ●●●   **133**

How does being a Christian affect a person's views about sex? What is the purpose of marriage? Why does the Bible say that sex and marriage go together?

In what way is *agapē* (God's love) better than *eros* (sensual or self-centered love)? What would happen to human love relationships if God's love were part of them?

What does sex imply in a relationship? Why does the Bible present marriage as the only relationship in which these sexual implications can be fully implemented?

The Bible defines love as self-giving. How would self-giving love benefit relationships between sexes? How would your relationships with members of the opposite sex be affected?

What is the Bible's view of sex?

Why are sex and the Gospel linked together?

In what way does *agapē* combat *eros*? Is *eros* always bad? Can *eros* be transformed by *agapē*? How would such a transformation affect a person?

Can Christians justify racial prejudice? What does the Gospel say about racism? Does the Bible permit feelings of superiority because of racial, ethnic, or national backgrounds? Carl F. H. Henry was one of several speakers at the Congress who discussed race and the Gospel. Henry stressed our common humanity with regard to race.

Racial variations are a fact of human existence, but they are subordinate to a common humanity. The notion that any single race is the special carrier of human destiny involves a demonic pretense of divine election. It thus becomes a prideful revolt against God's creation-purpose for all mankind and His redemption-purpose in Christ.

The Bible assuredly indicates that Jehovah chose the Jews. But it was not because of their superiority. He elected to give them special advantages as a witness to the world of the blessings of serving the living God. Jesus of Nazareth, the promised Son, manifests God's ideal for all humanity. He breaks down the wall even between Jew and Gentile.

Scripture condemns racism, and God judges it in history. The God of grace exalts the humble and topples the proud. The Church is a multiracial body. Racism is therefore anti-Christ in spirit, arbitrarily implying an election that Scripture disowns.

Christians should see themselves in the mirror of history whenever any minority is deprived of equal rights before the law. Christians may always be a minority and may well be the next target of abuse. More fundamentally, racial injustice to any minority should be considered implicitly a threat not simply to one's own kind but to all humanity. The Christian has double motivation for identifying with the victims of race discrimination. First, he knows that God created all men of one flesh. Second, Christ died for all and is Head of a body transcending racial distinctions. The Gospel is therefore rejected in principle wherever and whenever the church practices racial exclusion instead of exhibiting the spiritual and moral unity of the whole family of the redeemed.

Francis Schaeffer stresses that God made *all* people in His own image. Christians are to treat all men with dignity.

If you ask me why the evangelical church has been so often weak in the question of race in the past, I think it was because we have destroyed the absolutes of the Word of God by making something else equal to God's absolutes. We were surrounded by a culture that had racial prejudices and did not look at all men as equal, and we allowed this to infiltrate the church. We made taboos apart from and even against the Word of God, and we held them to be equal with the absolutes of the Bible.

We are to show something to the watching world on the basis of the human relationships we have with other people, not just other Christians. Christians today are the people who understand who man is. We say man is different because he is made in the image of God (Genesis 1:26–27). But we must not say man is made in the image of God unless we look to God and by God's grace treat every man with dignity.

The first commandment is to love the Lord our God with all our heart and soul and mind, and the second is to love our neighbor as ourselves (Luke 10:25–28). After Jesus commanded this someone said, "Who is our neighbor?" And Jesus then told the story of the good Samaritan (Luke 10:29–37). He was not just talking about treating Christians well; he was talking about treating every man we meet well, every man whether or not he is of our social status, every man whether or not he speaks our language, every man whether or not he has the color of our skin. Every man is to be treated as truly being made in the image of God, and thus there is to be a beauty of human relationships. This attitude is to operate on all levels.

135

●

What causes racism? Why does the Bible say racism is sin? Why is it necessary to apply what the Bible says about racism to every kind of feeling and action of superiority?

Do you ever feel superior to others? How does this harm your witness?

Where have you seen racism or other kinds of superiority practiced?

What can a person do to overcome his own racism? Why is this study unit called WORTH?

●●

How can we apply the idea of common humanity and creation in the image of God to racial and ethnic relationships?

How does racism affect evangelism?

Why is the dignity of the individual an important factor in evangelism? Where have you seen racism or superiority feelings demonstrated? What can you do to help solve these problems?

●●●

What insights come when we apply the Henry and Schaeffer position on racism to other social relationships?

In what ways do racism and other forms of superiority feelings harm the Gospel message?

How are dignity and common humanity demonstrated in your church?

Committed

Is Christ concerned with man's material aspirations? How can the Gospel relate to man's drive for material possessions? What about dependence on technology for salvation from our problems? At Lausanne, C. René Padilla stressed the dramatic change of values in Zacchaeus' life. The importance of this commitment of our resources as a vital aspect of salvation is emphasized in the following statement:

Padilla

> Salvation is man's return to God, but it is at the same time *also* man's return to his neighbor. In the presence of Jesus Christ, Zacchaeus the publican renounces the materialism that has enslaved him and accepts responsibility for his neighbor ("Behold, Lord, the half of my goods I give to the poor; and if I have defrauded any one of anything, I restore it fourfold" — Luke 19:8). This renunciation and this commitment Jesus calls "salvation" ("Today salvation has come to this house" — Luke 19:9). Zacchaeus' response to the Gospel call could not be expressed in more concrete terms. It is not merely a subjective but a moral experience — an experience that affects his life precisely at that point at which the Great Lie materialism had taken root, an experience that brings him out of himself and turns him toward his neighbor.

136

Carl F. H. Henry describes the depersonalization of modern technology and two possible solutions, one found in the youth counterculture movement and the other in Christianity. Henry uses the term "technocratic scientism" to refer to the belief that truth and knowledge can be found only through science. According to this belief, the best way for man to improve his life is through technology, which is the application of science to the problems of society and individuals. For example, mental disorders, energy problems and

even "spiritual" problems are seen as matters that can be solved through science and technology alone. This belief in "scientism" dispenses with any need for God.

Henry

Discerning Christian theologians have long pointed out that a culture based on technocratic scientism inevitably undermines personal values. The church in the twentieth century has not, however, related its preaching effectively to this contemporary phenomenon. Nor has it powerfully demonstrated the difference of life-style involved in the evangelical alternative.

The quest for a realm of reality that goes beyond scientific-empirical data explains, in part, youth's growing interest in Oriental mystery religions, hallucinatory drugs, spiritism, and demon possession. The youth counterculture outside the Jesus movement tries to confront the technocratic myth of ultimate impersonal reality by emphasizing mystical consciousness. This, however, merely counters one myth with another. The myth of technocratic scientism cannot be eradicated by a simplistic substitution of the myth of superrational mysticism. The only firm transcendent basis for moral values is God as an intelligible religious reality. As far as values are concerned, the secular counterculture concentrates on social values to the neglect of personal righteousness, and despite its emphasis on love for neighbor neglects the first and great commandment, namely, love for God.

137

Read Matthew 6:19–33. This Scripture teaches the place of material things in our lives in relation to the importance of the Kingdom of God, the rule of Christ as Lord of our lives in this world now, and His eventual rule over all things throughout eternity.

When we put science in the place of God how does this affect the way we treat people? How does materialism show what is first in a person's life?

Why is the Gospel better than materialism and a reliance on science as the answer to all problems?

If all your material possessions were taken away from you, how would you feel?

When Christ rules your life, how does He change your attitude towards material things?

Why are materialism and "technocratic scientism" similar in what they do to people?

Does the Gospel provide a better alternative than these?

If all your possessions were removed, except those most necessary to life, how much would you have left? How much would you miss these nonessential possessions?

How important are even the "essentials" like food and clothing?

If you seek the Kingdom of God first, what changes in reference to material things will come into your life?

What effect does materialism and "technocratic scientism" have on a person's view of man and interpersonal relationships?

In what ways is the Gospel a better alternative?

Why are materialism and scientism so widely accepted? How can the Gospel message satisfy the needs of those engrossed in materialism and technocratic scientism?

138

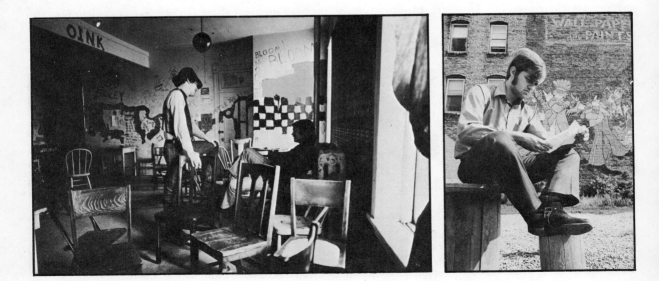

Men have intellectual needs. They have unanswered questions about the Gospel. Should this concern the Christian as he tries to witness? Francis Schaeffer points out that the responsible Christian tries to answer the honest questions of other people.

Schaeffer explains that some evangelical Christians have an attitude that says:

"Don't ask your questions, just believe." This sort of attitude was always wrong. It is not more spiritual to believe without asking questions. It is not more biblical. It is less biblical and eventually it will be less spiritual because the whole man will not be involved.

God made the whole man; the whole man is redeemed in Christ. After we are Christians, the Lordship of Christ covers the whole man. That includes his so-called spiritual things and his intellectual, creative, and cultural things. It includes his law, his sociology, and psychology. It includes every single part and portion of a man and his being.

There is nothing in the Bible which would say, "Never mind the intellectual, never mind the cultural. We will follow the Bible in the spiritual realm, but we will take the intellectual and the creative and put them aside. They are not important."

Many Christians think that 1 Corinthians speaks against the use of the intellect. But it does not. What 1 Corinthians speaks against is man pretending to be autonomous, to draw from his own wisdom and his own knowledge without recourse to the revelation of the Word of God.

Consider the ministry of our Lord Jesus Himself. He was a man who constantly answered questions. But someone will say, "Didn't He say that to be saved you have to be as a little child?" Of course, He did. But did you ever see a little child who didn't ask questions? My four children gave me a harder time with their endless flow of questions than university people ever did. What Jesus was talking about is that the little child, when he has an adequate answer, accepts the answer.

Not everybody is called to answer the questions of the intellectual, but when you go down to the shipyard worker you have a similar task. My second pastorate was with shipyard workers. They have the same questions as the university man. They just do not state them the same way.

Christianity demands that we have enough compassion to learn the questions of our generation. The trouble with too many of us is that we want to be able to answer these questions instantly. It cannot be. Answering questions is hard work. Can you answer all the questions? No, but you must try. Begin to listen with compassion, ask what this man's questions really are, and try to answer. If you don't know the answer, try to go some place or read and study to find some answers. Our responsibility is to have enough compassion to pray and do the hard work which is necessary to answer the honest questions. Of course we are not to study only cultural and intellectual issues. We must also study the Bible, and in both studies ask for the help of the Holy Spirit.

Why should questions about the Gospel be answered? Why does Schaeffer emphasize that Christianity involves mental as well as spiritual things? What questions are non-Christians asking you?

How well can you answer them? What should you do to try to answer them?

Why is answering the questions of non-Christians an important part of evangelism?

How can we listen with compassion to a person's questions?

What kinds of questions are non-Christians asking you? How could you answer them more adequately?

What are the cultural and intellectual questions that non-Christians are asking today? What are the forces at work in today's society that cause men to ask them?

How is the Gospel related to these questions?

What can you do to more adequately answer them?

People's needs are great. Christ can meet these needs in individuals and in society.

In this study we have looked at some of the major needs of mankind: problems of wealth, the poor, the masses, politics, sex, race, materialism, technology, and intellectual questioning. How does the Gospel apply to all areas of life? Samuel Escobar describes three different kinds of living situations and how a Christian can apply his faith to each.

In *situation one*, Christians are a small minority and their presence is felt on a small scale. If Christians are faithful to the integrity of the Gospel, their way of life usually provides a vivid contrast with that of society around them. Though their number and influence is limited in terms of social or political action, their dynamism as a model of social relationships, reconciliation, and coexistence under the Lordship of Christ is very powerful.

For Christians living in this situation, *service* is the main avenue of obedience to the social and political demands of the Gospel. Service is first in the context of the Christian community.

One of the most missionary-minded churches in Korea is also a church that has shown outstanding concern for the poor and needy. The linguistic and literacy work of the Wycliffe Bible Translators has many service avenues that have open doors to the Gospel. All these forms of service should continue hand in hand with concern for the announcement of the Gospel.

The other way open for Christians in *situation one* is that of *personal excellency*. The operative principle behind the witness of Joseph in Egypt, Esther in Persia and Daniel in Babylon is that an individual member of a small minority under God can achieve a position of power and be used as a witness in that situation for the sake of God's glory and for the sake of His people. Only when the church is strongly rooted in the truth of God will there be an original Christian contribution to society. Weak churches will produce communities that instead of transforming society will adapt themselves readily to a pagan pattern. Many Latin American young people were motivated by the Gospel to love their neighbors and be concerned for justice and freedom in their society. However, some have become Marxists either because their churches did not provide biblical instruction about Christian discipleship or because they were blind to clear demands from the Bible and opportunities and challenges provided by new social situations.

In *situation two*, society has a long tradition of definite Christian influence in government, legislation, politics, and social action. The vivid contrast between the Christian community and society around has disappeared. Responsible Christians have access to public office, to decision-making positions, and to action in the shaping of the social structures. In these cases there are many ways open to Christian action, and the contribution of Christians to the continuous reform of society is visible.

When the real spirit of Christ has been left out of a so-called "Christian" way of life, those who advocate commitment to Christ and obedience to His Lordship sound like revolutionaries. This would be the case in the Western world where secularism is rapidly displacing Christian influence, while Christians, including many evangelicals, watch indifferently in the name of commitment to evangelism. They do not realize the degree to which their so-called gospel is secularized and paganized by their passive acceptance of their society's pagan value system.

For Christians living in *situation two,* the call is to consistency. The evangelical community in the Anglo-Saxon countries has money, influence, and numbers that could really make it a decisive force for the reform of their society. Instead, many have let secularism take the initiative in education, politics, the media, and international relations. Christians in the Third World expect from their brethren in the West a word of identification with demands for justice in international trade, for a modification of the patterns of affluence and waste that are made possible because of unjust and exploitative trade systems, and for a criticism of the evils of the arms race and of the almost omnipotent maneuverings of international intelligence agencies. Christians in the West can do all that without in any way decreasing their missionary and evangelistic fervor. It is only a matter of taking seriously the Gospel that we profess to believe and that we are willing to defend against heresy. It is recognizing that Satan is alive and at work everywhere, and that some Western leaders who are eager not to offend Christians nevertheless are leading their nations by the route of abuse, injustice, and evil, bringing destruction and judgment from God in history. The worst danger for Christians in this situation is that they will use the model of the New Testament church incorrectly to justify inaction, conformism, and silence.

In *situation three,* power has been achieved by a definitely anti-Christian force. In these cases an ideology or a religion becomes the "official creed" of society, and Christians are treated as second-class citizens. Persecution and even martyrdom for the faith are a constant threat, and Christians are forced to observe the maximum neutrality in political and social affairs. This is the situation of Christians in some countries where Islam or Marxism is the official creed.

For Christians living in *situation three* the call is also to *faithfulness* to the Lord. The Word is there; it cannot be modified. The cost of obedience can be death. Those who enjoy the freedom of the West too easily overlook the necessity of refusing to "render unto Caesar" what belongs to God.

The Church has lived in very different regimes and situations and has survived even at the cost of martyrdom. The hope of evangelization of the world does not lie in the possibility that some nation will impose some political or economic regime favorable to the Gospel. It rather rests in the hands of Jesus Christ the Lord who has used emperors and tyrants as well as humble slaves and poor itinerant preachers to take His Word to the uttermost parts of the earth in unexpected, surprising, divine ways.

Escobar's three situations can be applied to your activities: church, work, social or sports activities, and home. List the different areas of your involvement and try to decide whether they are like situation 1, 2, or 3. Then decide which is the most effective way to live as a Christian witness in each of them. What changes does this suggest in your approach?

You could call Escobar's three types of situations minority, majority, and hostile. Examine your various activities, e.g., school, work, home, neighborhood, recreation, etc., and fit them into the three situations. How can you effectively live as a Christian witness in each?

●●●

Which of Escobar's three situations parallels the societal situation in which you live? How could you live an effective Christian witness in each?

Is resistance or revolt against government acceptable from a biblical perspective?

Complete your list of reasons for relating evangelization and social action, as begun in the first section of this study. Discuss the list in terms of the needs of mankind. Which needs can be met by individual Christians operating independently? Which by a community of believers? And which require a large-scale agency?

We have considered some of the great needs of mankind and how the Gospel of Christ can meet them. We have also seen how personal salvation implies involvement in the needs of humanity, not just far away but as close as our own neighborhood and family. How can your group within your local church demonstrate its faith in Christ through the good works which Christians are to do? How can you get involved *together* in expressing Christ's love and compassion so that others, seeing your good works, will glorify your Father in heaven (Matthew 5:16)?

Contents - 5

Acknowledgements

Authors and papers of the International Congress on World Evangelization used in this chapter are as follows:

William R. Bright, "Personal Evangelism";

Michael Cassidy, "Evangelization Among College and University Students";

John Chapman, "Dialogue/Debate Evangelism";

A. William Cook, Jr., "The Meaning of Depth In Evangelism";

Edward R. Dayton, "Planning Workbook";

James F. Engel, "The Audience For Christian Communication";

Noel C. Gibson, "Open Air Evangelism";

Michael Green, "Methods and Strategy in the Evangelism of the Early Church";

Roger S. Greenway, "Urban Evangelism";

David Ho, "Mobilize A Local Church in Evangelism";

Marge Alcala Isidro, "Teaching Families to Witness in the Community";

J. V. Manogarom, "Evangelization Among Secondary School Students";

Missions Advanced Research and Communication (MARC), "Status of Christianity County Profiles";

Stephen Olford, "Mobilize to Evangelize";

Ernest W. Oliver, "Mission Strategy";

Gottfried Osei-Mensah, "The Holy Spirit in Evangelism";

George W. Peters, "Contemporary Practices of Evangelism";

John Peters, "Training Believers to Evangelize Their Communities";

Donald K. Smith, "The Mystery of Hidden Words";

Herman ter Welle, "Evangelization of Children";

C. Peter Wagner, "Introduction to Church Growth Strategy, Principles, Methods and Movement."

Spiritual Planning

"I have become *all things* to *all men*, that I might by *all means* save some" (1 Corinthians 9:22). Paul's words are the key to the study of *Reaching By All Means*. The International Congress on World Evangelization was designed to help people all over the world develop and adapt various methods and means of evangelization for their own situations. It was the position of the Congress that God uses people, and people use methods; people *and* methods must be dedicated to Him. This study will begin with a general overview of the place of planning and strategy in evangelization. Next, it will deal with basic planning questions to be answered while deciding on methods. Finally, it will describe some of the important methods of evangelism reported to the Congress.

A continual theme throughout the Congress was the need for planning and strategy development, to make effective use of limited resources of personnel, money, and time. How to approach a problem or task is a matter of strategy. Strategy is concerned with the choice of goals and the selection and use of resources. Since evangelization is God's business, we need more than clever ideas. In this first part of the study we will consider the spiritual aspects of planning. If our strategy for evangelization is under the Holy Spirit's control, it will accomplish what God intends.

Ernest W. Oliver, Executive Secretary of the Regions Beyond Missionary Union, and Secretary of the Evangelical Missionary Alliance of Great Britain, gave helpful insight into the spirituality of strategy.

Oliver

149

Let us be clear that the creation and sustaining of the motivation for strategy remains the prerogative of the Holy Spirit. Methods and means must be justified by their availability to the Spirit to fulfill the divine purpose. In his book, *Missionary Principles*, Roland Allen wrote, "Refusal to study the best methods, refusal to regard organization as of any importance, is really not the denial of matter, but the denial of the Spirit. It is sloth, not faith." If the Holy Spirit is recognized as the motivator and the sustainer of the mission of the church, then He will give the wisdom for planning the methods and means to meet those needs in a way that witnesses to the power of Christ.

Gottfried Osei-Mensah, from Kenya, Africa, pastor of the Nairobi Baptist Church, provided additional understanding of the Holy Spirit's role in planning.

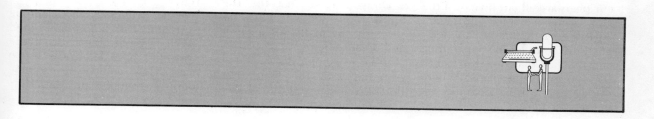

To keep a spiritual vision in focus and to use wisely our God-given resources requires careful planning and some degree of organization. There are dangers with every human organization including Christian ones. The chief danger with every Christian organization is the loss of spiritual vision. But the alternative is not the abolition of organization, it is the setting of wise and spiritual goals and objectives — wise because biblical, and spiritual because the Holy Spirit's help (rather than human techniques) is counted on as the dynamic for their achievement. Nothing is more calculated to check our tendency to sloth than a clear spiritual vision articulated in concrete objectives and well-defined principles for action. Spiritual goals give meaning to commitment, inspire perseverance in prayer, and promote self-discipline for their realization.

The apostle Paul taught these things by precept and example: "Do you not know that in a race all the runners compete, but only one receives the prize? So run that you may obtain it. Every athlete exercises self-control in all things. They do it to obtain a perishable wreath, but we an imperishable . . . I do not run aimlessly, I do not box as one beating the air" (1 Corinthians 9:24–26).

Underlying Paul's missionary effort was a definite plan and strategy. His plan was open-ended and completely disposed to the Holy Spirit's intervention at any point. He showed that there is no conflict between sound spiritual planning and the immediacy of the Holy Spirit's working (Acts 16:6–10). When the Holy Spirit intervenes sovereignly in our plans, He helps us achieve more than we had hoped for, not less. Through His intervention the Good News reached Europe, while Asia and Bithynia were not forgotten (1 Peter 1:1). That was Paul's strategy. We must work out our own strategy under the inspiration, guidance, and fellowship of the same Spirit.

150

●

Why is strategy so important? How can we make sure that the Holy Spirit is not left out of our planning?

What difference does it make if our plans are all our own or if the Holy Spirit is involved in them?

How does the life of Paul demonstrate both his own planning and the way that the Holy Spirit steps in to change plans? Where could you put these ideas to work in your own life?

●●

What results from lack of planning in evangelization?

Why is the Holy Spirit a necessary part of our personal and organizational plans?

Do you agree that the Holy Spirit is pleased when we take seriously the matters of methods and organization?

What principles do you see for planning with the Holy Spirit demonstrated in the life of Paul? How do they apply to your life?

●●●

Why is strategic planning part of the Holy Spirit's work in our lives?

Do you agree that lack of planning is a denial of the Holy Spirit? Why?

What principles for planning were demonstrated in Paul's life?

What implications do these principles have for the way you plan? How could you become more dependent on the Holy Spirit as you make plans?

The church described in Acts illustrates strategy and planning. Michael Green, an Anglican theologian and educator, Principal of St. John's College, Nottingham, England, pointed out that the strategy of the early Christians was very ordinary. Note that his teaching appears to differ somewhat from what Osei-Mensah said about Paul's strategy. Note also his contrasts between the early church and the church today.

There does not seem to have been anything very remarkable in the strategy and tactics of the early Christian mission. Indeed, it is doubtful if they had a strategy. I do not believe they set out with any blueprint. They had an unquenchable conviction that Jesus was the key to life, happiness and purpose, and they simply could not keep quiet about Him. The Spirit of Jesus within them drove them into mission. The initiatives in evangelism that we read of in Acts are consistently laid at the door of the Spirit Himself; effective mission does not spring from human blueprints. No, the nearest to a strategy those early Christians had was, perhaps, as follows:

1. *They worked from the center outwards.* "Beginning from Jerusalem" was the key word in Jesus' farewell charge to His disciples. Acts traces briefly the spread of the Gospel from Jerusalem into Judaea, then to Samaria, and from there to the uttermost parts of the earth. Always the policy seems to be to get the heart of the group "hot" and only then will it be ready for fresh additions. The policy of so much modern evangelism is to drag people from the outside inwards; their policy was the opposite — to move from the inside outwards, and to evangelize, not on their own ground, but on other people's.

2. *They were involved, yet mobile.* They were indeed involved, totally involved in the mission. We see this graphically portrayed when Stephen was killed. The believers scattered, and "those that were scattered abroad went everywhere preaching the message" (Acts 8:1–4). Celsus, a second century writer and critic of Christianity, complains of the Christians at work, in the laundry, in the schoolroom, and on the street corner who were always jabbering away about their Jesus. Could any leading critic of Christianity today make the same charge?

3. *They used their influence.* Many of these men planned their time with some care, conscious that they had but one life. They were determined to use it to the full for God. They entered spheres where their influence would be felt to the maximum. That, presumably, helped to dictate the direction of the Pauline missionary journeys. Antioch was the third city in the empire. Philippi was a Roman colony and administrative capital. Thessalonica was the administrative center of Macedonia. Athens was the cultural center of the world. Corinth was the capital of the province of Achaea. Ephesus, where Paul spent three years, was the largest city in Asia. Rome, his goal in the west, was mistress of the world. It is hard to escape the conclusion that Paul was determined to use his talents to the full in the places where they would do the most good. Of course, such planning can degenerate into worldly ambition, but it need not if the guidance of the Spirit is sought.

4. *They exercised oversight.* This is one of the intriguing factors in ancient evangelism which is not always looked after so well today. They were out, from the start, to consolidate gains. New

disciples needed to be strengthened. Converts needed to be added to the church as well as to the Lord. They continued in the apostles' fellowship, teaching, worship, and evangelism. There was, at least in some circles, some communalism of goods and life-style which bore eloquent testimony to the oneness in Christ which they talked about. That unity was maintained even as the church grew. The ancient splits between Jew and Samaritan, Jew and Gentile, bond and free, male and female, were not allowed to spoil the unity given by the Spirit. To this end, the apostles revisited their converts, they set up elders to look after them, they wrote letters to them, they sent messengers to them, and they prayed for them. From the most diverse backgrounds they came together to form one new humanity in Christ. Wise, diligent Christian oversight was instrumental in maintaining this God-given unity.

5. *They produced witnesses.* It was the normal thing, not the pleasurable exception, for a Christian to become so thrilled with Christ that he had to find ways of expressing it to his non-Christian neighbors. Indeed, in contrast to much of our own effort these days, the early evangelists seem to have set themselves to increase the number of witnesses to Christ, rather than the number of those they could persuade to listen to sermons about Christ. They were out not to gather hearers, but to equip missionaries. This may not have been very self-conscious on their part, but it was a strategic decision of the utmost importance, and one which the modern church has scarcely begun to appreciate.

What appears to be contradictory between Green and Osei-Mensah's viewpoints about strategy in the early church? What evidence is there that the early Christians made plans? How did the Holy Spirit use human planning? Under what conditions does human planning become God's hand of leading?

Assume that you and your group want to develop a strategy to evangelize those around you. Use the chart below to consider how to apply the general strategies of the early church to your own situation.

STRATEGY	WHAT THIS STRATEGY WOULD MEAN IN OUR SITUATION	STEPS WE COULD TAKE TO APPLY THIS STRATEGY
Worked From Center Out		
Were Involved, Mobile		
Used Their Influence		
Provided Oversight		
Provided Witnesses		

Green described seven methods used successfully by the early Christians. He stated that no one method was in itself very remarkable.

1. *Speaking.* Like us they spoke in church. Like us — they spoke in the open air, though more frequently and with more directness, humor, and response from the audience than is common in the West.

2. *Visiting.* Like us — they visited. It is a method used less often today. Ministers persuade themselves that it cannot be done, by themselves or by laymen. But it *can* be done and it must.

3. *Literature.* Like us — they made use of literary evangelism. In particular, they employed the Old Testament Scriptures. We would be foolish to underestimate the converting power of the Word of God even in the absence of a human interpreter.

4. *Fellowship.* The importance of Christian fellowship is plain to see. These early Christians embraced all the colors, all the classes, and all the untouchables of ancient society into one. Unless the fellowship in the Christian assembly is far superior to that which can be found anywhere else in society, Christians can talk about the transforming love and power of Jesus till they are hoarse, but people are not going to listen.

5. *Homes.* In Acts we read of homes being used, sometimes for a prayer meeting, sometimes for fellowship and instruction, sometimes for a communion service, sometimes for a meeting of new converts, and sometimes for an impromptu gathering.

6. *Explanation.* The early evangelists used their minds to relate the Gospel to the intellectual and cultural concerns of their day. Words that describe Christian preaching in the New Testament denote a high intellectual endeavor. The writers used such words as "to instruct," "to proclaim like a herald," "to proclaim good news," "to make careful announcement," "to testify," "to convince by argument," and "to argue." They spent time on this intellectual commendation of the Good News. They were prepared to argue and go forward on either neutral or hostile ground.

7. *Personal conversation.* This was a method that Jesus used a great deal. In every personal encounter, Jesus found a way into people through their own view of their needs. This also was Philip's way when he led the Ethiopian eunuch to Christ, and it was Paul's way when he brought Onesimus to the faith.

Which of these seven methods do you use for evangelization?

Which one is used *least* in your activities? Should you be using it more? Are there any you feel should definitely be omitted from your evangelization? Why?

How would you change or adapt some of these methods to apply to your own situation?

Information

Planning is an important step in God's overall design to evangelize the world. In this study you will find specific suggestions and outlines to help you in planning.

Several participants at the International Congress on World Evangelization gave helpful planning principles and suggestions. The process of communication — getting the message of evangelism from the sender to the receiver — was considered basic to planning evangelization strategy.

Both Donald K. Smith, executive director of Daystar Communications in Kenya, Africa, and James F. Engel, professor of communications and director of the Billy Graham Program in Communications at Wheaton College Graduate School in Illinois, sought to lay the foundation for effective planning through an understanding of communications principles. Smith, in a paper prepared for the Congress, stated the problem faced in communicating the Gospel.

Smith

Communication is what is *heard*, not only what is said. The really difficult part of communication is the gap between physical hearing of the message and mental comprehension of the message. In communications we are concerned about the understanding of ideas.

Many Christians assume that once the message is in the ear, their responsibility has ended. Too often we throw the message at a person and assume that because he has heard the message, he now understands it.

That is not communication. That is simply transmission. It is our obligation, in effective evangelism, to know what is being heard by the person we want to bring to Christ, and then to shape the message so that he will understand. When he understands the rudiments of the Gospel, he is then able to make his decision.

It is our basic obligation to do all within our ability to ensure that the Gospel is heard, and not only spoken. Our speech, our campaigns, and our sacrificial efforts may be heard as gibberish if we do not work to impart understanding.

There are definite causes for misunderstanding. Knowing these causes can help overcome misunderstanding by changing the way in which the message is sent. Two kinds of related causes lead to much misunderstanding: *selective perception* and *reinterpretation*.

Selective perception means that only a particular part of the total message is picked up or perceived by the receiver. The rest of the message is ignored and lost.

There are so many signals in the world around us that we defend ourselves by selective perception. We simply cannot take in all of the things that are clamoring for our attention, and so we select out of the mass of signals those things that interest us and promise to help us meet our personal needs.

Engel talked about selective understanding resulting from a person's "perceptual filter" — the process of making meaning out of what one hears or sees.

Engel

A perceptual filter is part of the God-given psychological equipment of every human being. Psychologists have demonstrated conclusively that exposure to a message is only the first stage in communication. The message input then must be processed through a filter which contains the accumulated experience, information, values, attitudes, and other dispositions of the individual. Furthermore, it is now known that this filter can function to prevent the entry of unwanted messages into the central nervous system and, conversely, to enhance the probability that compatible information will be processed and acted upon.

It is possible that the message may not be heard through disinterest, or that the message will be completely misunderstood, or that it will not be retained in memory. The key lies in whether or not the filter is open, and whether or not the message is phrased in such a way that it is compatible with the person's needs, interests, and background. To disregard the functioning of the perceptual filter is to raise the very real possibility that communication will not occur.

Is such a communication theory biblical? While the Bible obviously is not a textbook in psychology, it is interesting to learn from the example of Jesus. He invariably approached people in terms of their own view of their needs. He based his messages on an awareness of His audiences. For example, it would have been absurd for Him to tell the woman at the well that she should sell all she owns and give it to the poor while telling the rich young ruler that he needs living water. On the contrary, Jesus recognized that filters are open at the point of felt need and the individual is receptive to messages which speak to these issues.

Notice, however, that Jesus did not only contend with the need of the moment. Rather, He took occasion to capture the attention and interest of His audience and to move from that point to present necessary spiritual truth.

Smith described a second problem. People hear but still misunderstand the message. Why?

Smith

Supposing we have gained a listener's attention, and he receives the message that we give him; how can he still misunderstand? A process of *reinterpretation* very often occurs. The original message may be received, but it is altered in the mind of the receiver by a subconscious process, usually to conform to something he already knows or believes. For example, the man who leans heavily on his family or society for personal security may reinterpret a message stressing individual commitment to Jesus Christ. His reinterpretation may cause him to think that the Gospel would destroy his relationships with his family or his society.

We must anticipate reinterpretation before it occurs and shape the way in which we present the unchanging message if we are to avoid this misunderstanding.

Why don't people "hear" with their minds and hearts? Why is getting out the message not enough? What else must be done? What is the difference between transmitting a message and having that message understood? What parts of the communication process can we control? How can we help people to avoid problems in receiving our message about Christ?

We need to ask people what they are hearing when we think we are communicating the Gospel.

Why is it our responsibility to know what is being heard by the person we want to bring to Christ? What are some of the things we can do to shape our message to meet others' needs? How will starting with people's needs help in communicating the Gospel to them?

Selective perception and reinterpretation are likely to distort a person's understanding of the Gospel.

Engel

The basic principle is that people process communication messages in such a way that they "see and hear what they want to see and hear." This has profound implications for communication strategy. The communciator who bases message and media on his own ideas of what the audience should hear is pursuing an approach which is full of danger. The audience, in effect, is disregarded, and the message may be avoided, not comprehended, not retained, or not acted upon. Communicating effectively, on the other hand, begins with an understanding of the audience and utilizes both messages and media which are more likely to be understood. It is recognized that those in the audience have full ability to screen out unwanted or inappropriate messages.

All biblical content, especially the commands, should be viewed as a constant which never changes. The people of God are commanded to worship, for example, and so this is a constant. The program or strategy implementing that constant, however, is a variable which changes as circumstances change. The Christian message never changes when it is expressing biblical truth, but there is ample latitude to express that message in such a way that its phrasing, emphasis, and practical application relate uniquely to the hearer.

Why is it so important to recognize the ability of the audience to filter and reinterpret? What does a communicator do when he is acting on the principle that the audience's perceptions are important?

Information about people to be evangelized is of the utmost importance in planning. Information should give answers to the following: 1) What do you need to know about a group of people you are trying to reach with the Gospel? 2) Where could you obtain information about them? 3) How would you get that information? 4) How can you use what you learn about the audience to adapt the communication for better understanding?

On the international level two valuable sources of information were compiled for the International Congress on World Evangelization by the Missions Advanced Research and Communications Center (MARC) in Monrovia, California. Together, these provide a clear picture of the tasks involved in evangelization of a given group of people. One of these information sources is a survey of unreached people in the world. "Unreached people" refers to any ethnic, racial, religious, social, economic, or national group of which less than twenty percent have responded to the Gospel.

The second information source is called a "country profile." Fifty-two countries were surveyed by Marc.[1] The kinds of information which the country profiles provide illustrate one important approach to large-scale planning. You may be able to use the general approach for local planning for evangelization. It would need to be scaled down to fit the particular situation with which you are concerned. While your sources might be based on your own experiences rather than more formal data, you may be able to use this outline to help you in your planning.

1. Who are the unreached people?
2. What is the current status of Christianity among them?
3. What church influence already exists? That is, what denominations and religious bodies are organized and working with the people?
4. What missions are working with the people?
5. What major Christian programs and activities are going on?

These include a description of the following activities:

evangelism   education
broadcasting   social concerns
literature   Bible translation and distribution

6. What are the people like? This would include a description of the following:

population figures for the particular group   geography and climate
ethnic composition   history of people and nation
degree of literacy   government and political condition
language spoken   economy of the region
religious affiliations

When you have gathered as much information as possible in each of the suggested categories, you will then need to analyze it. You may want to use the following questions to guide you.

1. What new opportunities for evangelization exist?
2. What problems are revealed in the present work?
3. What trends do you discover?
   Consider population movements, population increase or decrease, improvement or decline of social conditions, etc.

_____

[1] A price list and copies of individual country profiles and the *Unreached Peoples Survey* may be obtained from MARC, 919 Huntington Drive, Monrovia, CA 91016, U.S.A.

158

4. Who is responding well to the Gospel? Why? How could their responses be increased even more?
5. What are some of the prominent characteristics of the people? Consider these factors:

historic background	number of males and females
ethnic background	large age groups
economic situation	vocational activities
religious background	educational levels
geographic location	leadership ability

6. What are some of the prominent needs of the people? Consider these factors:

economic needs	spiritual needs
social needs	medical needs
physical needs	educational needs

7. What plans do you need to make in order to reach these people? (See the details in the following unit on "how to plan.")
8. What methods will you use? (Details in the last three units of this study describe various methods.)

Another way to obtain information for planning is through church growth methods. C. Peter Wagner, professor at the School of World Mission, Fuller Theological Seminary, Pasadena, California, emphasized the need for strategy.

Wagner

The most basic principle of strategy is to know exactly what your goals are. Confusion, fuzziness, and imprecise thinking must be eliminated, just like the trees of a forest must be cleared away before a field of corn can be planted. The goal of evangelism, according to Matthew 28:19, is to make disciples. This does not reduce in the least the importance of employing biblical and practical means — such as sending, going, witnessing, preaching, signing decision cards, baptizing, translating the Bible, or whatever else is necessary. But it does emphasize that if your evangelistic program fails to result in making disciples, to that extent it is not accomplishing the true goal of evangelism.

In the past, many evangelistic programs have been evaluated as successful because many persons heard the preaching of the Gospel, many hands were raised, or many decision cards were signed. But this is a rather superficial basis for evaluation because the efforts are not being measured in terms of the final goal of evangelism. Results are better reported in terms of how many disciples are made.

You are encouraged to gather information about the people whom you want to reach effectively for Christ. This will help you plan an evangelistic approach that will reduce the major communication "hang-ups" — selective perception, and reinterpretation.

How to Plan

Many people talk about planning, but few know how to do it. In order to provide basic guidelines on how to plan, Edward R. Dayton, Director of Missions Advanced Research and Communications (MARC), Monrovia, California, provided the Congress with a workbook for planning. Portions of Dayton's workbook are presented here as a series of steps for your group to follow in planning a group outreach. As you go through the steps, use the information collected and analyzed in the preceding section.[1]

1. THE PEOPLE GOD WANTS YOU TO REACH

The people God wants you to reach may be the family living next door, a particular group of people in your city or neighborhood, or a group of people living in a distant land.

It is important to understand people within their *need*. The Good News must always be applied to the life and needs of the individual. The Gospel does transform societies. But the way in which it is communicated and the strategy we use to reach a particular people should specifically reflect *their* situation and *their* need. The place to begin is not with the *method* of evangelism, but rather with an understanding of the people whom God loves and for whom Christ died.

a. Describe the people you believe God wants you to reach. Where are they? What are their special characteristics? What makes them a special group of people? What is their language, location, class, religion, age, etc?

b. What are some of the major spiritual, physical, educational, social, and emotional needs of these people, as *they* perceive their needs, and as *you* perceive their needs?

c. Who else might have information about these people? How can you discover what they already know? What are their interests? What do they value and appreciate?

2. WHAT THEY ALREADY KNOW ABOUT THE GOSPEL

In order to evangelize, we need to know where people are in relationship to the Gospel.

Here are some of the various levels at which we find people. We ought to discover how many are at these stages:

No real knowledge of the Gospel
Some awareness and interest
Awareness of the fundamentals of the Gospel
Understanding of what the Gospel can and should mean to them
Recognition of their own need
Open and willing to receive Christ
Already accepted Christ
Growing in Christ

We should also attempt to discover how many have knowingly rejected Him.

---

[1]*Planning Strategies for Evangelism — a Workbook*, by Edward R. Dayton, Copyright 1974, World Vision, Inc., used by permission.

3. THE FORCE FOR EVANGELISM TO REACH THESE PEOPLE

As we think about evangelizing a particular group, it is easy to overlook other members of the body of Christ who are also interested in them and may be of help in reaching them. All of these people can be called the "force for evangelism." This force includes the existing Christians who are within a particular community or location, the organized church there, other Christian organizations working there, or organizations outside the area which have a potential interest in this group.

4. DISCOVERING GOD'S STRATEGY FOR PEOPLE

If we have developed an understanding of the people we are trying to reach, if we have an adequate understanding of the force for evangelism potentially available, and have examined various means and methods that God might use to reach them, we are now ready to attempt to discover God's strategy for them.

As we make this first analysis of how the force for evangelism might be used, we should first identify some key elements suggested in the following questions:

a. Who are the ones most likely to be open to the Gospel among those we will try to reach?

b. Which churches are most likely to receive converts from this group?

c. Which ministries have been or are now particularly effective with this group?

d. Which church leaders might be helpful in their influence to unite a force for evangelism to reach this people? How can we gain their support?

e. Having thought about the people, the force for evangelism, the need, and available methods, what overall strategy or approach might be best?

f. When will we begin? How will we contact these people? What will our message be to these people, considering their needs?

g. Would a "trial run" to test the methods and approach with a smaller portion of the people provide valuable understanding? How will we go about this?

5. ANTICIPATED OUTCOMES

God expects us to exercise our faith in deciding where He would have us go and what He would have us do. He expects us to think about the possible outcomes of the activities in which we are going to become involved. This will give us a way to communicate with each other about what we hope to do. It will also help us know whether or not we are reaching the goals to which God has pointed us. In order to tell what is being accomplished, outcomes need to be measurable.

As you plan strategy, design an evaluation procedure. Consider these questions:

a. What do we expect God to do as a result of this strategy?

b. How will we know if anything worthwhile has happened so that we can build on the results and re-plan as necessary?

6. YOUR ROLE IN GOD'S STRATEGY

It does not always follow that because we have a concern for another individual or group, we will be the most effective ones in reaching those people. We need to understand what gifts God has given us. We need to understand how we fit into the total task of evangelization.

We should continually ask ourselves if there are others who would be more effective with these people or who should work along with us.

    a. What roles or jobs are necessary to carry out our strategy?

    b. Which of these do I fit into best?

    c. Which roles can our group, agency, or church best fulfill in carrying out this strategy?

7. FROM POSSIBLE OUTCOMES TO ACTION-PLANNING

The last step in planning is to move our prayers and faith into action. If, through planning, we come to believe that we are part of God's resource of love to people, we must now decide what steps of obedience to take.

    a. What steps should be taken to reach the planned goals?

    b. Who should take these steps and when?

8. RESOURCES NEEDED TO CARRY OUT THE PLAN

Plans won't work if we don't have the resources to carry them out. Resources include the various people who are going to be needed, the financial support that may be required, the various tools, such as radio, literature, recordings, etc., and the prayer support that is needed to undergird all of this. Look back at each step of the plan: What resources are going to be needed for each step? What cooperation will be needed from each of the various groups that will participate?

    a. What people, how much money, and what other resources, such as other organizations and churches, are needed to carry out these plans?

    b. What cooperation are we expecting from others?

9. BEFORE WE BEGIN

Some final questions: Is the plan practical? Do we really have a basis for believing that this is God's best for us? If not, what next? How should we modify what we have done so far? Go back over the plan; prayerfully consider each decision and each assumption that you have made.

    a. Is the plan workable? If not, what next? How should it be modified?

    b. If the plan looks like God's best, what is our first step?

Approaches-1

This unit and the next two in the study describe various methods and means of evangelization which have been used successfully. Some methods probably could be modified to fit your needs. But it is unlikely that someone else's methods can be totally accepted without some modification. As you read and study each method, consider whether it could be modified to fit your own particular needs. Some methods may stimulate you to think of original ways to meet your needs.

Use the chart below as a checklist to consider the methods described in these three units. By going through the checklist as you read each review, you will have a handy reference to methods which might be helpful in your evangelization tasks. Additional sheets of paper may be necessary, especially as you write down modifications of promising methods.

APPROACHES	NOT FOR US NOW	WE CAN USE NOW	MODIFICATIONS TO BE MADE	WE MIGHT USE LATER
PERSONAL EVANGELISM Direct Friendship Dialogue				
FAMILY Silent witness Verbal witness Active Creative				
CHILDREN Cell				
YOUTH Secondary University				
CHURCH Evangelistic programs Men in Action In-Depth Evangelism				
URBAN CHURCHES Chapel-to- church Mother- daughter Apartment House-church Open-air				
CRUSADES				
ADDITIONAL METHODS				

The comments of George W. Peters, professor of World Missions at Dallas Theological Seminary, introduced the first review of methods and procedures.

PERSONAL EVANGELISM

Effective personal evangelism is well illustrated and demonstrated in the New Testament. Christ is our foremost example, instructor, and inspiration in personal evangelism.

In direct confrontation evangelism, the Gospel is offered to the *individual*, and the claims of Christ are made known in a face-to-face meeting and without lengthy introductions.

Direct Confrontation Evangelism. William R. Bright, founder and President of Campus Crusade for Christ International, reviewed the approach used in many countries by Campus Crusade.

From our experience in more than twenty-five years of personal evangelism, we have reached the following conclusions:
1. Personal evangelism is the task of every Christian — not just a specialized few.
2. A Christian should take the initiative in sharing Christ with others.
3. The Christian must be filled with the Holy Spirit when sharing his faith.
4. Love must be the principal motivation in the Christian's heart when he shares.
5. The Gospel should be communicated simply, in a way that speaks to the heart as well as to the head.
6. The person with whom a Christian shares should be given an opportunity to receive Christ by faith.
7. God, through the Holy Spirit, draws a person to Christ. Therefore, the one witnessing should encourage a decision, but should not press for one. He should leave the ultimate results to God. Success in witnessing is simply sharing Christ in the power of the Holy Spirit and leaving the results to God.
8. Tens of millions will respond if Christians everywhere will present the Gospel clearly and simply.
9. Every Christian should be trained and motivated to share his faith and challenged to help fulfill the Great Commission in this generation. This is primarily the task of the local church.
10. The best way to train others in personal evangelism is through basic instruction, followed by field experience.

George Peters discussed two types of personal evangelism:

Friendship Personal Evangelism. The purpose of friendship personal evangelism is as definite as that of direct confrontation evangelism. The procedure, however, differs greatly. The cultivation of genuine and concerned friendship constitutes an integral part in the presentation of the Gospel and the claims of Christ. It seems a more natural approach than the direct confrontation.

Peters

Bright

164

However, it is beset with some difficulties. It is admitted that to gain the confidence and friendship of unsaved people is not as easy as is often imagined. To make the transition from friendship to actual personal evangelism demands a good measure of tact and divine wisdom.

Dialogue Personal Evangelism. Dialogue is a two-way conversation rather than a one-way presentation or proclamation. The meeting of Christ and Nicodemus may be taken as a biblical pattern of dialogue personal evangelism. The purpose is evangelism; the procedure is dialogue with a view toward dissolving obstacles, and prejudices in the unsaved person.

John C. Chapman, director of the department of evangelism, the Church of England, Diocese of Sydney, Australia, described his dialogue evangelism methods to the Congress.

The Dialogue Meeting. The outreach is designed to encourage Christians to invite friends to their homes so that they can hear an explanation of Christianity and have the opportunity to ask and discuss questions. The informal atmosphere of the home fosters contacts with people who would not come to a church building.

Host and Hostess. These people take responsibility for inviting friends, entertaining them, and engaging in some follow-up. They are given a one-night training session. The following are excerpts from material given at the training session.

A. *The Invitation*
   1. These can be printed, but we suggest that they *not* be sent, but personally delivered. The emphasis is on person-to-person contact.
   2. When the invitation is given, it is important that people know exactly what will happen, e.g., "Our church is holding a special series of meetings called Dialogue Meetings. In connection with these we have invited a few friends in to discuss Christianity. Would you be able to join us?"
   3. When wives do the inviting, women come; when husbands *and* wives do the inviting, husbands come, too.
   4. A day or so before the meeting a phone call is made as a reminder.
B. *When Your Guests Arrive*
   1. *Climate.* It is essential that the guests be made to feel at home and at ease. It is important not to be shocked at anything they might say and not to attack them or their views.
   2. *Introduction.*
      a. People can be introduced to the dialogue leader as they arrive.
      b. When all the guests have arrived, the host can introduce the proceedings with something like, "You know why we are here. We've asked John Smith here tonight so that we can talk together about Christianity. I'll ask John to introduce our discussion with a short talk, and then there will be plenty of time for discussion."

C. *Talk*
1. It will be brief and to the point, about ten minutes.
2. It will present the Gospel and will be thought-provoking.

D. *Discussion*
1. The host and hostess should make normal contributions to the discussion with other members, but they should not dominate. The guests should be made to feel free to speak.
2. The discussions should be strictly honest, rather than attempts to impress.
3. There should be constant prayer about the discussion.
4. The host or hostess may want to have a useful opening question ready, carefully based on the ideas in the talk given. For example, the unconverted person often wonders if *good* people are necessarily Christians. A possible question you might ask to start the discussion could be, "What would you say to a person who says, 'I believe that all good people are Christians'?"

E. *Before the Guests Leave*
1. Before the guests leave, see that they are reminded about weekend meetings at the church. There may be an opportunity to invite them to attend along with the host and hostess.
2. In the event of people expressing a desire to meet again, see that another night is arranged fairly soon, perhaps within a month.
3. Each person is given a small pack of material to take away. It contains a Gospel of Mark, an application for the Anglican Information Center's correspondence course, "The Christian Faith," and a copy of the first study from that course,

F. *Whom to Invite*
1. It is preferable that those invited not be churchgoers. We are reaching out to uncommitted people rather than to Christians.
2. It is important to consider the ages and interests of the people to be invited. Will they, in fact, form a group?
3. Numbers at a meeting should not exceed twenty, or be less than six.

G. *When It's All Over*
Follow-up is designed around the handout material. These are the options:
1. Follow-up Bible studies on Mark's Gospel. There are three Bible studies on Mark's Gospel available. The guests can be invited back to do these studies. Each study is designed to take one hour.
2. Follow-up dialogue meeting. Invite your dialogue leader back, and continue where you left off.
3. Christian Faith course. Each person in the group could enroll in the correspondence course and get together to discuss the lessons each week. There is a study guide available.
4. Prayer. Continue to pray for the people who attended the meeting.

Approaches-2

FAMILIES

The Christian family was described as a potent tool in evangelization by Marge Alcala Isidro, chairman of the Christian education department of Febias Bible College, Manila, Philippines. She enumerated several ways that the church could involve its families in witness for Jesus Christ.

1. *Silent witness.* The eloquent but silent witness of the Christian family living, playing, working, and serving the Lord together in loving harmony will be used of God to draw others to Himself. The family does not shout out, but shines out, the transforming power of God. This is not a "tongue-tied" kind of silence. Tongue-tied silence has been used as a cloak for timidity and unconcern for the lost. This silent witness is really a transformed life wrapped up in a person or family, walking and living in the community for the Lord Jesus Christ. The home is the showcase of God's grace, and a godly family is a silent witness to God's goodness. It is more eloquent than a torrent of words.

2. *Verbal witness.* To teach families how to give a brief verbal testimony, the following are suggested as topics for content: 1) What we were before we became Christians, 2) How we became Christians, 3) What Jesus means to us now, 4) Why we call ourselves Christians, 5) What is our authority for calling ourselves Christians? 6) How do we know that we are saved? This last topic is recommended as a way to help make the testimony coherent and clear.

Write a friend about your experience, invite a non-believer to read the letter and find out whether or not he understands the message. Then practice verbalizing it to your family. After you have gained some confidence, share it with an unchurched family. These ideas have been taught to individuals, but now we must try to teach them to families as a whole.

Teach families to memorize Scripture. Families should be encouraged to underline and memorize some witnessing verses. When a family knows some of these functional things, fear of verbal witness will be alleviated.

3. *Active witness.* Active witness implies putting legs to our witnessing. The pastor can teach active witness by his personal example. He can also take families along with him during his visitation. He should teach them how to visit among their own friends first, and then visit the folks who are friendly with people in the church. These are low-threat sorts of witness. Then he can teach them how to go "prospecting" among the unsaved.

Teach families to be friendly to their neighbors. Suggest a vase of freshly-cut flowers, a book, shared food, or any small gift personally carried to the family for which it is intended. Watch the "For Sale" or "For Rent" signs or ads and be the first to welcome a new family to the community. Assign families to watch for guests in the worship service and follow them up at home. When families go calling, they might take along a church handbook with pictures of the activities in the church. Pictures will catch attention. Teach families to find avenues to people's hearts and then to show care and concern in practical and visible means. This is active witness.

4. *Creative witness.* This means innovative or unique approaches to family witnessing. For example, share a cassette tape of music and messages. Also, capitalize on the relevance of cultural values to Christian life.

Encourage a family to adopt an unchurched family. Then sponsor a "Come Double" Sunday when this adopted family comes to a special service at church with the foster family.

With the present energy crisis, more families stay at home. Take advantage of this opportunity. Share hobbies and other wholesome activities together. Try joint gardening, fixing a fence, painting, crocheting, knitting, or sewing. Take this opportunity to "gossip the Gospel." View slides or filmstrips together and draw some lessons from them.

In the Philippines, families put great emphasis on special days and thanksgiving occasions such as graduations, promotions, moving into a new house, completing a successful venture, or a family homecoming. Christian families who have built bridges of friendships with unchurched families have an open door into homes and a tremendous opportunity for witness.

The more affluent Christian family may take advantage of vacations, weekends, or other holidays by planning to travel with an unchurched family. The close association during the few days together will provide avenues of witness. The privacy of the occasion will contribute to a greater openness to the Gospel. A creative family may also use a one-day or a few-hour trek, like riding, walking, cycling, or picnicking with another family.

CHILDREN

Herman ter Welle, founder and director of a national children's ministry in the Netherlands, suggested that a way to evangelize children was through "children's cells."

This plan is open to any believer willing to become a substitute spiritual mother or father for neighborhood children who do not come from Christian families. "Cells" or clusters of children are thus established in homes where they feel at ease about learning to pray. There they can love the Bible, and learn to know and trust the Savior.

What is the aim of such a children's "cell"? To win children to Jesus Christ by offering them instruction in the things of God in the atmosphere of a Christian home.

Who can create such a "cell"? All those who personally know the Lord revealed in the Scriptures, and have a heart wide open for children. They may be married or single, young or old, any occupation, either able to offer their own home or help in the home of another.

Which children should be invited? Those who live in your immediate neighborhood.

How many children ought to be invited? At least one! No rule, of course, can be laid down, but the idea is to set up small groups of five or six children.

How do you go about starting a children's "cell"?

1. Invite the children at the most convenient time for them. The actual meeting need only be a short one, thus not taking too much of their playtime or time set aside for homework. It is better to meet for a short time once a week than for a long time every three or four weeks.

2. Contact the parents of children you have invited and explain clearly your objective. Ask them how their children enjoy the little group.

3. Welcome them as you would your own children. Refreshments help make them feel at home.

4. Take time to get to know them, to listen to them, and take an interest in their news.

5. Pray with them and teach them to pray. Bring to the Lord the things which have been shared together. Let them discover that God is alive, that He loves us, and is interested in each one of us. Teach them that He intervenes in our lives in response to prayer.

6. Read verses from the Bible with them. Let them discover that the Bible is a living book in which God Himself speaks. Avoid reading the same passages over and over; use a plan of your own, or one of an existing Bible reading program. Think over the passage with them and ask them questions about what has been read. Make a simple and practical application.

7. Transform into prayer what God has said in His Word. Show how He speaks through His Word, and how we answer in prayer.

8. Let the leader of your church know about your initiative and the existence of a children's cell in your home.

9. Know that God has promised in Matthew 18:20, "For where two or three are gathered together in my name, there am I in the midst of them."

10. Pray daily for each child personally, that God will give an increase (1 Corinthians 3:7).

169

Evangelization of secondary school youth on a teenager-to-teenager basis is a method suggested by J. V. Manogarom from Madras, India. He is the Central Asia Area Director of Youth for Christ, International.

Manogarom

A few years ago young people used to run after the popular preachers, but that trend is changing. Now they listen to the person who is available to listen to them. The person who communicates with young people is one who is available to answer their questions and help them in their practical needs.

Whenever we think of the qualified messenger, we usually have in mind the adult — such as pastor, evangelist, teacher, or layman — who is interested in the work among teens. But we often forget a group which could be the real key to communicating with teens. We fail to tap a legion of resource personnel if we do not give serious consideration to the Christian teenagers themselves!

May I suggest some ways of winning non-Christian teens and helping Christian teenagers to communicate with other teenagers?

1. *Challenge teenagers.* Teenagers can be challenged to make their school campuses their mission fields. They need guidance and counsel regarding methods to use.

2. *Organize teen musical teams.* Using teen musical teams can often overcome barriers in reaching teenagers with the Gospel. Musical teams are able to gain entry and share the Gospel without much difficulty even in countries ruled by Hindus, such as Nepal and Burma which have closed their doors to foreign missionary activities. They are often warmly welcomed by administrators of institutions, even those of other religions.

3. *Conduct youth congresses.* These congresses give opportunity for young people to participate in musical talent contests, preaching contests, quiz contests, and music festivals. We find that when young people know that other young people will be present, they are there.

4. *Conduct youth camps.* Camps play a vital role in evangelizing teens, encouraging Christian teens to witness to non-Christian teenagers.

5. *Conduct clubs in homes.* Club ministries in homes have become more and more a necessity as government regulations in many countries do not permit religious activities on school campuses. Conducting clubs in homes is effective for evangelism among secondary students. Home clubs make it easier for teenagers of other faiths to come more freely, rather than going into a church or into a Christian religious instruction class in a school.

6. *Conduct evangelistic missions.* In many countries the door is still open for conducting evangelistic missions in schools. Scripture Union and Inter-School Christian Fellowship have experienced great blessings through such missions for many years. These missions make use of the Christian teenagers who work with their non-Christian friends to influence and help them.

7. *Conduct vacation Bible schools.* Vacation Bible schools when schools are on holiday have been greatly used to bring teens to Christ.

Methods of evangelizing university and college youth were described by Michael Cassidy, Director of African Enterprise.

1. *A fellowship must be built and trained.* Early church evangelism and growth were the outflow and overflow of fellowship (Acts 2:42–47). As they continued in the apostles' doctrine, fellowship, breaking of bread, and prayer, people were added to the church daily. Evangelism is born not just out of "me and God" but "us and God." There is therefore in student evangelism no greater priority than building a strong, local body of student believers who will incarnate the Gospel and give it credibility in the eyes of the whole campus. A quality fellowship of believers not only authenticates the Gospel, it proclaims it. The fellowship is both medium and message.

2. *A vision must be conveyed.* The vision which must be caught is that of the total body of believers, students and staff, reaching the total campus with a comprehensive penetration at every level of the institution. Christians should not be a ghetto group, but a band of infiltrators, witnesses, and caring agents.

3. *A strategy must be planned, tested, and evaluated.* The fellowship of believers will need to analyze their task of evangelizing the campus, break it down into manageable units, brainstorm on relevant strategies, mobilize the forces, and assign the tasks. The overall strategy should be diversified, comprehensive, and inclusive.

4. *Outreach must be undertaken.* All of the fellowship, analyzing, and planning is of no avail until or unless evangelization actually happens. Following are some tried and tested methods of outreach:

    1) Individual and personal student witness.

    2) The witness in private and in class of the Christian professor or lecturer.

    3) The special thrusts aimed at freshmen.

    4) Films and multimedia presentations, e.g., InterVarsity Christian Fellowship's "Twenty-One Hundred."

    5) Visitation evangelism.

    6) The straight lecture on themes of apologetic interest, e.g., the resurrection, the New Testament documents, science and faith, freedom and meaning, etc.

    7) Symposia. In our recent university missions we have used symposia extensively. The symposium often has far more drawing power than the monologue lecture. Giving a voice to the "opposition" is appreciated by dialogue-oriented and anti-doctrinaire students. The Christian view will authenticate itself impressively when juxtaposed with alternatives.

    8) Local church proclamation and teaching. Blessed indeed is the campus located close to a church with a vigorous preaching and teaching ministry! Christian students can take inquiring student friends into these contexts.

9) The Christian home. Committed Christians in a university town can use their homes for effective outreach, not just through discussion evenings, but in friendly caring. This ministry can be particularly meaningful to international students.

10) Literature. Every group of Christian students in every university hall or residence should have a book ministry. They should operate a book table at every meeting for outreach or discussion. A strategically located book table outside a dining hall produces surprising interest and significant sales. The excellent range of InterVarsity and IVCF books and booklets, plus the fine Campus Crusade tools should be in constant use. *HIS* magazine, *Collegiate Challenge*, and other student magazines have further usefulness. At Cape Town university the Christian students started their own campus newspaper called *"COMMENT."* It has had a vital impact on the entire university. Christians should also submit articles regularly to the secular campus newspapers.

11) Music and drama. The folk singer or folk group and the dramatist or drama group can make an impact, particularly in pre-evangelism, where more conventional approaches sometimes fail.

12) The student center. In great cities, where students are often upset and dissatisfied with the dismal atmosphere of the overcrowded campus and cramped student housing, a well-equipped student center can be very attractive.

13) The university mission. Some universities have a tradition of evangelistic meetings every three years so that each generation of undergraduates should have the opportunity of facing the claims of Christ in a special way. This is a useful tradition. Our experience is that the "success" of university evangelistic meetings is directly related to the quality and vitality of the student fellowship out of which it flows.

5. *Follow-up must be sustained.* Follow-up must be integral to the overall strategy of campus evangelization. To catch fish and let them go is the height of folly. Campus Crusade summarizes their philosophy — Win, Build, Send.

Approaches-3

Church-centered evangelization was discussed by several participants at the International Congress on World Evangelization. John Peters, a Canadian teacher in Switzerland and Germany, listed numerous evangelization methods for the church.

The church that wishes to become involved in evangelizing its community has a great potential both in its membership and in its use of different agencies and programs of outreach. Some means that have been successfully used in many areas are listed here:

1. *Systematic Bible teaching for all*
   –Sunday School
   –Cottage Bible study groups
   –Vacation Bible schools
   –Deeper Life seminars
2. *Visitation programs*
   –Surveys
   –Literature distribution
   –Invitation distribution
   –Cradle roll
   –Home department
   –Absentee follow-up
3. *Prayer Meetings*
   –Prayer breakfasts
   –Neighborhood prayer cells
4. *Camping and retreats*
   –Children's camps
   –Youth retreats
   –Family camps, etc.
5. *Club work*
   –Good News Clubs
   –Christian Service Brigade
   –Pioneer Girls
   –Awana Clubs
6. *Film ministry*
   –Evangelistic films
   –Moody Science Films
   –Filmstrips
7. *Coffee house ministry*
8. *Missions*
   –Foreign missions
   –Rescue missions
9. *Street meetings*
10. *Telephone ministry*
    –Dial-a-Message
11. *Hospitality*
    –Teas, luncheons
12. *Ministry in institutions*
    –Jails
    –Senior citizens homes
    –Homes for the retarded
    –Children's homes
    –Nursing homes
13. *Travel*
    –Guided tours
    –Study tours
14. *Music*
    –Bands
    –Choirs
    –Orchestras
15. *Recordings*
    –Records
    –Cassettes
16. *Family education*
    –Seminars
    –Counseling
    –Training for family devotions

J. Peters

Stephen Olford, former pastor of Calvary Baptist Church in New York City and now minister-at-large of Encounter Ministries, listed fourteen ways to contact people through a church evangelization program.

1. *Telephone calls.* List the names of people you have thought and prayed about. Find their telephone numbers and call them regularly, inviting them to evangelistic services. Where calls prove unfruitful, substitute new names and work with them prayerfully and consistently until they become regular attenders.

2. *Car service.* If you have a car, call the people and drive them to the services. Refreshments before or after can be an incentive.

3. *Bus parties.* With other interested friends, hire a bus and fill it up with interested people. Here again, refreshments or a meal can be planned to make the evening more pleasant.

4. *Other churches.* If you know ministers who offer no evening service, contact them tactfully to ask if they would announce your evening service in their church.

5. *Every member evangelism.* Pray with fellow church members as you talk over ways that each member could bring at least one individual each Sunday to the evangelistic service.

6. *Street meetings.* It is good to have a permanent group ready to do this work.

7. *Prayer list.* Have a loose-leaf notebook in which you enter the names of people you want to see converted: for example, mother, father, brother, sister, office colleagues, etc. As you regularly pray for them, you will find that God will give you inspirational ideas on how to help them hear the Gospel.

8. *Publicizing the services.* Contact the church office for suitable publicity material and then make it your business to see that attractive notices concerning the services of your church are placed in hotels, offices, apartment houses, public rooms at YMCAs, YWCAs, and similar hostels.

9. *Names and addresses.* If you have the names and addresses of people who would like to be informed about the church's program, send such information to the pastoral office with a suitable explanation about who the person is and how best to write them.

10. *Cottage prayer meetings.* Invite Christian people together for prayer in your home. There is great need for a praying band who will regularly seek God's blessing upon the ministry.

11. *Coffee klatches.* This is a splendid way to get to know neighbors and unconverted friends. Invite them for a time of refreshment and friendly informality, and then tell them about your church's program. If your church has a tape ministry, a tape of one of the services or a special meeting can be played.

12. *Tract distribution.* This ministry can be done individually or by organized parties of tactful, prayerful men and women committed to tract distribution every week. The material used and the areas covered should be organized by the pastor.

13. *Radio ministry.* Have you ever thought of inviting neighbors and friends to listen with you to a Gospel broadcast when you cannot be in church? A ministry such as this could affect a great number of people.

14. *Letter writing.* There are hundreds of lonely people who rarely receive a letter. For these people to receive a nicely written letter from you inviting them to church, or to tune in to a Gospel broadcast, could have far-reaching effects.

One church-oriented approach to evangelization was presented by David Ho, the Jamaica coordinator for Men in Action.

The goal of Men in Action is to assist the church in a continuing program of evangelization. During the first year, churches receive the help of the Men in Action team. In the second year the churches and denominations carry through a simplified version of the first year's program.

Our goal is church growth in three dimensions: quantitative growth, qualitative growth, and organic growth.

Quantitative growth refers to winning new people. Numbers are important! They represent people reached for Jesus and trained for His service!

Qualitative growth refers to the spiritual growth of the church members. We desire that they pray and witness more effectively, study the Bible with more earnestness, and be more faithful members of the church.

Organic growth refers to the organizational efficiency of the local church. We find that much church work tends to be "busy-work" and contributes little to the Kingdom of God. The team desires especially that the pastor use his time wisely, set priorities, and follow them so that he may be a more efficient servant of Christ. The program of Men in Action contains five basic building blocks for church growth.

1. Forming prayer cells to encourage every Christian to pray. A prayer cell is two or more people meeting together for fellowship, Scripture reading, and prayer. Every church member should be challenged to participate in a prayer cell.

2. Teaching Christians to build bridges of love and friendship with non-Christians. Participants learn methods of friendship evangelism through a six-fold teaching technique: lecture, literature, role-playing, films or film strips, personal training, and small group sharing. After a period of cultivation, friends are personally brought to friendship activities to hear the Gospel.

3. Special activities and crusades to win individuals to Christ through group presentations of the Gospel. Christians bring guests to special activities. The guests are contacts made through friendship evangelism. These activities are held in restaurants, resorts, camps, etc. At these occasions the atmosphere is relaxed. The program includes fellowship, a meal, a special feature, music, and a presentation of the Gospel. In the first year a united community crusade is sometimes used. Later, the church can sponsor a local preaching mission.

4. Initiating a direct witnessing training program for a special core of workers. This evangelistic team of men and women is trained by the lay coordinator. Learning takes place during actual evangelistic visits where the pastor presents the Gospel and the trainees observe.

5. Teaching and discipling through an emphasis on the growth of each new Christian as he uses his gifts in the church. This emphasis includes the dynamic of Christian friendship, new ideas from the Word of God, personal experience and practical application, and Christian prayer and worship. The groups meet weekly. Sharing and discussion are emphasized to facilitate participation. Every new Christian has a study companion who also attends the friendship group.

Men in Action also seeks to accomplish its goal through management training. We have found that most ministers have never had any training in management skills.[1]

A. William Cook, Jr., Coordinating Secretary of the Institute of In-Depth Evangelism, São Paulo, Brazil, described In-Depth Evangelism's approach. This approach has been used with some modification in several dozen countries in Asia, Africa, Europe, Latin America, and North America.

1. *Preparation.* An open-ended period for building bridges, establishing a simple organizational structure, and beginning to lay a spiritual foundation, especially among pastors and key leaders.

2. *Reflection.* Probably the key to the success of the entire program is the involvement in Reflection Groups of leadership at every level — interdenominational, denominational, city-wide, and local church. The goal is to involve every Christian in small prayer cells of five or six people. These small groups meet for prayer and praise, inductive study of the missiological themes of the Bible, analysis of research and observation, and, eventually, for goal-setting and planning. The members of these groups become leaders of prayer cells, action groups, or evangelism task forces.

3. *Action.* Based on the motivation, prayer, reflection, analysis, planning, and training that springs from the reflection groups and research teams, members coordinate activities and lead specialized task forces to specific ethnic, social, and geographical groupings.

4. *Consolidation* of gains and evaluation of methods. Once again the Reflection Groups have a vital part to play. This review becomes the springboard for a new cycle of preparation, reflection, action, and consolidation.

At the heart of in-depth evangelism is the *what*, the message of our communication — the Gospel of the Kingdom of our Lord. Guiding it on four sides are the four *hows* or channels of our communications: 1) meditation and prayer; 2) the observation and research of responses, attitudes, and needs; 3) analysis, goal setting, planning, and evaluation; and 4) strategic action.

---

[1]Additional information is available from Men in Action, P.O. Box 325, Coral Gables, FL 33134, U.S.A.

Its four cornerstones are 1) *who* — The communicators, i.e., God and the church — every Christian using every available resource; 2) *to whom* — The receivers, i.e., the whole world — people in political, ethnic, social, and geographic relationships; 3) *where* — The locus of the receivers; 4) *what for* — The goals of our communication — the multidimensional growth of the body of Christ. The aim of in-depth evangelism is to change the life-style of the church.[1]

URBAN CHURCHES

Roger S. Greenway, Latin American director of the Board of Foreign Missions of the Christian Reformed Church, described five basic ways to start city churches.

1. *The chapel-to-church method.* A mission board or committee chooses a promising location, erects a chapel, and appoints a missionary or evangelist to conduct services and develop the chapel into a church. When the group of believers has grown sufficiently, it becomes an organized church. Denominational mission work often follows this method. The high price of land in the city, plus the rising cost of labor and materials, makes this method increasingly difficult since it requires a large outlay of money for land and building. Indigenous churches can seldom afford to use this method without receiving outside funds.

2. *The mother-daughter method.* An established, indigenous church encourages the development of "daughter" churches in growing areas of the city where some of its members have gone to live. Services usually begin in private homes with laymen playing a leading role. The "mother" church helps with some of the expenses. Many older, well-established churches have in this way fostered the growth and development of scores of young churches.

3. *The Bible school approach.* Bible schools train evangelists and future church leaders. A large part of this training is in the practical experience of evangelization. Biblically defined and goal-oriented evangelization goes beyond personal evangelism to the planting of churches and community witness. Teachers and students canvass new areas of the city — selling Bibles and witnessing to entire families in their homes. When doors are opened, they organize family Bible studies. Neighbors are invited in and Sunday services begin. Eventually, some of these groups become organized churches.

4. *Apartment house evangelism.* The apartment house has been called the "modern frontier of the church's mission." Unfortunately, no widely successful method has yet been devised for reaching apartment dwellers and planting churches among them. However, in cities such as Singapore and San Juan, missionaries and evangelists have successfully established a witness in large apartment complexes. They have started Sunday Schools in private residences within the buildings, and in some cases certain apartments have been set aside as Christian day-care centers.

---

[1] Additional information is available from Institute of In-Depth Evangelism, Apartado 1307, San Jose, Costa Rica.

One key to successful apartment house strategy is to determine the type of apartment which you plan to evangelize. Not all apartment houses are alike. There are low-rent apartments which attract poorer families and are the most accessible for evangelization. There are also the middle-class apartments designed for better-paid office workers and business people. These are harder to approach. Finally, there are the upper-class, high-rise apartments where affluent families, single persons, or childless couples find the independence, privacy, and personal comfort they seek. This group is the hardest to reach, and the family orientation of most churches does not appeal to them.

5. *The house-church method.* The church is not a building but an assembly of believers organized according to biblical patterns and meeting regularly around the Word and sacraments. Any house, apartment, or rented facility can serve as the meeting place. House-churches generally develop out of Bible study groups, which in turn result from house-to-house visiting and personal invitation. Not all groups survive to become real house-churches. As a rule of thumb, during the early stages it takes fifteen to twenty calls to get five persons to a meeting. Services begin with six to eight persons.

It is important that house-churches be related to a wider Christian community for fellowship and mutual support.

OPEN-AIR EVANGELISM

Noel C. Gibson, training superintendent for Open-Air Campaigners International, described how to evangelize outdoors in cities and other locations.

The open-air preacher must go where people gather. His best opportunities will be found in these sorts of places:

parks and reserves

beaches, resorts, camp groups
  picnic areas

shopping centers, plazas

agricultural shows, fairgrounds

industrial centers, dockyards, mines,
  etc. (lunch hours, breaks)

workers' camps of all varieties

seaside fishing communities

village markets

indigenous meetings, particularly on
  festive occasions

streets and roads in housing
  and commercial areas

open air festivals and public
  events

football and sports grounds

racecourses

outdoor season workers in tobacco,
  wine, fruit, hop industries, etc.

high-rise housing settlements

street bazaars

railway stations, wharves, bus
  depots, airports

To reach adults:

1) One or two dedicated persons may conduct effective open-air evangelism.

2) Groups should appoint one capable person to be team leader.

3) The attention and interest of people can be attracted by music and singing, recorded music, or an artist with his sketchboard in a prominent place.

4) Introduce yourself, and then explain what organization you represent, and the purpose of the program.

5) Present the Gospel by testimony, teaching, preaching, and music — supported by sketchboard, graphics, object lessons, etc. Explain the implications of the Gospel for the whole person.

6) Challenge listeners to receive Christ as Savior and Lord. Use a simple prayer of faith.

7) Invite people who have responded to Christ by faith to make some public witness to their faith.

8) Offer literature to interested people at the conclusion of the program.

9) Maintain personal and/or written follow-up contact with the people who indicated that they trusted Christ as Savior.

To reach children:

1) Attract their attention and interest by using musicians or recorded music, a ventriloquist doll or puppet, or by personal invitation. Make sure the children are shaded in hot weather and seated comfortably.

2) Introduce yourself, your group, church or mission, and explain the purpose of your program.

3) Where possible, sing some children's songs with words clearly displayed and explained.

4) Teach the children a Bible verse. This should lead into a sketch or illustrated story which unfolds the Gospel.

5) Explain the way to receive Christ as Savior, inviting those interested to return for personal counsel after the program has concluded.

6) Use literature with discretion.

CRUSADE EVANGELISM

George W. Peters, professor of World Missions at Dallas Theological Seminary, summarized the method of crusade evangelism.

Crusade evangelism is a serious organized attempt to communicate the Gospel of Jesus Christ in an intelligible and meaningful manner to masses of people in public gatherings.

Crusade evangelism may follow various patterns. It may be national in scope, and present a program of evangelism that encompasses a whole nation.

United city-wide and area-wide campaigns have become a part of the heritage of the evangelical churches. In recent decades evangelistic campaigns have become a worldwide phenomenon through the efforts of such instruments as the Billy Graham Evangelistic Association, the World Vision endeavors, and the Good News Crusades of the Assemblies of God.

EVALUATION

Evaluation should be a part of evangelistic work. Peters suggested four criteria for evaluation based on what he calls "New Testament ideals." Use these criteria plus any others you may want to add, to evaluate your evangelization efforts.

1. Has the evangelism effort and endeavor brought renewal, revitalization, and a new pulsation of the Holy Spirit to the local church communities?

2. Has the evangelism effort added new converts to the local churches? Has the Gospel message penetrated sufficiently to change the direction and relationships of the individual, or has the "conversion" stopped short at a profession or decision?

3. Has the evangelism effort resulted in an ongoing movement, or has it remained one solitary event in the community? It is not too difficult to bring a great and impressive event to pass. It is a different matter to generate a movement that will increase in strength and intensity and enlarge in scope and dimension. Such an event was Pentecost!

4. Has the evangelism effort facilitated the continued ministry of the local churches in the community? Paul's practices and patterns of evangelism unlocked whole areas and communities which others were able to enter and effectively evangelize. This must be accepted as a biblical norm in evangelism strategy.

In summary, then, I conclude that ideal New Testament evangelism must build into its efforts dynamic factors that will bring renewal to the churches, add new converts to local congregations, transmute the event into a movement, and facilitate the continued Gospel ministry of the local congregations in the communities.

Contents - 6

Acknowledgements

Authors and papers of the International Congress on World Evangelization used in this study are as follows:

Thomas Houston, "The Holy Spirit in Evangelism";

Nilson A. Fanini, "Deacon Stephen: A Man Full of the Holy Spirit";

Billy Graham, "The King Is Coming";

Billy Graham, "Why Lausanne?";

Festo Kivengere, "The Cross and Evangelism"; Lausanne Covenant;

Donald McGavran, "Ten Dimensions of World Evangelism";

Gottfried Osei-Mensah, "The Holy Spirit in Evangelism";

Francis A. Schaeffer, "Form and Freedom in the Church";

Howard A. Snyder, "The Church as God's Agent of Evangelism."

Ralph Winter, "The Highest Priority: Cross-Cultural Evangelism";

In All of Me

The Holy Spirit is the necessary power for effective evangelization. Personal dedication is also necessary for effective evangelization. Without the Holy Spirit and personal dedication of Christians, evangelization is only a human effort without divine presence and power or personal commitment. The Holy Spirit's power and our personal commitment, "All power in all of me," is the focus of this study. It is based on excerpts from several papers presented at the International Congress on World Evangelization held in Lausanne, Switzerland.

The Holy Spirit is God's power in our lives. Do we have a specific part to play in His work or are we merely passive "tubes" through which the Holy Spirit blows? Gottfried Osei-Mensah, a pastor in Nairobi, Kenya, sketched two different views concerning the Holy Spirit's role in evangelism.

Christian thinking and practice with regard to this subject varies between two extremes. The one extreme regards the Holy Spirit as an impersonal divine energy or influence. You plan your evangelistic program, devoting time and thought to every detail and using all the known techniques that should guarantee success. Then you call upon the Holy Spirit, God's power, to take care of the unforeseen factors in your plans and to boost the anticipated success. That is one extreme.

The other extreme disparages every human initiative in planning for evangelistic outreach as vain striving. You must not attempt anything until you are moved irresistibly and spontaneously by the Holy Spirit. Only then can you be sure you are filled with the Holy Spirit and expect lasting spiritual results.

The first extreme denies the personality of the Holy Spirit; the second denies the responsibility of the Christian. But the Bible affirms both the personality of the Holy Spirit and the responsibility of the Christian.

Osei-Mensah then described the general nature of the Holy Spirit's power and work. Read Acts 1:8 and continue with the following:

"You shall receive power. . . ." If you received an explosive device you would have to decide what to do with it. But if you have the privilege of receiving some dignitary into your home, he more or less decides what to do with you! You are at his disposal. The Lord Jesus promised His people not packages of power but the powerful personality of the Holy Spirit to live in them.

The coming of the Holy Spirit was proof that God had exalted Jesus to the position of highest authority, honor, and rule. God had thereby vindicated Jesus' claim to be both Lord and Christ (Acts 2:33, 36). The supreme work of the Holy Spirit is to witness to this reality in and through Christians. It is chiefly for this reason that the Lord referred to Him as the Spirit of Truth (John 14:17). The Holy Spirit communicates spiritual truth to people by a two-fold process. First, He reveals what lies hidden from human search and understanding. Second, He opens our minds to know and understand. The Spirit gives greater understanding of how precious the exalted Savior is and how unsearchable His riches and merits are to meet the needs of all who trust in Him. What He taught the apostles is embodied in the Scriptures for us. When we come to the Bible, the same Holy Spirit must again illuminate the written Word and enlighten our understanding if we are to profit by the Truth.

The work of the Spirit begins with bringing to our understanding the truth as it relates to our exalted Savior, enthroned at the right hand of God. But it does not end there. He then helps us to know consciously the presence of our Lord in our daily lives. To enjoy this, we must trust and love Him and show it by our ready obedience to His expressed will. To be the object of God's love and also to be a place where God feels at home is a deeply satisfying result of fellowship with the Father and the Son (John 14:20–23).

The Lord assured the disciples and He reassures us that this fellowship will enable us to face both the loneliness and alienation of a world that cannot understand us (John 14:18–19) and the antagonism of a world that crucified our Lord (John 15:18–20). In the confidence of our Lord's presence we can also in love boldly plead with people to give up their hatred and return to the Lord who is ready to pardon them and fulfill their deepest need (Acts 2:38–39; 3:17–19).

The ability to understand, experience, and boldly proclaim Jesus as the One exalted by God to be the Christ, our Savior and Lord, and the effectiveness of this proclamation in those who hear, are all the result of promised power. We are deeply involved in its exercise, but only as we are in fellowship with the powerful Spirit who lives within us — not independent of Him.

● If people think of the Holy Spirit only as an impersonal force they do not have to think about His will for their lives. On the other hand, if they make Him totally responsible for everything they do not have to accept responsibility for what they do. Why do people take one of these positions to the exclusion of the other? Do you ever do that? Why are these two extremes dangerous to evangelism?

Based on Acts 1:8, why do we say that the Holy Spirit is not a thing but a Person? How would your relationship to God be affected if the Holy Spirit was only a "power"? How does He as a Person affect your relationship to God?

List several things that the Holy Spirit does.

Why does the Holy Spirit's work center so much on Christ? What should be the results of the Holy Spirit in your life? Do you see these results in your life? How can you experience greater effects from the work of the Holy Spirit?

●● When people explain the Holy Spirit as an impersonal force, what do they overlook in evangelism? If they put all responsibility on the Holy Spirit, what are they denying?

Do you ever find yourself wanting to escape from either committing yourself to the Holy Spirit's leading or from accepting personal responsibility for your own decisions and actions in evangelism? Why?

What difference does it make when a Christian views the Holy Spirit as a Person and not just as an impersonal power?

List several things that the Holy Spirit does. Why is His work so important for our continued spiritual growth? Why is Jesus the central focus of the Holy Spirit's work in us?

How should you respond to the work of the Holy Spirit in your life?

●●● What happens when a Christian views the Holy Spirit as just an impersonal influence or as the sole responsible agent in evangelism? Why do people think of the Holy Spirit in terms of either extreme? What sort of escapism is inherent in both extremes?

What difference does it make when a Christian views the Holy Spirit as a Person rather than as an impersonal power?

What are the major tasks of the Holy Spirit?

The two major factors in the Holy Spirit's work are Jesus Christ and the person of the Christian. In what ways does the Holy Spirit cause these factors to interact?

What should be the response of a Christian to the Holy Spirit's work in his life? How do you normally respond?

How can you help others respond more positively to His work in their lives?

187

One of the Christian's responsibilities is to evangelize. How does the Holy Spirit help with this task? Osei-Mensah suggested several ways. In the following section he focused on the role of the Holy Spirit in our life and witness.

"You shall be my witnesses. . . ." The Holy Spirit indwelling us witnesses to the authority, honor, and rule with which our exalted Savior is now invested. The dwellers of heaven proclaim His worth as One entitled to all power, riches, wisdom, strength, honor, glory, and blessing (Revelation 5:12). One day the whole created order will say, "Amen" to that and bow in worship to King Jesus (Revelation 5:13–14; Philippians 2:9–11). But now it is the privilege of the Christian to know this truth and to live his life in the light and experience of its reality. When we take care to enjoy this privilege, we become effective witnesses to our exalted Savior in two respects, namely by life (sanctification) and lip (proclamation). In both these respects, the power of the Holy Spirit living in us takes issue with our real weakness in order that the hidden worth and preciousness of Christ may be seen in and through us.

It is the work of the Holy Spirit, living in us, to free us from the rule of sin in our daily lives, and to help us live the new life we share with Christ. In this process, He may use the strong attraction of Christ's love to help us aspire to a greater devotion to Him. He may also use a painful discipline of some trial to return us to submission and obedience. There is no better witness to the authority, honor and rule of our Savior among men than to see us gladly and thankfully subject to His authority and rule, thereby upholding His honor. If they see us free from the rule of sin in our lives, they have the evidence that Jesus Christ is powerful to save.

Submission to the rule of Christ's Holy Spirit is no easy matter in this permissive and materialistic age. Every Christian must make a conscious effort to "lay aside every weight, and sin which clings so closely," and refuse to be "conformed to this world " (see Hebrews 12:1; Romans 12:2). The practical discipline of regular fasting and stricter stewardship of our resources of time, money, and materials may be salutary in our age. Somehow or other, the evangelical Christian's reverence and submission to Christ's authority in every aspect of life needs to be more evident than it is today.

188

●

Do you ever have a desire to act like Jesus and then do just the opposite? Why do you not act like Christ? Why does the Holy Spirit have to point out to us that power over sin comes from Jesus?

How does "trusting in the Lord" lead us to victory over sin?

How well does your life demonstrate Jesus' power over sin? How can your life be a better witness?

●●

The Holy Spirit sanctifies us, that is, helps us to become morally and spiritually like Christ. But how is Christ the example, pattern, and source of victory? Why does trusting Him lead to victory? How do we "trust Him"?

How does your *life* demonstrate Christ's power to free from the rule of sin? What can you do to increase His power in your life?

●●●

How does one "enjoy this privilege" of knowing the worth of Jesus? How does such "enjoying" lead to effective witness? Explain why effective witness is or is not the same as evangelization.

What is the place of Christ in our sanctification?

What does "trusting in the Lord leads to victory" mean? How does one "trust in Him"? How do you know when you trust Him?

What is a Christian's personal responsibility in evangelism? Should a Christian use his mind to think, plan, and pray, or just let the Holy Spirit "lead" him to do evangelism? Osei-Mensah answered these questions.

Osei - Mensah

Both the Holy Spirit and the Christian are deeply involved in the Lord's command to evangelize. The Christian's practical obedience to the "heavenly vision" (God's call to serve Him, Acts 26:19) involves him in the exercise of his renewed mind and committed will (Romans 12:1–2). The Holy Spirit leads by inspiring us with a life and disposition out of which right purposes and decisions come forth. But the right purposes must be carefully thought out by us. How else can we be certain that they are right? Decisions must be taken responsibly. Every Christian is automatically a witness for the Lord Jesus Christ. In the matter of evangelism, as in all other aspects of his life for Christ, he must find out what his specific role is. When he knows this, his response in love to the Lord must be with all his heart, mind, soul, and strength. However, this is only possible as the Christian has fellowship with the Holy Spirit, both in discerning the will of his Lord and in the doing of it (Philippians 2:12–13). There is therefore a balance between the inspiration of the Holy Spirit and Christian initiative which denies neither the sovereignty of God nor the responsibility of man.

●

●●

●●●

189

Who inspires, leads, and guides a Christian as he makes decisions? Why are a renewed mind and committed will important to a Christian?

How can you allow the Holy Spirit to do His part? How can you be sure to do your part?

How can a Christian achieve a balance between his own responsibility and the Holy Spirit's? Why is such balance necessary? Why is doing the will of God so important?

How would you go about working out a balance between the Holy Spirit's responsibility and your own?

What are the roles of the Holy Spirit and the individual Christian in decision-making?

How do a renewed mind and a committed will relate to the decision-making process?

Why is *doing* the will of God a vital factor in achieving the balance between the Holy Spirit's responsibility and human initiative?

What else is involved? How "balanced" are you?

The Holy Spirit is a divine Person of the utmost importance to our spiritual life and therefore to our witness. One of the Holy Spirit's major roles is to tell us about Christ's greatness. Everything the Holy Spirit does is to show that Christ is preeminent — "Jesus is number One"!! When we give Jesus this high position in our lives, we can more adequately demonstrate that He is Lord. How we do this witnessing is left to us to determine under the Holy Spirit's guidance.

Consider again Acts 1:8, "But when the Holy Spirit has come upon you, you will receive power to testify about me with great effect, to the people in Jerusalem, throughout Judea, in Samaria, and to the ends of the earth. . . ." What does the Holy Spirit do? What does He give us? What do we do? How do we testify? In what power?

In My Message

When we proclaim the Gospel, are we doing so on our own, or is the Holy Spirit the one who does the proclaiming? What does the Holy Spirit do in the heart and mind of a non-believer who hears the Gospel?

Gottfried Osei-Mensah sought to answer these questions when he focused on the relationship of the Holy Spirit to the Christian's proclamation of the Gospel.

As human beings, we are limited in what we can do; we have weaknesses. In proclamation, the Holy Spirit takes hold of our weakness. We can see the necessity for this when we remember that the grand objective of our proclaiming is that Christ may write His divine nature in people's hearts as the principle of their lives (2 Corinthians 3:2–3). The Spirit is Christ's ink; the proclaimer's tongue is Christ's pen! Divine power takes hold of our weakness and qualifies us to minister the Good News through the Holy Spirit (2 Corinthians 3:5–6). "Everyone can see that the glorious power within must be from God and is not our own" (2 Corinthians 4:7).

There are two parts to the proclamation of the Good News. Both must bear the stamp of the Holy Spirit if the proclamation is to bear fruit.

The Holy Spirit must interpret the message we preach. By the Holy Spirit "God opens the eyes of those called to salvation to see that Christ is the mighty power of God to save them; Christ Himself is the center of God's wise plan for their salvation" (1 Corinthians 1:24).

The Holy Spirit must give the boldness to preach the message. Then the Good News comes to the hearers not in a word only, but with full conviction (1 Thessalonians 1:5; 1 Corinthians 2:4).

You do not have to become a learned theologian to proclaim boldly. But you must be filled with the Spirit (Acts 4:13, 31). Utterance is a gift from God (Ephesians 6:19).

●

In what way does human weakness tend to hinder or prevent our proclaiming the Gospel? How does the Holy Spirit overcome these weaknesses?

What difference does the Holy Spirit make in how fearlessly you speak?

Why is "utterance" a gift from God? How do you receive such a gift?

●●

Why does our human nature cause weakness in our proclamation of the Gospel?

How does the Holy Spirit enter into the message we proclaim and make it more than just a human message? Is the message or the hearer affected, or both?

How can you be sure that the Holy Spirit is truly present when you witness?

●●●

Why do you think Osei-Mensah equates proclamation with preaching? What else could proclamation include besides preaching?

Is "proclaimer" or "preacher" the better word in this section?

How does the Holy Spirit affect the message, the proclaimer, and the hearer?

Are certain conditions necessary to assure that the Holy Spirit's power is operative in proclamation?

Osei-Mensah explained the way the Holy Spirit works on non-Christians when they hear the Gospel proclaimed to them:

Effective witness by life and lip is the Holy Spirit's tool in appealing to the consciences of men and women about the truth of Jesus Christ (John 16:8–11). He does this work, first of all, by bringing to light the relationship between sin, righteousness, and judgment. Sin is a state of rebellion against God's rule in a life. In this state a person deeply resents God's interference, especially in his moral life. But, at the same time, he would admit to a nagging sense of emptiness and failure. Righteousness refers to the will of God which man should be doing in order to please God and to enjoy His friendship. Judgment is the inevitable result of a holy God's attitude toward man's rebellion. The sinner's present state of guilt, emptiness, and failure is only a foretaste of what is in store for him if he persists in his rebellion against his Maker. The relationship of sin, righteousness, and judgment is brought into light through the Christian's life, primarily by contrast. The non-Christian can see the Christian's submission to God's will and his apparent freedom from a sense of emptiness, failure, and condemnation.

If, in the strength and grace of the Holy Spirit, the Christian follows this witness of life with a "reason for the hope" that is in him, the Holy Spirit takes His work a step further. He presses the truth home to the conscience by showing how sin, righteousness, and judgment relate to the Person of Jesus Christ.

Jesus showed God's nature in His life, teaching, miracles, death, and resurrection. God is holy, just, merciful, loving, wise, and almighty. Jesus showed us the Father: "He who has seen Me has seen the Father" (John 14:9). He also showed the way into God's friendship. We please God and enter His friendship by a decisive trust in Jesus Christ and an equally decisive break from our rebellion against God's rule.

God counts our faith in Him through His Son Jesus Christ as righteousness (Romans 4:22–25). Our faith in the Lord Jesus not only brings us into God's friendship, it also frees us from the power of Satan (Acts 26:18). Satan is the "ruler of this world" who incites unbelieving men and women to rebel and disobey God (Ephesians 2:2). One aspect of the Lord's mission was to destroy Satan's works and place him under judgment (1 John 3:8). When the Holy Spirit relates these realities to our exalted Lord and presses the truth home on the conscience, the non-Christian must decide for or against God. Unbelief then becomes the greatest of all sins (John 3:19). It despises not only God's truth, but also God's love.

It is a sheer miracle of grace that some who rationalize away the impact of God's truth for a long time, suddenly break down under the conviction of God's love for them personally through Jesus Christ. The conversion experience is the crowning of the Holy Spirit's convincing and convicting work in a person's life.

Why does the Holy Spirit emphasize sin, righteousness, and judgment in dealing with non-believers?

Why is it necessary for the Holy Spirit to show how sin, righteousness, and judgment are related to Jesus Christ?

Why is Jesus Christ the focal point of the Holy Spirit's work in non-Christians? How is Satan's power defeated? Does this mean that all Christians have power to defeat Satan and sin in their lives? How successful are you in defeating Satan and sin in your life?

How does successful Christian living influence your witnessing for Christ?

Who or what is the main focus in the Holy Spirit's work in non-Christians? Why is this so?

What makes sin, righteousness, and judgment such good topics to emphasize to non-Christians? How does Jesus provide the way out of sin and judgment, and the way to righteousness?

Why does faith in Christ bring the possibility of victory over sin and Satan? Is unbelief the greatest of all sins? Who rules the unbeliever's life? How can Christ rule more and more in your life? What will happen to your witness for Christ when He is truly ruling in your life?

How do Christians cooperate with the Holy Spirit in His work in "convincing the world"?

Is a verbal testimony necessary for the Holy Spirit to "take His work a step further" and press home the message about Christ?

How do sin, righteousness, and judgment relate to Christ?

Why is unbelief the "greatest of all sins"?

Why is conversion "the crowning of the Holy Spirit's convincing and convicting work"? Is this the ultimate goal of the Holy Spirit's work or is it something else?

Is the Holy Spirit limited to the witness of believers?

Osei-Mensah, in his concluding remarks at the Lausanne Congress, outlined five areas in which the Christian is dependent upon the Holy Spirit.

Osei - Mensah

The church is dependent upon the Holy Spirit for the fulfillment of Christ's command to evangelize the world. This dependence must be thankfully acknowledged in five specific areas.

1. *Perspective:* There is a need for an evangelical world view, dominated by the anticipation of our Lord's soon return. A love for "His appearing" gave motivation, direction, and urgency to the missionary activities of the early church. The Holy Spirit can help us set our minds on the heavenly things that bring honor to our exalted Lord. We must appeal to Him for a clear, constant, and consuming vision of our blessed Lord and His plans.

2. *Prayer:* Through prayer the Holy Spirit makes the will of our Lord personally known to us, commits our will to it, and strengthens us to actively obey. A life of prayer is brought about by intimate fellowship with the Spirit of prayer. In this way Christ shares His burden for men and women with us, as well as His resources for reaching them effectively for Him (John 20:21–22). Some of His strongest promises about answered prayer are in connection with our obedience in evangelism (John 14:12–14; John 15:16; Acts 4:29–31; Matthew 9:37–38).

3. *People:* "God so loved the world that He gave His only begotten Son" (John 3:16). "From now on, therefore, we regard no one from a human point of view," but from God's

(2 Corinthians 5:16). Men and women are the objects of God's love in Christ and of the Spirit's patient wooing for Christ. Both realities must be evident in our approach to people. We must get alongside them and cultivate their friendship and thus earn the right to communicate to them the Good News in a relevant way. Where there is a false sense of security, we must expose it in love and seek to help them see their real need of the Lord. We must be interested in their objections to belief and try to remove them.

Ultimately, it is the reality of the Holy Spirit's working through us that brings conviction, repentance, and faith in the Lord Jesus. The command to be separate is not to be isolated but rather to be involved without being contaminated. Our involvement with people is the Spirit's opportunity to draw them to the Savior who died for them.

4. *Partnership:* In a shrinking world of jet travel and satellite communication, evangelical cooperation is not only desirable but vital for the goal of world evangelization. Our evident oneness is a powerful witness to Christ's divine mission and His power to save (John 17:21). But it is also wise stewardship in a world of rising costs of resources for training and outreach. Duplication and even competition among evangelicals contradicts our message and confuses those whom we seek to reach for Christ.

5. *Power:* "God, by the power at work within us, is able to do far more abundantly than all that we ask or think" (Ephesians 3:20). Our plans should be made under His Spirit's guidance. Therefore we must be open to His sovereign intervention in revival and renewal within the church as well as the consequent large-scale ingatherings of Christ's redeemed people in preparation for His coming.

193

What difference does it make to his outreach when a Christian thinks about Christ's returning soon?

Why do you think promises of answered prayer are often connected with evangelism? What does this suggest about the importance of evangelism?

People are the object of God's love and the patient work of the Holy Spirit; how should *we* treat people? In what ways do you think your witnessing would change if you treated people as God does?

With which groups of Christians in your church or community could you become "partners" to do a more effective job of witnessing?

How much spiritual power is available to you? How much do you use? Remember that obedience to God is the beginning of spiritual power. How will you know when you receive it?

What should an anticipation of Christ's return do to your attitude and manner of outreach?

What relationship between God and a Christian does prayer suggest? What should prayer produce in you?

Knowing how God treats people, how should you treat them? What would the results be in your outreach?

How can you be "partners" with others in your church or community to evangelize more effectively? How does lack of cooperation among Christians hinder the Gospel?

What would happen if the Holy Spirit's power was really unblocked in our world? In you? Should you be asking Him for power?

How does the Holy Spirit influence each of these five areas?

Why does an eschatological perspective help the Christian in evangelization?

Does an absence of such a perspective hinder evangelization?

What elements related to evangelization are involved in the communication of God and man through prayer?

How does one "earn the right to communicate" the Gospel?

In what sense is evangelical cooperation vital to world evangelization? In what kinds of cooperative efforts could you become involved?

Why do you think Osei-Mensah equates God's power with His sovereign intervention? Although God is sovereign and has all power, yet it is our responsibility to evangelize. How can this seeming contradiction be reconciled?

Choose one of the following: the Gospel message is (a) ours, (b) God's, or (c) God's message in us but through our personality. What reasons do you have for your choice? How much *personal* responsibility do *you* have in fulfilling the command to "make disciples of all nations"? What will you have to do to determine your next tasks in obeying the Lord? What will you do after you have discovered your next tasks?

In My Church

What does the Holy Spirit do in and through a group of believers, known as a "local church," and through the entire family of all believers called the "universal church"? Several leaders at the International Congress on World Evangelization talked about the Holy Spirit's relationship to the church. Howard H. Snyder, Dean of the Free Methodist Theological Seminary in São Paulo, Brazil, said that the church must be viewed as a dynamic group of God's people who have received gifts from the Holy Spirit. As you read, consider this question: How does the Holy Spirit make the people of God, the church, a special agent for evangelism in the world?

Snyder

The Bible describes the church in charismatic, rather than institutional, terms. According to the New Testament, the church is a charismatic organism, not an institutional organization. It is through grace that members of the church are saved (Ephesians 2:8), and through the exercise of spiritual gifts of grace (*charismata*) that the church is edified (Romans 12:6–8; Ephesians 4:7–16; 1 Corinthians 12:4–11, 27–31, 14:1–5; 1 Peter 4:10–11).

God gives His gracious gift of salvation on the basis of Christ's work and through the agency of the Holy Spirit. This provides the basis of the church's community life. The pure light of God's "varied grace" (1 Peter 4:10) then shines through the church, as light through a prism, producing the varied, many-colored *charismata*, or gifts of the Spirit. Thus the church is a diversity within unity. The church is edified through the exercise of spiritual gifts as "the whole body, joined and knit together by every joint with which it is supplied, . . . makes bodily growth and upbuilds itself in love" (Ephesians 4:16).

195

●

What does the word "organism" mean? How is the word "organization" different? What does "charismatic" mean? Why is the church called a "charismatic organism"?

Why does the Holy Spirit provide spiritual gifts?

● ●

Why is the church a "charismatic organism" and not an "institutional organization"?

Why does God give spiritual gifts to the church?

● ● ●

What benefits occur when the church is seen as a "charismatic organism" rather than an "institutional organization"?

What are the roles and goals of spiritual gifts in the church?

Read Romans 12:6–8; 1 Corinthians 12:4–11, 27–31, 14:1–5; Ephesians 4:7–16; 1 Peter 4:10–11. As you study these passages, list the spiritual gifts according to their functions: i.e., teaching, leading (include pastoring), and other ministries. According to Scripture, does every believer have some spiritual gift? How can a Christian discover his gift or gifts?

The church is more than just another organization. Snyder's view of the church as a charismatic organism, built on the gifts of the Holy Spirit, has direct implications for evangelization.

The New Testament relates evangelism to spiritual gifts (Ephesians 4:11–12). Yet it is significant that the word "evangelist" occurs only three times in the New Testament. The apparent reason for so few references is that the New Testament church did not see evangelism as primarily the work of specialists. Evangelism was the natural expression of the life of the church. There was no need to exhort believers or to raise up a special class of evangelists to insure that evangelism occurred.

Why, then, does Paul even mention "evangelists" as a spiritual gift? Simply because men who were strictly evangelists, and recognized as such (as distinct from apostles and prophets, with whom they presumably had much in common) had arisen in the church — for example, Philip. Paul recognized these men as being a part of God's plan for the church. The normal life of the Christian community will produce growth, but God especially calls and raises up men with a particular evangelistic gift, sometimes for evangelism within the same culture and sometimes for cross-cultural evangelism. These are God's special gifts in order that new frontiers may be crossed and the Great Commission be fulfilled.

In order for the church to be alive and growing, it must be based on a *charismatic model*, not an *institutional model*. The question of a charismatic or institutional model for church life and structure is becoming urgent in contemporary society. Technological development, the population explosion, and other factors are speeding up the pace of change. This acceleration puts new strains on all institutional structures. Alvin Toffler analyzes these trends in *Future Shock*, and argues that "the acceleration of change has reached so rapid a pace that even bureaucracy can no longer keep up." This means that "newer . . . more instantly responsive forms of organization must characterize the future."

Whether this is good or bad for the church depends on whether the church is structured according to a charismatic model or an institutional model. Biblically, it is clear that the church should be structured charismatically, and any church so structured is already largely prepared to withstand "future shock." But churches which are encased in rigid, bureaucratic, institutional structures may soon find themselves trapped in culturally-bound forms which are fast becoming obsolete.

196

●

Why is the church which is built on the gifts that the Holy Spirit gives better able to make changes?

●●

Why is it important for evangelization to view the church as a charismatic organism rather than an institutional organization?

●●●

For what purpose are the spiritual gifts given? How does the purpose of the spiritual gifts relate to evangelization?

Will such a church be more effective in evangelization?

Is your group organized on the basis of the special abilities (spiritual gifts) that God has given? How can a person be sure that his group leadership is based on the gifts of the Holy Spirit? How can you apply these principles to your own group in your church?

As you consider such factors as ability to change, receiving new directions from Christ, the Head of the church, meeting people's needs, what are the evidences that your local church is a charismatic organism?

What can you do to help your group and your local church be organisms controlled by the Holy Spirit?

Do you agree with Snyder that the church must be based on a charismatic model? Why?

What procedures could move a church from an organizational structure to a charismatic organism?

It could be argued that if a church is based on the leading of the Holy Spirit then all human thinking, planning, strategies, and organization are unnecessary! But this idea that no human responsibility is needed when the Holy Spirit is in control is not biblical. Gottfried Osei-Mensah pointed out the need for human planning and the Holy Spirit's relationship to those plans. Why does he teach that organization is necessary? How is the Holy Spirit involved in our planning?

Osei - Mensah

The stewardship of God's grace (time, money, spiritual gifts, or personnel) requires some degree of organization, even when only one person is involved. The invisible church of Jesus Christ is an organism, but the local church functions as an organization (Ephesians 4:11–16).

There are dangers in every human organization, including the church. The chief danger with Christian organizations is a loss of spiritual vision. But the alternative to this is not lack of organization, but rather in the setting of wise spiritual goals and objectives. Nothing is more calculated to check our tendency to sloth than a clear spiritual vision articulated in concrete objectives and well-defined principles for action.

Spiritual goals and objectives give meaning to commitment, inspire perseverance in prayer, and promote self-discipline. The apostle Paul taught these things by precept and example. "Do you not know that in a race all the runners compete, but only one receives the prize? So run that you may obtain it. Every athlete exercises self-control in all things. They do it to obtain a perishable wreath, but we an imperishable. Well, I do not run aimlessly, I do not box as one beating the air" (1 Corinthians 9:24–26).

If anyone demonstrated that there was no conflict whatever between sound spiritual planning and the immediacy of the Spirit's working, it was the apostle Paul (Acts 16:6–10). Underlying Paul's missionary effort was a definite plan and strategy. The immediacy of the Spirit's working may not be made an excuse for lack of spiritual planning. The Spirit helps our weakness, but not our laziness. When He intervenes sovereignly in our plans, He gives us more than we had hoped for, not less.

●

Read Acts 16:6–10 to see how the Holy Spirit steps into our planning.

Why do you think the Holy Spirit allowed Paul to make his decisions twice and be corrected each time?

What was Paul's attitude toward the Holy Spirit?

How can you have this same attitude toward God's will in your life?

Was God's will a blueprint for all of Paul's life or just the next major step?

What does your answer suggest about knowing God's will for your life?

●●

Osei-Mensah said that a local church is an organization and the invisible church is an organism.

Snyder indicated that the people of God, the church on both local and universal levels, should be considered an organism. With which do you agree? Is it possible to be an organized organism?

What principles about the guidance of the Holy Spirit can you learn from Acts 16:6–10?

Why didn't God reveal His will for Paul at his conversion rather than piece by piece.

What do you know of God's will for your life?

●●●

Is a local church an organization or an organism? Why is it quite consistent to think of a local church or denomination as an organized organism? What definition of "church" is implied by Osei-Mensah and Snyder's usages of the word? With which do you agree, and why?

In what ways can setting wise and spiritual goals overcome lack of spiritual vision? What is the source of these goals?

What observations about divine guidance are implicit in Acts 16:6–10?

How open to new input from God are you? How flexible are you to His will?

The Holy Spirit is at work in the world today. Does He work just in individuals one by one or in large groups also? Does He change only a person's inner life, or does He have an impact on that person's society as well? Osei-Mensah had this to say:

We have considered the nature of the Holy Spirit's power and how it relates to evangelism. In all of this we have emphasized the Spirit's work in and through the individual. I believe this is primary. But the Spirit also moves on a large scale in different communities and cultural groups. The first city crusade outside Jerusalem was conducted by Philip the evangelist at Samaria and it was a great success (Acts 8:4–25). There were mass conversions and one notable false profession of faith. The follow-up was personally supervised by two apostles.

Ephesus is a biblical example of the impact of the Good News on every aspect of community life (Acts 19). Paul made a few converts there, trained them in discipleship for two years, and the result was that "all the residents of Asia heard the Word of the Lord, both Jews and Greeks" (verse 10). The Word of the Lord converted deficient, nominal Christianity (vv. 1–7), challenged Jewish traditionalism (vv. 8–9), condemned religious syncretism (vv. 11–17), conquered occultism (vv. 18–20), and undermined questionable trade and industry at Ephesus (vv. 23–27). Individuals entered a deep spiritual experience; the name of the Lord Jesus was extolled and the Word of the Lord grew and prevailed mightily (see vv. 6, 17, 20).

Men and women filled with the Holy Spirit have "turned the world upside down" many times since those apostolic days. Tribe after tribe has become disenchanted with the unjust, immoral, and wasteful aspects of their traditional beliefs and practices. Through the activities of small witnessing communities, Christian educators, Bible translators, medical missionaries, literature and radio evangelists, etc., they have found the concepts and virtues of the Christian faith fulfilling. And true conviction has led many to turn to God from idols to serve a living and true God (1 Thessalonians 1:9).

However, in any mass turning to the Christian faith, the need for sound individual conversions should not be forgotten. "All we like sheep have gone astray, we have turned everyone to his own way" (Isaiah 53:6). In bringing us back to the Lord, the Holy Spirit follows everyone "in his own wicked way" to convince and woo us with Calvary love!

Donald McGavran, professor at the School of World Mission of Fuller Theological Seminary, Pasadena, California, listed some modes of church growth that God is blessing.

The first mode of growth is *one-by-one-against-the-family*. In this, converts come to Christ one by one, regardless of what other members of their families do. This form of growth has taken place across all lands of earth. God uses it to begin the process, but He blesses other modes to better and greater growth.

The second mode of church growth is the *family movement to Christ*. In this, several members of a family accept the Lord at the same time. The New Testament tells of many family conversions. "He and his household" accepted the Lord, is frequently recorded. "One-by-one-against-the-family" should normally progress to where decisions are being made family by family. The church grows better when this happens.

The third mode of church growth is the *people movement to Christ*. A people movement results from the joint decision of a number of individuals — whether five or five hundred — all from the same people, which enables them to become Christian without social dislocation, while remaining in full contact with their non-Christian relatives, thus enabling other groups of families across the years, after suitable instruction to come to similar decisions and form Christian churches made up exclusively of members of that people. People movements are today bringing multitudes to Christian faith in all the continents. Tomorrow, the great surges of church growth are likely to come from people movements of which there are many different varieties.

The fourth mode of church growth being blessed of God is the multiplication in cities and villages of *house churches*. Tens of thousands can now be established. Evangelism will be more effective as it finds ways to organize converts into small congregations in homes.

●

Why does the Holy Spirit work through different modes? What does this tell you about the Holy Spirit's wisdom? What are some different ways for you to witness?

Refer to Acts 19 for some general ideas and principles on how salvation affects you and your daily life.

●●

Why does the Spirit use various ways to do His work? What can we learn from Him about flexibility and fitting the mode to a particular situation?

Using Acts 19 as background, how should your salvation affect your daily environment?

●●●

Why does the Holy Spirit use various modes to accomplish His work? What does this suggest regarding the Spirit's character?

Why does salvation affect more than just an individual and his own inner life? How is your salvation affecting your society?

McGavran suggested several conversion modes that God is blessing to help the church of Christ grow. There are many modes, means, methods and procedures that God is blessing today. Look over the following list. Add your own ideas to it. Which do you recognize that He is blessing? Which mode could you use in your area as an effective tool with people you know? (Be sure to include means suggested by the four McGavran modes and the others mentioned by Osei-Mensah.)

200

Communications media modes: radio, television, tape recording, print (newspapers, books, pamphlets, etc.), crusades, person-to-person.

Language modes: national, tribal, regional languages, trade languages, dialects, specialized "languages" such as "street people language."

Cultural modes: national, regional, and ethnic cultures; foreign culture standards; Western, Eastern, Northern, Southern cultures; etc.

Organizational modes: small house churches; large, medium, and small churches; rural, urban, and suburban churches; churches with their own buildings, churches without their own buildings; etc.

Age-group modes: children, youth, college age, young adult, adult, middle age, elderly.

Briefly state the Holy Spirit's relationship to the church, the people of God. Why is human planning and praying important in God's plan for the church? How well is your group or church listening to God's direction? How can you and your group plan and pray in order to be more effective in your witness for the Lord Jesus Christ?

Because of the Cross

The Cross of Jesus Christ, representing His death in our place, is the focal point of all the history of salvation. It is from the Cross that man's new eternal relationship with God is established. At the International Congress on World Evangelization in Lausanne, Switzerland, the importance of the Cross of Christ to evangelism was pointed out by Donald McGavran. His statement stands as the keynote on this extremely important and personal matter: the Cross of the Lord Jesus Christ, evangelism, and me.

McGavran

The apostle Paul wrote, "For the word of the cross is folly to those who are perishing, but to us who are being saved it is the power of God. . . . For since, in the wisdom of God, the world did not know God through wisdom, it pleased God through the folly of what we preach to save those who believe. For Jews demand signs and Greeks seek wisdom, but we preach Christ crucified, a stumbling block to Jews and folly to the Gentiles, but to those who are called, both Jews and Greeks, Christ the power of God and the wisdom of God" (1 Corinthians 1:18, 21–24). World evangelism goes forward, not in the power of men, but in the power of God; not in the wisdom of men, but in the wisdom of God; not by philosophy, but by the Cross of Christ. This is the ultimate dimension of world evangelism.

Tremendous forces are arrayed against world evangelism; but in the sign of the Cross, the mission of healing and redeeming sinful, alienated men and their societies will overcome all adversaries. The Cross is the dynamic of renewal, revival, and awakening within the church. The Cross is also the dynamic of evangelization across cultural barriers outside the church. Evangelism continues until there is a cell of committed Christians in every community, in every city, and in every country throughout the whole wide world. This will prepare the way for our Lord's triumphant return.

If a very good friend was hanged on a gallows because he was found guilty of an awful crime, would you be very proud of that friend? But, if you had committed the crime, and your friend took the punishment, how would you feel about your friend? Whenever you saw a gallows or heard of someone being executed, would you think about your friend? Does this illustrate to you why the Cross of Jesus is so important to Christians?

Why did Paul say the Cross was folly to some people? What kind of person can appreciate the meaning of the Cross of Christ? Why do you think the Cross showed not the defeat of God but the power of God? How can evangelism go forward in the power that was shown through the death of Christ? Is this part of what unbelievers call "foolishness"?

As you think about the Cross of Christ and what it means to you, thank Jesus Christ for dying for *you* personally. And thank Him for the whole new way of living that He has made available to all people. It is also important to think about what the Cross means in terms of your responsibility to share Christ with others.

Festo Kivengere, a bishop in the Anglican Church in Uganda, Africa, related the meaning of the Cross to our own lives and to evangelization.

Man, the upward-looking-one, became a creature in dilemma when he lost his bearings (his life-direction). This tragic experience happened when the upward-looking-one turned away from the direction of life and became the downward-looking-one or the inward-looking-one. Away from the life-direction he turned to death-direction. Away from light he turned to darkness. Away from the center he became eccentric. No wonder the Bible describes man in this state as lost!

His life since has always been lived in the midst of conflicting pulls: (1) the upward pull towards the original ideal; (2) the downward pull towards deterioration into the base kind of living — of slavery to violent appetites and passions; (3) the outward pull towards things and people against him; and (4) the inward pull towards his own likes, feelings, and ambitions. The cry of his heart seems always to have been, "Oh for a balanced existence in the midst of these great pulls!" It is into these life-breaking contradictions that God in Christ came. For man in such conflicts was destroying himself.

Therefore, God took up the rescue in His self-sacrificing love! "God was personally present in Christ, bringing his hostile world of men back into friendship with Himself" (2 Corinthians 5:19). Thus Jesus was baptized in the river Jordan among sinners — sinless as He was — refusing to be counted apart from those He came to rescue. Jesus Christ, who is God's Good News, with outstretched arms in a mighty embrace took hold of our broken lives on *the Cross*. His almighty act of love condemned the hostility to death, releasing the captives.

So the Cross of Christ became God's almighty salvation for us sinners. (a) *In its divine origin*, it ended the despair of ever reaching God through futile man-made endeavors at goodness, and provided the fresh and life-giving way to fellowship with God (Galatians 4:4–5). (b) *In its downward reach*, it went beyond the very roots of our depravity and helplessness, thus dealing with our deepest moral dilapidation and releasing us who were cripples. (c) *In its inward penetration*, our wrong center which made us self-centered was replaced by the new and right center, Christ. He makes us "Christ-centered" and so rescues us from our inner fragmentation. The Cross brings inner wholeness. (d) *In its outward reach*, it removed the conflicting elements from our relationship with our fellowmen and our world as a whole.

Here then in the self-sacrificing love of God in Christ is the centrality, the all-roundness, the cruciality of the Cross. It is this sharing of God's Good News with His world that is evangelism.

What do you think Kivengere had in mind when he described man as the upward-looking one? Was man made for upward-looking, downward-looking, or inward-looking? Why is it that when man stopped being upward-looking, his life fell apart?

What holds people captive? How would you describe man's lostness? How do you express your feelings about man's plight without God to a non-Christian? Do you think most people consciously recognize that they are lost? If they do not, how can they be reached with the Gospel?

What does the Cross of Christ do for mankind? What has Christ's death done for *you* personally? Isaac Watts, the hymn writer, responded to his own meditation on the Cross of Christ with these words:

"Were the whole realm of nature mine,
That were a present far too small;
Love so amazing, so divine,
Demands my soul, my life, my all"
(from "When I Survey the Wondrous Cross").

Jot down your inner feelings about Christ's death for you. Then, thank Him for dying for you. Consider using some of these ideas you have just written to communicate God's love to someone who does not know Jesus Christ personally.

Kivengere tied the Cross directly to evangelization. He said the Cross is (1) the message, (2) the motivating power, (3) the inspiration, (4) the price, (5) the uniting power, and (6) the drawing power of evangelization. We will look briefly at each of these to see the relationship of Christ's death to evangelization.

Kivengere

1. *The Cross is the message of evangelism.* Without the Cross there is no Christian faith. Christianity was born *on the Cross*. It was love on the Cross of Calvary that broke down all the barriers of *cultural, national, racial,* and *intellectual pride.*

The Cross spells out the desperate moral need of man. Nothing less than the love that God demonstrated in Christ on the Cross could have come anywhere near to meeting our deep-seated *guilt*. The Cross primarily deals with human moral guilt, the divine judgment of it, and God's forgiveness. The Cross is, therefore, *Good News* to all men everywhere.

2. *The Cross is the motivating power of evangelism.* It is by the light shed from the Cross that scales fall from our eyes and we begin to see the wonder of His incredible redeeming love as well as the utter wretchedness of our sinfulness.

All people are welcome. There is no one too far gone in the light of this tremendous love! In the midst of *chaos, tumult, philosophies of despair,* and *sad divisions* among professing Christians, we can lift our voices still, and point to the only place of healing — the Cross. God was present in Christ removing the barriers between us and Him, and bringing us into friendship with Himself and with each other.

3. *The Cross is the inspiration of evangelism.* If this is what God went through to bring us into a right relationship with Himself, then we are left no room for aloof attitudes toward any of His children! There is no justification whatsoever for any other attitude than of the love He demonstrated on Calvary's Cross for the world. Evangelism flowed directly from the Cross toward those who were in the very act of crucifying the Lord and to the desperate criminals crucified with Him! The Cross inspires evangelism — there is no other inspiration for it.

Why can't the Christian faith exist without the Cross? Why is the Cross, the death of Christ, singled out as so important?

Why is the Cross *the* message of evangelization? Write the message of the Cross in your own words. How well would your statement be understood by a non-Christian? What changes can you make in your statement to make it communicate more effectively? After you have finished this study, look for someone with whom you can share the message of the Cross.

What is it about the Cross that makes us want to evangelize? Why is there nothing else in the life of Christ that makes us want to evangelize so much as the Cross?

We continue now to Kivengere's last three statements on the relationship of the Cross to evangelization.

Kivengere

4. *The Cross is the price of evangelism.* According to the biblical record, the "Good News" became a living, practical reality for us when He who was equal with God "emptied Himself" of all glory in order to come and share our humanness (Philippians 2:6–8). It cost Him His life to reach us in our misery. According to Isaiah, "He has poured out His soul unto death; He was counted as a sinner among sinners" (Isaiah 53:12). The Cross spells out in shining letters that there was no limit to which God would not go in His redeeming love.

As we see the extent of what God was willing to undergo on our behalf on Calvary, all our values are re-evaluated and our outlook is changed. This is what Paul meant when, in the light of impending danger to his life, he burst out, "But life is worth nothing unless I use it for doing the work of telling others the Good News about God's mighty kindness and love" (Acts 20:24). The only way we can look at our lives, our possessions, our gifts, our status, and our abilities is in the light of the Cross in evangelism.

5. *The Cross is the uniting power of evangelism.* Only through the constraining vision of Christ and Him crucified can the Christian church repent of its unfortunate weakening *divisions* and *divisiveness in its ranks*, the *wastage of its manpower*, and the corrosive *hoarding of its material means*. We need to catch a fresh vision of our Lord's words, "He who spares, loses, but he who lets go, gains" (Luke 9:24–25). The commentary on these words seems to come from Paul's words in Romans 8:32, "He did not spare even His own Son but instead of sparing Him, He gave Him up on our behalf."

At the Cross there can never be justification for hoarding or withholding. Such selfishness, not only regarding money and property but also concerning ourselves as persons, is inconsistent with the Cross. It is our physical lives which are to be offered as a living sacrifice to God (Romans 12:1–2).

6. *The Cross is the drawing power of evangelism.* It is the Lord Jesus Himself who drew the attention of His bewildered disciples at the end of His earthly ministry. He said, "When I am lifted up (on the cross) above the earth, I will draw all men to Me" (John 12:32). No matter what methods we may use in sharing the Good News with men, still the drawing power is the Cross of Christ. It is Christ, the one crucified, who wins rebellious lives, melts stony hearts, brings life to

the dead, and inspires stagnant lives into unsparing activity. It is the crucified who makes us see the world alive with need for forgiveness. It is the crucified Christ who crosses out our own fancies and introduces us to the value of people. It is the crucified Christ who destroys our prejudiced evaluations of our fellowmen as racial cases, tribal specimens, social outcasts or aristocrats, sinful characters, and religious misfits by giving us the fresh evaluation of all men as redeemable persons on whose behalf Christ died.

Evangelism fails miserably when its only purpose is to draw men to its programs of preaching or social concern. Men are to be drawn by the power of the self-sacrificing love of God in Christ into new life in Him. The Cross gives flesh and bones to evangelism. It is in the Cross that the truth becomes incarnate and reaches us where we are and as we are. It is the Cross which encourages us to cross over the barriers of our particular camps to meet God's world. The Cross of Christ is the panacea for the deep troubles of the human race. It is the hope for my beloved country of Africa with all its conflicting problems. It is the solution for the "richer" nations of the West with their disturbing disintegration of lives in the midst of material plenty.

The Cross demonstrates the great price paid for our salvation. What do you think the Cross means to God the Father? What did it mean for God the Son to become human, live as a man, and die in the manner of a criminal? What did the Lord Jesus Christ leave behind in heaven when He became a man (Philippians 2:6–8)? Knowing the price paid for our forgiveness helps us to commit ourselves unreservedly to God. How do people make such a commitment? Is it a commitment done once and never again or is it an ongoing commitment? How can we show by our behavior that we are committed to Christ?

Is it possible for the Cross to unite all people in Christ? Most personal distinctions remain after a person becomes a Christian — a white person is still white, a poor man is still poor, a Chinese is still Chinese. To what degree are these distinctions overcome through the Cross?

According to Kivengere, the Cross shows that God gave His Son. He let go of Christ, and so gained. Kivengere equated this with the unifying power of the Cross in evangelization. How does "giving up" lead to uniting all things? In what way does the Cross of Christ do this?

What kind of practical results does the uniting power of the Cross suggest to you? How can this unity be expressed in your own evangelization? How can you begin to help the many Christians who do not have resources to do effective evangelism? What do you have that you could share with them to further their witness to the Gospel of Christ?

Many find it strange that the death of Christ as represented by His Cross should draw people to Him. What does the Cross demonstrate about the worth of a person?

What is it about Calvary that encourages and enables us to cross over all barriers of race, culture, language, and economics to reach out to people? What should characterize the life of one who has been to the Cross of Christ and received forgiveness, divine love, and new divine life? How do *you* measure up to that standard?

Kivengere's final remarks at the Congress led to the celebration of the Lord's Supper.

I plead that as we receive the bread and the cup that we will open our hearts to our estranged brothers and sisters. I plead that we will allow the Cross to lead us out of the spiritual ghettos of our security. And I plead that as we go out to Him we shall meet many who come to Him from other camps and shall have fellowship with them around the Cross. Then the communion with Him and with each other will be a life-liberating and satisfying experience. It will spark the fire of evangelism for which our churches are in desperate need. Our age is waiting for the redemption of God's children from the corroding influences of this world's power of evil into the glorious liberty of the fullness of life in the new kingdom of our Lord. Let us approach with boldness, and enter the presence of God through the Cross. Let us enjoy fellowship with God and with each other, and by the power of the Holy Spirit proclaim God's Good News to our age. "As for me, God forbid that I should boast about anything except the cross of our Lord Jesus Christ" (Galatians 6:14).

How can the Cross of Christ cause you to reflect to all persons, Christian and non-Christian, the love of Christ that was summed up in the Cross? Take steps now to share the meaning of the Cross with one person who is a Christian, and with one who is not.

In Practice

Doctrine is basic to true Christianity. We cannot be "wishy-washy" about the full authority and infallibility of the Bible, the existence of God, the deity of Christ, Christ's death and resurrection for us, or the deity and work of the Holy Spirit. At the International Congress on World Evangelization, Francis A. Schaeffer, founder of L'Abri Fellowship in Switzerland, pointed out some major implications of doctrine in several areas of our lives.

When we talk about content, we are talking about something very practical indeed. We must have a strong doctrinal content. And we must practice the content, practice the truth we say we believe. We must exhibit to our own children and to the watching world that we take truth seriously. It will not do in a relativistic age to say that we believe in truth and fail to practice that truth in places where it may be observed and where it is costly. We, as Christians, say we believe that truth exists. We say we have truth from the Bible. And we say we can give that truth to other people in propositional, verbalized form and they may have that truth. This is exactly what the Gospel claims and this is what we claim. But then we are surrounded by a relativistic age. Do you think for a moment we will have credibility if we say we believe the truth and yet do not practice the truth in religious matters?

Consider an example in the academic world. A Christian young woman was teaching sociology in one of the major universities of Britain. Her department chairman told her that she had to teach in the framework of behaviorism or lose her post. Confronted with the question of the practice of truth, she said no. She lost her post. This is what I mean by practicing truth when it is costly.

It will also come in the area of sexual life form. Surrounded by permissive sexualists and asexuality, we must be careful by the grace of God to practice what we say the Bible teaches, the one-man, one-woman relationship, or we are destroying the truth that we say we believe.

But nowhere is practicing the truth more important than in the area of religious cooperation. How will we have credibility in a relativistic age if we practice religious cooperation with people who in their books and lectures make very plain that they believe nothing or practically nothing of the content set forth in Scripture? We must have the courage to take a clear position.

But beware! We certainly must not take our secondary distinctives and elevate them to the point where we refuse to have fellowship with those who do not hold them. It is the central things of the Word of God which make Christianity distinctive. These we must hold tenaciously, and, even when it is costly for us, we must maintain that there is not only an opposite of truth but an opposite that is observable in practice. Out of a loyalty to the infinite-personal God who is there and who has spoken in Scripture, we who are evangelicals dare not take a half-way position concerning truth or the practice of truth.

There must be a strong emphasis on content and there must be a strong emphasis on the practice of truth. We can talk about methods, we can stir each other up, we can call each other to all kinds of action, but unless action is rooted in a strong Christian base in the area of content and the practice of truth, we build on sand and add to the confusion of our day.

How is correct belief or doctrine the basis for correct action or practice? Why is correct belief not good enough by itself? Why must we practice truth as well as believe it?

Think of at least one area in your life in which what you believe should have a greater effect on your actions.

How is correct doctrine the basis for correct practice? Why is correct doctrine useless if we do not also practice it in life?

Do you consider your beliefs about basic Christianity to be correct? On what basis? Do your beliefs usually show in your actions? How can you increase the likelihood that what you believe will be part of how you act?

How should what you believe determine your participation or cooperation with others?

How does truth imply action, or doctrine imply practice? Why is doctrine foundational to practice, yet incomplete without practice?

How do you apply the principle of "correct doctrine must imply correct practice" to religious cooperation? With whom could you cooperate in religious matters such as shared evangelistic activities?

What are some of the "central things of the Word of God" which make Christianity distinctive? Are these the factors which determine your willingness to cooperate in religious matters?

208

Schaeffer

We believe with all our hearts that Christian truth can be presented in propositions. But, the end of Christianity is not the repetition of mere propositions. Without the proper propositions you cannot have that which should follow. But after having the correct propositions, the end of the matter is to love God with all our hearts and souls and minds. The end of the matter, after we know about God in the revelation He has given in verbalized, propositional terms in the Scripture, is to be in relationship to Him. A dead, ugly orthodoxy with no real spiritual reality must be rejected as sub-christian.

If Christianity is truth, as the Bible claims, it must touch every aspect of life. At every point in our lives Christ must be our Lord and the Bible must be our norm.

Back in 1951 and 1952, I went through a very deep time in my own life. I had been a pastor for ten years and a mssionary for another five, and I was connected with a group who stood very strongly for the truth of the Scriptures. But as I watched, it became clear to me that I saw very little spiritual reality. I had to ask why. I looked at myself and realized that my own spiritual reality was not as great as it had been immediately after my conversion. We were in Switzerland at that time, and I said to my wife, "I must really think this through."

I took about two months, and I walked in the mountains whenever it was clear. And when it was rainy, I walked back and forth in the hayloft over our chalet. I thought and wrestled and prayed, and I went all the way back to my agnosticism. I asked myself whether I had been right to stop being an agnostic and to become a Christian. I told my wife if it didn't turn out right I was going to be honest and go back to America and put it all aside and do some other work.

I came to realize that indeed I had been right in becoming a Christian. But then I went on further and wrestled deeper and asked, "But then, where is the spiritual reality, Lord, among most of that which calls itself orthodoxy?" And gradually I found something that I had not been taught, a simple thing but profound. I discovered the meaning of the work of Christ. I learned the meaning of the blood of Christ, moment by moment in our lives after we are Christians — the moment-by-moment work of the whole Trinity in our lives — because as Christians we are indwelt by the Holy Spirit. That is true spirituality.

I went out to Dakota, and spoke at a Bible conference. The Lord used it and there was a real moving of God in that place. I want to tell you with all my heart that I think we could have had all the intellectual answers in the world at L'Abri, but if it had not been for those battles in which God gave me some knowledge of spiritual reality — a relationship with God moment-by-moment on the basis of the blood of Jesus Christ — I don't believe there ever would have been a L'Abri.

Do we minimize the intellectual? I have pled for the intellectual. I have pled for the propositional. I have pled against doctrinal compromises, specifically at the point of the Word of God being less than propositional truth all the way back to the first verse of Genesis. But at the same time there must be spiritual reality.

Will it be perfect? No, I do not believe the Bible ever holds out to us that anybody is perfect in this life. But it can be real, and it must be shown in some poor way. I say poor because I am sure when we get to heaven and look back we will all see how poor it has been. And yet there must be some reality. There must be something real of the work of Christ in the moment-by-moment life, something real of the forgiveness of specific sin brought under the blood of Christ, something real in Christ bearing His fruit through me through the indwelling of the Holy Spirit. These things must be there. There is nothing more ugly in all the world than dead orthodoxy.

209

●

What did Schaeffer realize was true spirituality? How did it change his life?

What have you discovered about behavior as a spiritual person? Why do Christians not always live a spiritual life? Why do you sometimes not want to live a spiritual life? How can you overcome this problem?

● ●

If you were trying to explain true spirituality to a new Christian friend, what would you say?

How well are you demonstrating true spirituality in your life? What changes must you make with God's help?

● ● ●

What is the content of the true spirituality that Schaeffer discovered?

How does this spirituality become a reality in daily living?

How much of your life shows true spirituality? How can your life demonstrate more spiritual reality?

True spiritual living could be characterized by one word. Schaeffer called it "beauty."

True Christianity produces beauty as well as truth, especially in the specific areas of human relationships. I am talking now about beauty, and I have chosen this word with care. I could call it love, but we have so abused the word that it is often meaningless. So I use the word beauty. There should be beauty, observable beauty, for the world to see in the way all true Christians treat each other and the world.

Read the New Testament carefully with this in mind; notice how often Jesus returns us to this theme, how often Paul speaks of it. We are to show something to the watching world on the basis of the human relationships we have with other men, not just other Christians.

Read the following Scripture to determine what love is. The love the Bible commands has been defined as self-giving love. How do these verses support that idea?

Luke 10:25–37	Romans 13:8–10	Galatians 5:14	1 Peter 4:8
John 13:34–35; 15:12–13	1 Corinthians 13	Ephesians 5:2	1 John 4:7–12

I meet a man in a revolving door. How much time do I have with him? Maybe ten seconds. I am to treat him well. Because he is made in the image of God, we will treat him well in those ten seconds which we have.

We approach a red light. Perhaps we will never see those other people at the intersection again, but we are to remember that they have dignity.

And when we come to the longer relationships, for example, the employer-employee relationship, we are to treat each person with dignity. The husband-and-wife relationship, the parent-and-child relationship, the political relationship, the economic relationship — in every single relationship of life to the extent to which I am in contact with a man or woman, sometimes shorter and sometimes longer — he or she is to be treated in such a way that, if they are thinking at all, they will say, "He treated me well."

Now, if we are called upon to love our neighbor as ourselves when he is not a Christian, how much more — ten thousand times more — should there be beauty in the relationships between true Bible-believing Christians. This should be something so beautiful that the world would be brought up short!

We must hold our distinctives. Some of us are Baptists, some of us hold to infant baptism, some of us are Lutheran, and so on. But to true Bible-believing Christians across all denominational lines I emphasize: If we do not show beauty in the way we treat each other, then in the eyes of the world and in the eyes of our own children, we are destroying the truth we proclaim.

Every big company, if they are going to make a huge plant, first makes a pilot plant in order to show that their plan will work. Every church, every mission, every Christian school, every

Christian group, regardless of what sphere it is in, should be a pilot plant that the world can look at and see there a beauty of human relationships which stands in exact contrast to the awful ugliness of what modern men paint in their art, what they make with their sculpture, what they show in their cinema, and the way they treat each other. Men should see in the church a bold alternative to the way modern men treat people as animals and machines. There should be something so different that they will listen, something so different it will commend the Gospel to them.

Every group ought to be like that, and the relationships among our groups ought to be like that. Have they been? The answer all too often is *no*. We have something to ask the Lord to forgive us for. Evangelicals, we who are true Bible-believing Christians, must ask God to forgive us for the ugliness with which we have often treated each other.

Why was the early church able, within one century, to spread from India to Spain? When we read in Acts and in the Epistles, we find a church that held and practiced both correct doctrine and the beauty of relationship, and this could be observed by the world. Thus they commended the Gospel to the world of that day and the Holy Spirit was not grieved. There is a tradition (it is not in the Bible) that the world said about the Christians in the early church, "Behold, how they love each other."

211

●

From the Scripture which you have read and from Schaeffer's comments, describe the actions and attitudes of a loving person. Do you hold these attitudes and practice these actions?

In what way is love a very important part of evangelization? Why will non-Christians find it difficult to believe that God loves them if you do not show them love? Ask God to help you be loving toward some particular person who needs love.

●●

What sort of relationship can be called "beautiful"? Why is love or beauty of relationship always self-giving and unselfish? How can you increase your love toward others? Be specific and ask God to help you act lovingly toward at least one particular person who needs love.

In what way is love related to evangelization?

●●●

Why can love be called "beauty of relationship"?

In what form should love appear in your church, your group, and your life? Be specific and work with God to let love be more clearly expressed in at least one area of your life through what you are and do.

Why is love a prerequisite for evangelization? What form could love take in evangelization? Do you manifest these forms?

The King Is Coming

During the ten days of the International Congress on World Evangelization, 1,852,837 people were added to the world's population. Many of these people became part of the almost three billion people of the world who have been unreached by the Gospel of Jesus Christ. This large number demonstrated the tremendous need to evangelize the world. The final statement of the Congress, the "Lausanne Covenant," spoke of the urgency of the evangelistic task.

> More than 2,700 million people, which is more than two-thirds of mankind, have yet to be evangelized. We are ashamed that so many have been neglected; it is a standing rebuke to us and to the whole church. There is now, however, in many parts of the world an unprecedented receptivity to the Lord Jesus Christ. We are convinced that this is the time for churches and para-church agencies to pray earnestly for the salvation of the unreached and to launch new efforts to achieve world evangelization. A reduction of foreign missionaries and money in an evangelized country may sometimes be necessary to facilitate the national church's growth in self-reliance and to release resources for unevangelized areas. Missionaries should flow ever more freely from and to all six continents in a spirit of humble service. The goal should be, by all available means and at the earliest possible time, that every person will have the opportunity to hear, understand, and receive the good news. We cannot hope to attain this goal without sacrifice. All of us are shocked by the poverty of millions and disturbed by the injustices which cause it. Those of us who live in affluent circumstances accept our duty to develop a simple life-style in order to contribute more generously to both relief and evangelism. (John 9:4; Matthew 9:35-38; Romans 9:1-3; I Corinthians 9:19-23; Mark 16:15; Isaiah 58:6, 7; James 1:27; 2:1-9; Matthew 25:31-46; Acts 2:44, 45; 4:34, 35)

List the major ideas in this selection from the "Lausanne Covenant." Add any other Scripture references which also support these ideas. In what way should these ideas affect your personal life and the life of your group, local church, or organization?

Ralph Winter, professor at the School of World Mission, Fuller Theological Seminary, Pasadena, California, emphasized the importance of sending missionaries to people of other cultures.

> We must take seriously the immense responsibility that still remains for cross-cultural evangelism. Cross-cultural evangelism should have the very highest priority because at least 80 per cent of the non-Christians in the world today are beyond the reach of ordinary evangelism and cannot be reached unless at least initial contact is made by means of *cross-cultural* evangelism.

Winter explained that by ordinary evangelism, he means evangelizing people from within one's own culture; for example, an American middle class person communicating the Gospel to other middle class Americans, or Japanese businessmen to other Japanese businessmen. By cross-cultural evangelism, Winter means evangelism that involves communicating the Gospel to people who are different from the person who is reaching out; for example, an American middle class person evangelizing in the hill country of Taiwan or a similar American going to the Navajo Indians in the American West.

Billy Graham emphasized some of these same ideas in his opening address to the Congress.

In the last quarter of the twentieth century, the unevangelized world consists of two main blocs of people. The first are the superficially Christian populations. If you ask them their religion, they more than likely reply, "Christian," but they do not personally know Christ. A second part consists of large "unreached" populations which can be found in almost every country. For example, the Turks, Algerians, and Vietnamese in Europe constitute large unreached populations in the heart of Europe itself. In these unreached populations, Christians of any sort, "born again" or in name only, constitute only a tiny fraction.

While some people can be evangelized by their neighbors, others and greater multitudes are cut off from their Christian neighbors by deep linguistic, political, and cultural chasms. They will never be reached by "near neighbor" evangelism. To build our evangelistic policies on "near neighbor" evangelism alone is to shut out at least a billion from any possibility of knowing the Savior.

Churches of every land, therefore, must deliberately send out evangelists and missionaries to master other languages, learn other cultures, live in them as long as God wills, and thus evangelize these multitudes. Thus, we should reject the idea of a moratorium on sending missionaries.

●

Could people hear the gospel and be saved without cross-cultural evangelism? What makes cross-cultural evangelism different from "near-neighbor" evangelism?

How does cross-cultural evangelism lead to "near-neighbor" evangelism?

What can you and your group do to help increase cross-cultural evangelism?

● ●

How would you answer a person who said it was not necessary to send missionaries to people of different cultures?

Why is cross-cultural evangelism so important?

Why is cross-cultural evangelism difficult?

How does cross-cultural evangelism eventually lead to "near-neighbor" evangelism?

How could you and your group help to increase cross-cultural evangelism?

● ● ●

What makes the task of cross-cultural evangelism so important today? Why can we not rely on "near-neighbor" evangelism?

What is the difference between "near-neighbor" evangelism and cross-cultural evangelism? Why does Graham suggest that missionaries may have to be redeployed?

What are the reasons for rejecting a moratorium on sending cross-cultural missionaries?

The task of world evangelization, whether evangelism of one's next-door neighbor or of someone in a totally different culture, is not only a problem of correct plans. All evangelism involves a spiritual battle. The "Lausanne Covenant" speaks of a conflict with evil outside and inside the church.

> We believe that we are engaged in constant spiritual warfare with the principalities and powers of evil, who are seeking to overthrow the church and frustrate its task of world evangelization. We know our need to equip ourselves with God's armor and to fight this battle with the spiritual weapons of truth and prayer. For we detect the activity of our enemy, not only in false ideologies outside the church, but also inside it in false gospels which twist Scripture and put man in the place of God. We need both watchfulness and discernment to safeguard the biblical Gospel. We acknowledge that we ourselves are not immune to worldliness of thought and action, that is, to a surrender to secularism. For example, although careful studies of church growth, both numerical and spiritual, are right and valuable, we have sometimes neglected them. At other times, desirous to ensure a response to the Gospel, we have compromised our message, manipulated our hearers through pressure techniques, and become unduly preoccupied with statistics or even dishonest in our use of them. All this is worldly. The church must be in the world; the world must not be in the church. (Ephesians 6:12; II Corinthians 4:3, 4; Ephesians 6:11, 13–18; II Corinthians 10:3–5; I John 2:18–26, 4:1–3; Galatians 1:6–9; II Corinthians 2:17, 4:2; John 17:15)

The power to win the spiritual battle is in the Holy Spirit. The "Lausanne Covenant" stated the absolute necessity of the Holy Spirit.

> We believe in the power of the Holy Spirit. The Father sent His Spirit to bear witness to His Son; without His witness ours is futile. Conviction of sin, faith in Christ, new birth and Christian growth are all His work. Further, the Holy Spirit is a missionary spirit; thus evangelism should arise spontaneously from a spirit-filled church. A church that is not a missionary church is contradicting itself and quenching the Spirit. Worldwide evangelization will become a realistic possibility only when the Spirit renews the church in truth and wisdom, faith, holiness, love, and power. We therefore call upon all Christians to pray for such a visitation of the sovereign spirit of God that all His fruit may appear in all His people and that all His gifts may enrich the body of Christ. Only then will the whole church become a fit instrument in His hands, that the whole earth may hear His voice. (I Corinthians 2;4; John 15:26, 27, 16:8–11; I Corinthians 12:3; John 3:6–8; II Corinthians 3:18; John 7:37–39; I Thessalonians 5:19; Acts 1:8; Psalm 85:4–7, 67:1–3; Galatians 5:22,23; I Corinthians 12:4–31; Romans 12:3–8)

List the major ideas in these two selections from the "Covenant." Which Scripture references support each idea? What other Scripture would you include? What do each of the ideas mean to you?

What is a person like when God's Spirit fills him? Nilson A. Fanini, pastor of the First Baptist Church of Niteroi, Brazil, used the life of Stephen in Acts 6 and 7 as an example of a person who is filled by the Holy Spirit. Fanini said a person who is full of the Holy Spirit is. . .

Fanini

1. One who is a channel through whom God performs His signs and miracles here on earth (Acts 6:8).
2. One who reacts graciously when provoked (Acts 6:15).
3. One who is powerful in the Scripture (Acts 7:2–53).
4. One who is sustained by God (Acts 7:55).
5. One who is similar to Jesus in the days of his flesh (Acts 7:59).
6. One whose death is greatly lamented (Acts 8:2).
7. One who not only is full of power, but also is ready to do things for God (Acts 6:3, 8).

Read Acts 6:1–15; 7:1–2, 54–60. How does your life compare to the seven characteristics Fanini listed? How will your life be different if you show these seven characteristics? What power is available to help you become more like Stephen?

The Holy Spirit is probably the most misunderstood Person of the Trinity. Some people want the Holy Spirit's power for wrong reasons. Thomas Houston, communications director of the British and Foreign Bible Society, London, England, gave insight into this problem of misusing the power of the Holy Spirit.

Houston

The work of the Spirit is not to build me up but to reduce me to size so that Jesus can be seen. The Bible suggests two contrasting ideas about the Holy Spirit. There are pictures of rushing mighty winds, floods, baptisms by fire, places shaking, and so on — all symbols of power, force, violence, coercion, crashing, breaking, burning, overwhelming — all big and great and grand. In contrast, there are statements about God not being in the wind and the fire and the earthquake but in the still small voice.

I have to avoid seeing myself in the grand metaphors of fullness and baptism because they swamp me and like their counterparts in nature cause damage instead of fertility. In my hands the spirit of power would do violence to the free response that is the very essence of the Good News of Jesus. Instead I need a modest check-list approach.

1. Am I lying to the Holy Spirit by being dishonest and professing more than is true, as Ananias and Sapphira did (Acts 5)?

2. Am I resisting the Holy Spirit by refusing the truth, as the Jerusalem Jews did (Acts 7)?

3. Am I grieving the Holy Spirit by having a bad relationship with others as the Ephesians did (Ephesians 4:1–6, 5:21–6:9)?

4. Am I quenching the Holy Spirit by preventing the development and use of God's gifts in other people or in myself as the Thessalonians did (I Thessalonians 5:19–22)?

What is the Holy Spirit's work in the life of the believer? Why is "power" a problem to some people? How is the "Spirit of truth" an answer to the "power" problem? Use Houston's check list to determine your relationship to the Holy Spirit.

Psalm 12:1 is translated in the *Living Bible*, "Lord, help! Lord! Help! Godly men are fast disappearing. Where in all the world can dependable men be found?" Are you a godly man, a godly woman? Are you a dependable man, a dependable woman? Our whole world is in a crisis of leadership at this moment. We want some person to come on the stage of world events with a formula for world peace. The world is waiting for a leader. Some day that leader is going to step on the world's stage; that leader is the Lord Jesus Christ! He alone has the solution to our complex problems. You must be an instrument prepared for the hand of God.

Yes, the King is coming. Some day we shall see the Son of Man, seated at the right hand of God and coming in the clouds of heaven. The Lord himself shall descend from heaven. Phillips translates Colossians 3:4, "One day Christ, the secret center of our lives, will show Himself openly and you will share in that magnificent glory." But this doesn't make us complacent until that moment. Critics of those that believe in the Second Coming say that we lose our incentive for work. It has been my experience that those who believe the coming again of the Lord are the hardest workers, the most zealous and the most dedicated.

The King is Coming! "In the twinkling of an eye" — one thousandth of a second. That leaves no opportunity for a Christian to re-commit his life; it leaves no opportunity for the thief to repent or the prodigal to come home. Now is the moment. The King is Coming! We do not know that these are the last days. We do not know the day nor the hour. Even if He were coming to-night and we were certain of it, we would be busy about our Lord's business.

A shoe salesman sat on a Boston park bench many years ago, thinking. He had heard a Christian brother say, "The world has yet to see what God can do with a man fully committed to Him!" And this man with hardly any education stood up and said, "By the grace of God, I'll be that man." Dwight L. Moody became one of the greatest evangelists of the Christian church.

Will you be such a person? In view of the world's need, in view of what we've heard and seen and felt here, and in view of the coming again of the Lord, I am asking, "Are you willing? Many of the problems that we wrestle with are not intellectual. They are deep down inside the will. Are we willing to deny self and take up the cross to follow our Lord? Are you willing?

The King is Coming.

Many of the Congress participants responded in renewed dedication and commitment to the task of world evangelization as God leads them. In the words of the "Lausanne Covenant,"

We enter into a solemn covenant with God and with each other, to pray, to plan, and to work together for the evangelization of the whole world. We call upon others to join us. May God help us by His grace and for His glory to be faithful to this our covenant! Amen, Alleluia!